Library of Shakespearean Biography and Criticism

I. PRIMARY REFERENCE WORKS ON SHAKESPEARE

II. CRITICISM AND INTERPRETATION
  A. Textual Treatises, Commentaries
  B. Treatment of Specal Subjects
  C. Dramatic and Literary Art in Shakespeare

III. SHAKESPEARE AND HIS TIME
  A. General Treatises. Biography
  B. The Age of Shakespeare
  C. Authorship

Series II, Part A

SHAKESPEARE VERSUS SHALLOW

The gifte of William Gardner Esquire

Library of Shakespearean Biography and Criticism

SHAKESPEARE

versus

SHALLOW

BY

LESLIE HOTSON

Shakespeare, that nimble Mercury, thy brain,
Lulls many hundred Argus-eyes asleep.

BOOKS FOR LIBRARIES PRESS
FREEPORT, NEW YORK

First Published 1931
Reprinted 1970

822.33
XH
69431
March, 1970

STANDARD BOOK NUMBER:
8369-5261-8

LIBRARY OF CONGRESS CATALOG CARD NUMBER:
74-109652

PRINTED IN THE UNITED STATES OF AMERICA

TO

M. M. P. H.

THE CONTENTS

LIST OF ILLUSTRATIONS

(*The Photographs are by Monger & Marchant.*)

xi

PREFACE

In this contribution to our knowledge of Shakespeare and his acquaintances in Southwark, I have confined my attention chiefly to the poet and to William Gardiner and his stepson William Wayte, reserving Francis Langley for fuller treatment elsewhere. For convenience to the reader, in reproducing Elizabethan documents I have for the most part modernized spellings, and added some punctuation. The intricacies and repetitions of obsolete legal language offer difficulties enough without the gratuitous obstacle of a chaotic orthography. For the chapter on Gardiner's life the documents of control will be found in the appendix chronologically arranged.

My obligations are various, and so numerous as to preclude detailed acknowledgment. I am most grateful for the encouragement given by my friends in England and America. The John Simon Guggenheim Memorial Foundation, in appointing me to a Fellowship for two successive years, has made possible the uninterrupted application which successful record-searching exacts; and the American Council of Learned Societies, by a generous grant,

has helped me to make the most of my opportunity.
For aid of various kinds in the collection and
interpretation of materials I am indebted to the
officers and staff of the Public Record Office, and
in particular to Mr. J. J. O'Reilly; to Dr. Hubert
Hall, Mr. J. H. Morrison, the Rev. C. A. Newdi-
gate, S.J., the Rev. Edward J. Newill, the Rev.
Arthur Sinker, Mr. George F. Sutton, and Miss
A. F. Wise; above all to Miss Nellie McN. O'Farrell,
who has been my right hand from the outset. I
have found the training in method given me by
my master Professor G. L. Kittredge to be invalu-
able. In preparing the manuscript I have profited
greatly by the suggestions of my friend Mr. David
Garnett. To my wife I owe the deepest debt—the
heart to undertake a task and the faith to persist
in it.

L. H.

JORDANS, BEACONSFIELD,
    June 1931.

SHAKESPEARE'S QUARREL

IF one wishes to feed a secret hope of discovering new facts about Shakespeare's life, one is not well advised to turn for nourishment to the standard biographies. It is the business of standard biographies not to stimulate research, but to capitalize its results; and ever about such books hangs an air of regretful finality dampening to the spirits.

Not so with the occasional observations of the pioneering record-searcher. His account of good hunting, and his description of promising territory to be explored, are not only fascinating but heartening. Encouragement of this expert sort was thrown out by one who was perhaps the greatest of all discoverers of Shakespeare material—Halliwell-Phillipps. In 1884, towards the close of his active career, he published 'for strictly private circulation' a suggestive paper entitled *Memoranda, intended for the use of amateurs, who are sufficiently interested in the pursuit, to make searches in the Public Record Office on the chance of discovering new facts respecting Shakespeare and the contemporary stage.*

In the course of his remarks in this paper, the author tempered encouragement with good advice:

1   B

"That there are undiscovered notices of Shakespeare amidst the millions of papers in our national Record Office may be fairly accepted as certain. Some, unfortunately, may remain concealed for many generations, but others, it is hoped, may be unearthed by inductive methods of research, that is to say, by carefully bearing in mind the names of his friends and professional associates, his dealings with property, &c., and in that way to trace out accounts of legal proceedings in which it is likely that he was interested. . . . More than one of my correspondents are under the delusion that I have already got everything of theatrical value that is to be found in the Record Office. That is beyond the power of any individual, however persistent he may be in his work. It would take a hundred people more than a hundred years to go through the records exhaustively."

Since the time of Halliwell-Phillipps, at least two sustained attacks have been made upon the records on the lines which he laid down. Professor and Mrs. C. W. Wallace, working chiefly among the documents of the Court of Requests, unearthed much new material of prime interest, and crowned their labours with the exciting discovery of a deposition of Shakespeare's—his testimony given under oath, and signed with his own hand. Mrs. C. C. Stopes, another indefatigable worker, contributed many notable additions to the skeleton fabric of fact.

When such lynx-eyed gleaners have gone before, it is easy to throw up one's hands in despair; especially easy when Professor Wallace tells us he has reason to believe that he has found everything of importance on the subject that exists in the Record Office. A re-reading, however, of the sturdy words of Halliwell-Phillipps, emphasized by a solemn tour through the great strong-rooms behind the scenes at the Record Office, with their thousands of Elizabethan rolls and bundles of documents, gives fainting hope a fresh hold on life. Inescapably one feels confident that somewhere, somewhere in this vast forest of parchment, there are further traces of Shakespeare still hidden. Among the millions of dusty answers there *must* be a few certainties. But how to get at them? Which way to turn first?

Here Halliwell-Phillipps comes once more to our assistance. His pamphlet suggests that the rolls of the Court of Queen's Bench should be sifted, both Coram Regina and Controlment Rolls; and although, since he wrote, Mrs. Stopes has evidently gone through many of the records in this series, yet the richness and diversity of the materials invite further investigation.

On the strength of this hint, I embarked recently on a careful search through the rolls of the Queen's Bench for the period covered by Shakespeare's lifetime. In the course of examining the Controlment Rolls, I was arrested by a special set of entries described as 'petitions for sureties of the peace'. These are brief records of proceedings on the peculiarly English plan of preventing crimes of violence: a method which obliges the person alleged to have threatened the petitioner to enter bond, which he will forfeit if he breaks the peace. Jacob's *Law Dictionary* (1729)[1] outlines the procedure as follows: "He that demands security for the peace, must make oath before the justice of blows given [him], or that he stands in fear of his life, or some bodily hurt, or that he fears the party will burn his house, &c., and that he doth not demand the peace of him for any malice or revenge, but for his own safety". If such sworn information were laid before a Judge of the Queen's Bench, he would thereupon command the sheriff

[1] *s.v.* 'Good Behaviour'.

4

of the appropriate county to attach and produce the person complained of. On his appearance, the latter was required to enter, with two bondsmen or sureties, into sufficient bonds, conditioned on his keeping the peace 'towards all Her Majesty's subjects and especially towards' the person complaining. If he should break the peace within the period specified (usually a year), he and his friends would forfeit their bonds.

It is easy to see that fascinating quarrels may lie behind judicial records such as these. Let me give a specimen quarrel, with its attendant 'binding to the peace', from a suit[1] in the Star Chamber, dated 1606. A grocer of Clerkenwell, one John Channon, wished to collect a debt from another grocer, Gawine Beare. Channon alleges that Beare not only refused to pay him, but out of malice, and wrongfully to vex him, "came unto Sir Francis Gawdy . . . one of Your Majesty's Justices of Your Highness' Bench . . . and did upon his oath . . . depose, say, and affirm that he . . . stood and was in danger and fear of his life by your said subject, whereby your said subject was . . . attached of the peace, and by the said Court . . . bound with sureties to the peace for a year then following; in which

[1] Star Chamber Proceedings, James I., 93/15.

5

his said deposition the said Gawine Beare hath committed most wicked, wilful, and corrupt perjury, for he . . . never was in fear of his life or other damage of your said subject".

Examined on this point, Beare swears that, on his refusal to pay, Channon had "whispered this defendant in the ear, saying . . . that it had been better this defendant had not done it, and that this defendant should be sped [*i.e.* killed], but should not know who hurt him. And afterwards this defendant, going towards Ratcliffe, was met by two seafaring men (whom this defendant had once before seen in the complainant's company)." One of them asked him why he would not pay the debt, and the other said "that if it were his case, he would chop this defendant's flesh, and presently drew out his dagger and offered to strike therewith at this defendant; whereupon he made sudden speed to get from the said persons".

For fear of death and mutilation of his limbs is the phrase used in the Elizabethan records of petitions for sureties of the peace, and the alleged threats against Beare—that he should be sped and his flesh be chopped—obviously fit the terms to a nicety.

A more modern instance of the procedure, under

date of December 8, 1763, involves the notorious demagogue John Wilkes. A portion of the writ issued at his petition by Sir John Eardley-Wilmot, as a Judge of the Court of King's Bench, runs as follows: "I have received information on the oath of John Wilkes Esq., Matthew Brown, and Matthias Darly, that one Alexander Dun, between eleven and twelve of the clock on Tuesday evening last, demanded entrance into the house of the said John Wilkes, and threatened violence to his person; and hath since, in the hearing of the said Matthias Darly, declared his intention to massacre the said John Wilkes the first opportunity; and therefore the said John Wilkes craves sureties of the peace against the said Alexander Dun, not out of hatred or malice, but merely for the preservation of his life and person from danger".[1]

With threats of flesh-chopping and massacre as their reason for being, the entries on the Elizabethan Controlment Rolls, brief as they were, laid hold on my imagination. At first glance it might seem a hopeless business to search among such violent quarrels for traces of Ben Jonson's 'gentle Shakespeare' and Anthony Scoloker's 'friendly Shakespeare', whose demeanour Henry Chettle

[1] K.B. 33/20.

7

had seen 'no less civil than he excellent in the quality he professes'. But we must remember that the gentle, friendly, and civil Shakespeare, like everyone else in those days, 'at his side wore steel'; and an Elizabethan gentleman of wit and courage had no need to be as violent in temper as Kit Marlowe to find himself at some time or other with an unsought quarrel on his hands. If Shakespeare was at some time in his life involved in a quarrel, the possible record of it in these Controlment Rolls might prove to be the outcrop of a vein which, if followed closely, might yield rich ore. I confess that the chance was slim, but it was sufficient to set me off on an extended search.

Pursuing my quest down through the years of Shakespeare's early life, I came to 1596—a year for which we have already three definite Shakespearean records: the burial at Stratford of the poet's young son Hamnet on August 11, a grant of a coat of arms to his father, John Shakespeare, on October 20, and an assessment for the subsidy, indicating the residence of Shakespeare in the parish of St. Helen's, Bishopsgate, London.

At this point in my search—in the roll of entries for Michaelmas term, 1596—the good angel of record-searchers must have favoured my rummag-

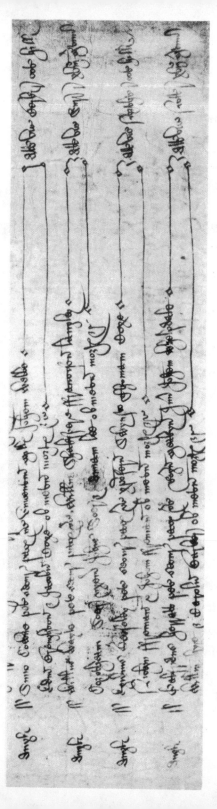

ENTRY OF PETITION FOR SURETIES OF THE PEACE

Transcription of second entry above: Angl ss Willus Wayte pet secur pacę vs Willm Shakspere Franciscū Langley Dorotheam Soer vxem Johis Soer & Annam Lee ob metū mortę &c Att Vic Surr r xviii Mtini

Expansion of above: Anglia scire scilicet Willelmus Wayte ṗetit securitates pacis versus Willelmum Shakspere Franciscum Langley Dorotheam Soer vxorem Johannis Soer et Annam Lee ob metum mortis etc. Attachiamentum Vicecomiti Surreie retornabile xviii Martini

Translation of above: England Be it known that William Wayte craves sureties of the peace against William Shakspere, Francis Langley, Dorothy Soer wife of John Soer, and Anne Lee, for fear of death and so forth. [Writ of] attachment [directed] to the Sheriff of Surrey, returnable on the eighteenth of [St.] Martin [*i.e.* November 29, 1596, the last day of Michaelmas term].

ing in his haystack, for at length I was guided to the precious needle:

Angl*ia* ss Will*elm*us Wayte pet*it* secur*itates* pacis v*er*sus Will*elm*um Shakspere, Franciscum Langley, Dorotheam Soer ux*or*em Joh*ann*is Soer, & Annam Lee, ob metu*m* mortis &c.

Att*achi*amentum vicecomiti Sur*reie* re*tornabile* xviii M*a*rtini.[1]

The legal Latin may be Englished thus:

England Be it known that William Wayte craves sureties of the peace against William Shakspere, Francis Langley, Dorothy Soer wife of John Soer, and Anne Lee, for fear of death, and so forth.

Writ of attachment issued to the sheriff of Surrey, returnable on the eighteenth of St. Martin [*i.e.* November 29, 1596, the last day of Michaelmas term].

Here was strange treasure-trove. Shakespeare, hitherto known only as a poet and player affable and unobtrusive, now for the first time steps out from the dusty records of the past as protagonist in a turbulent scene of raw Elizabethan life. To be sure, there is here no actual fight to the death, as in the cases of his fellow-playwrights Watson, Marlowe, Jonson, Day, and Porter; nevertheless

[1] K.B. 29/234.

9

this man Wayte swears that Shakespeare and these three other persons have threatened him with death. Who is William Wayte? What made Shakespeare threaten him? Who are these three persons who were arrested with Shakespeare? The two women are unknown, but in Francis Langley, the other man, we recognize a figure familiar to students of the Elizabethan stage.

Shakespeare's senior by fourteen years, Langley was a member of the Drapers' Company, and dealt in trade as a goldsmith. (By Elizabeth's time, the London livery companies had relaxed the strictness of the earlier rules of the craft gilds, and many a citizen of London dealt in a trade other than that of the company to which he belonged.) In 1582, Francis Langley had been admitted to the lucrative office of alnager, or inspector and sealer of woollen cloth in London. We may be sure that, in the years which followed, he made the most of the opportunities afforded by his office of extracting fines and fees from the clothiers; for not long after the date of our newly discovered document, I find that on behalf of several members of the clothing trade he was charged by Attorney-General Coke in the Star Chamber with violence and extortion.

Langley had purchased the manor of Paris Garden in the parish of St. Saviour's, Southwark, in 1589, planning no doubt to add to his sources of income by letting houses which he intended to build on his new property. In the winter of 1594–1595, as we know, he had set about building in his grounds a handsome playhouse, which he named the Swan. Langley would naturally seek to let his splendid new theatre, as soon as it was ready, to a good troupe of actors. It has not, however, been known what company or companies of players made use of the Swan before Pembroke's Men came to it in February 1597.

After this brief introduction to Francis Langley, let us return to our newly discovered document, in which he is associated with Shakespeare, and see what we can deduce from the date and place mentioned in this astonishing petition for sureties of the peace.

The writ of attachment, or order for the arrest of Shakespeare and the others, reveals the extremely interesting new fact that Shakespeare, as well as Langley, was living in the bailiwick of the sheriff of Surrey in November 1596. Langley's manor of Paris Garden adjoined the Southwark Bankside, or Liberty of the Clink, with its Bear-Garden and

Henslowe's playhouse, the Rose. For Shakespeare's residence in Southwark, this document is new evidence of prime importance, confirming as it does the uncorroborated statement made in 1796 by Edmund Malone, based on a source which no other scholar has seen: "From a paper now before me, which formerly belonged to Edward Alleyn, the player, our poet appears to have lived in Southwark, near the Bear-Garden, in 1596".

With this new certainty in hand, we are now in a position to ask why Shakespeare migrated from the parish of St. Helen's, Bishopsgate (where, in October 1596, we know he had been assessed a tax of five shillings on goods appraised at a value of five pounds), across the Thames to the Bankside in or before November of the same year. It was not, of course, to be near the famous Globe, his later headquarters, since that theatre was not built and ready for plays until the spring or summer of 1599. Hitherto it has been supposed that Shakespeare's company used Burbage's playhouse called "the Theatre" in Shoreditch into the year 1597. But of this there is no proof; and if it were so, why did Shakespeare move from Bishopsgate, a district within easy reach of Burbage's Theatre, to the Bankside in or before November

1596, and give himself a gratuitous daily journey of more than two miles each way over the water and through London to the playing-place in Shoreditch?

I wish to suggest that Shakespeare went to the Bankside because he and his fellow-actors had shifted their chief centre of operations from the Theatre in the autumn of 1596, and established themselves for a time in Langley's new playhouse, the Swan, in Paris Garden.

We shall see that the reasons for this move were urgent. At the period of our document, the inveterate opposition of the puritanical authorities of the City had been growing to a strength which threatened the livelihood of even the best protected companies of players. In November 1594, when Langley was preparing to build the Swan, the Lord Mayor, outraged by the construction of another of what he termed "the ordinary places of meeting for all vagrant persons and masterless men that hang about the City, thieves, horse-stealers, whoremongers, cozeners, connycatching persons, practisers of treason, and such other like, where they consort and make their matches, to the great displeasure of Almighty God, and the hurt and annoyance of Her Majesty's people", the

Lord Mayor, I say, had seized the opportunity to urge Elizabeth's chief minister, Lord Burghley, not only to forbid Langley to proceed, but also to put down "all other places" of acting in and near London. In September 1595, the Lord Mayor and the Aldermen followed up their attack on the theatres with a letter to the Privy Council, pressing for the final abolition of stage-playing. In the deliberations of the Privy Council, Henry Lord Hunsdon, Lord Chamberlain, who was of course at this time the patron of Shakespeare's company, must have had no easy task to protect the interests of his players against such assaults as these.

Unhappily for Shakespeare and his fellows, on July 22, 1596, Lord Hunsdon died. On the very day that death robbed Hunsdon's company of their powerful protector, plays were prohibited throughout London and the suburbs. "For that by drawing of much people together increase of sickness is feared", was the reason given, but we can find no evidence of plague.

In addition to the temporary prohibition of acting at the theatres, which were all in the suburbs or in Southwark, this order meant the closing of the inn-yard playing-places in the City proper, which had been important sources of revenue to the players. Once the inn-yards were closed to the actors, the new balance of power in the Privy Council gave the Lord Mayor and the Aldermen the means to prevent their reopening: for Hunsdon's successor as Lord Chamberlain, William Brooke, Lord Cobham, did not look with favour on the players. They reciprocated his dislike. It is probable that Shakespeare's first choice of the name *Oldcastle* for the fat buffoon who later was rechristened Falstaff was no accident. The historical Sir John Oldcastle, in the fifteenth century, had married into the family of the Lords Cobham. It may not, moreover, have been mere negligence on Shakespeare's part that the original name assumed in the *Merry Wives* by the jealous Ford was *Brooke*. The alteration of 'Oldcastle' to 'Falstaff' and of 'Brooke' to 'Broome' seems to indicate that offence was taken, and had no doubt been intended.

It is clear at any rate that with the death of Hunsdon and the advent of William Brooke, Lord Cobham, the members of the acting profession were exposed to the full force of official London's hostility. The gravity of the situation for Shakespeare's fellow-actors in particular is shown by a reference to them in a letter written by the poet

Tom Nashe to a friend late in the summer of 1596: "now the players . . . are piteously persecuted by the Lord Mayor and the aldermen, and however in their old Lord's time they thought their state settled, it is now so uncertain they cannot build upon it".

Cut off definitively from the lucrative City inn-yards, when acting in the theatres was once more allowed the troupes of players were restricted to the four playhouses in the suburbs—the Theatre and the Curtain in Shoreditch, and the Rose and the new Swan on the Surrey side. By this time two companies had risen to a dominant position in London: the Admiral's Men, with Edward Alleyn, acting at Henslowe's Rose, and their rivals, the late Chamberlain's Men, with Richard Burbage and William Shakespeare, who, as we have seen, had been using the Theatre. There were difficulties, however, with this house, for it had long borne the brunt of Puritan attack; and now James Burbage, its owner (father of Richard Burbage the actor), was involved in a dispute with Giles Allen, his ground landlord, over a renewal of the lease. Burbage was nearly two years behind with his rent. The Theatre was moreover an old building, found to be considerably decayed when

THE INTERIOR OF THE SWAN THEATRE

From the drawing after Johannes de Witt

it was pulled down two years later. Altogether, in 1596 it must have been a disadvantageous and uninviting place. As for the other possible house, the Curtain, in Shoreditch, there is no evidence that Shakespeare and his fellows used it in the autumn of 1596, the date of Shakespeare's arrest in Surrey. The Rose, the only other theatre, was of course out of the question, being pre-empted by the Admiral's Men.

Langley's Swan, in Paris Garden, on the other hand, was new, well-built, and was described as the largest and fairest of all the playhouses. Moreover, it was situated in a manor outside the limits of the borough of Southwark; and even Southwark, though attached to London, was never so strictly under the municipal control as the City proper. Southwark's notorious contempt for the civic authorities is referred to by John Donne in his first Elegy:

> There we will scorn his household policies . . .
> As the inhabitants of Thames' right side
> Do London's Mayor.

To players who had tasted the bitter hostility of the City, the advantages of the Swan were obvious. Shakespeare's fellows might well resolve to leave the older houses with their drawbacks to less important companies, such as the Queen's Men, who had passed their prime, and seek to establish themselves in the impressive new theatre in Paris Garden.

As we have seen, although the Swan must have been finished by the middle of 1595, it has not been known what company or companies of players used it before 1597. Professor Wallace discovered that in February of the latter year a newly formed group of actors, "servants to the right honourable the Earl of Pembroke", contracted with Langley to play at the Swan for one year following. But we also learned from this discovery that these were not the first actors at the Swan, for they later testified in a suit against Langley that the house had been used for plays "lately afore" February 1597. Our new document now points to Shakespeare's fellows, the late Chamberlain's Men, as the recent users in question. With this new light, we now see the force of the remark made by the character Tucca, in Dekker's play *Satiromastix*, which connects the earlier *Hamlet* (acted formerly by the Chamberlain's Men at the Theatre) with the Swan, as follows: "My name's Hamlet revenge: thou hast been at Paris Garden, hast not?" Finally, in my newly discovered document, Shakespeare, a leading member of the late Chamberlain's company, is found joined with Langley, the owner of the Swan.[1]

In short, there is no evidence that Shakespeare and his fellows acted at the Theatre or at the Curtain in the autumn of 1596. We now learn that Shakespeare had moved to the Bankside, and was associated with Francis Langley, the owner of the new playhouse, the Swan, in Paris Garden. The reasonable inference is that his company was then acting at the Swan.

So much of what our new document reveals is clear enough; but the mystery of the threats of violence and death remains. What was the irritating cause of them? And who was William Wayte?

Before seeking light elsewhere, I thought that the Controlment Roll which had already given me this document might yield something more. It was not uncommon, as I had learned, to find that the petitioner for sureties of the peace was retaliating on the person complained of for having

[1] The famous copy of Johannes de Witt's sketch of the interior of the Swan would now take on a new and absorbing interest if one could delimit the date of his visit to London to the autumn of 1596. We might then suppose with some confidence that the scene he there represents as in progress on the stage was enacted by Shakespeare's fellow-comedians.

previously sworn the peace against *him*. I might possibly find therefore that one of these persons complained of in my new document had at some previous time sworn the peace against the present complainant: that is to say, that Langley or Shakespeare might have already sworn the peace against Wayte. Other persons might be found involved, and their names be used as further clues.

Fortune again was on my side, for I now discovered that Langley had indeed previously asked for sureties of the peace against Wayte. Among the earlier entries for Michaelmas term 1596, I turned up the following:

> Angl*ia* ss Franciscus Langley pet*it* securi-*tates* pacis *versus* Will*elmu*m Gardener & Wil-*lelmu*m Wayte ob met*um* mortis &c.
> *Attachiamentum* vic*ecomiti* Surr*eie retornabile* C*rastino animarum*.

> England Be it known that Francis Langley craves sureties of the peace against William Gardener and William Wayte for fear of death, and so forth.
> Writ of attachment issued to the sheriff of Surrey, returnable on the Morrow of All Souls [November 3, 1596].

In our first document we had found Wayte testifying to his fear of Shakespeare and Langley.
Now we discover that Langley, more than three
weeks earlier, had already sworn that not only
Wayte but also a certain William Gardener had
first threatened *him* with death.

This new name, William Gardener, was another
possible source of light; and, as it proved, light
which was to grow in power until it illuminated
the dark region of the unknown.

The problem now set itself thus: I must find out
the identity of these men, Gardener and Wayte,
and with this new knowledge, re-create a hitherto
unknown episode in Shakespeare's life.

I began my search with Gardener's name as a
key. Turning to the rich and conveniently in-
dexed series of State Papers for Elizabeth's reign, I
found his name under the date 1584–85, connected
with the report of a search in a certain suspected
house for 'papists and papistical books'. The
search had been made by the constable and
bailiff of Paris Garden, and the report was taken
and signed by 'William Gardiner, Esquire'.[1]

Evidently this Gardiner was my man; and I suspected from this document that he was a Surrey

[1] State Papers, Domestic, Elizabeth, 176, f. 30.

21

justice of peace, with jurisdiction over the Bankside and Paris Garden. My suspicion was con-
firmed by a glance at the *Acts of the Privy Council*.
Here was the minute of the well-known letters
dated July 28, 1597 (sent by the Privy Council to
the justices of peace for Middlesex and Surrey):
orders elicited by the 'lewd matters' contained in
Tom Nashe's *Isle of Dogs*, a play recently acted by
Pembroke's Men at Langley's theatre, the Swan.
And among the Surrey justices who are hereby
ordered to take harsh steps to suppress the playhouses on the Bankside, we read the name of
'William Gardyner'. Not only therefore is our
William Gardener here proved a justice, but we
find him ordered to cause the stage of the Swan
to be torn down by its owner Langley: Langley,
with whom, as our new document shows, Justice
Gardiner had had a violent quarrel in the autumn
preceding.

The terms of the Privy Council's letters are
severe. The first, addressed to the justices of
Middlesex, commands them in the Queen's name
not only to prohibit all plays until November 1,
1597, but also to "send for the owners of the Curtain Theatre or any other common playhouse and
enjoin them by virtue hereof forthwith to pluck

down quite the stages, galleries, and rooms that are made for people to stand in, and so to deface the same as they may not be employed again to such use; which if they shall not speedily perform, you shall advertise us, that order may be taken to see the same done according to Her Majesty's pleasure and commandment". The second letter is addressed to "Mr. Bowier, William Gardyner, and Bartholomew Scott, esquires, and the rest of the Justices of Surrey, requiring them to take the like order for the playhouses in the Bankside, in Southwark, or elsewhere in the said county within three miles of London".[1]

Less than a year, then, after Langley's violent quarrel of 1596 with Justice Gardiner, we find that the latter was under orders from the Council to send for the theatre-owner and command him to wreck his playhouse. No unwelcome duty, in the circumstances! Luckily for theatrical London, however, the harsh order for demolition was reconsidered in season, and the stages and galleries were suffered to stand. Langley was nevertheless punished for having allowed the 'slanderous and seditious' *Isle of Dogs* to be acted in his house. For in the autumn, when Henslowe was permitted to

---

[1] Dasent, *Acts of the Privy Council*, xxvii, 313.

reopen the Rose, we know that Langley could get no licence to show plays at the Swan.

But this is to anticipate. Our business at present is not with the brush between Justice Gardiner and Francis Langley in 1597 over the *Isle of Dogs* and the Privy Council's order, but with their quarrel of 1596, involving Wayte and Shakespeare.

Thus far I had shed more light on Langley, and established the identity of Gardiner, but Wayte remained a *tertium quid*. It seemed from the document that he should be connected somehow with Justice Gardiner. In search of evidence in this direction, I had recourse to the records of the equity side of the Exchequer, which in due time gratified me by yielding a suit dated 1591, brought by Thomas Heron, gentleman, an under-marshal of the Court of Exchequer, against William Gardiner of Southwark, Surrey, and William Wayte.[1] Gardiner is described in Heron's bill of complaint as "a justice of the peace", and Wayte is slightingly set down as "a certain loose person of no reckoning or value, being wholly under the rule and commandment of the said Gardiner". This unflattering description of Wayte simplified the situation for me. As a hanger-on and tool of Gar-

[1] Exchequer Bills and Answers, Eliz. and James I., Surrey, 40.

diner's, Wayte now took a properly subordinate position in the picture. Evidently the central figures in the quarrel were Gardiner on the one side and Langley and Shakespeare on the other: local justice of peace against theatre-owner and player. Thus defined, the problem emerged not only absorbing but challenging. I should have no peace until it was solved.

At this point the proper move seemed to be to go through the chief series of judicial records for 1596 in search of some clue to the quarrel. The courts of Queen's Bench and Common Pleas, because of the richness of their materials, commended themselves for this purpose, and I plunged hopefully into their docket rolls. Once more I was not disappointed, for they led me to no less than three separate suits, which Justice Gardiner brought against Francis Langley, for slander. All three were recorded in Michaelmas term 1596, the very term of the already discovered petitions for sureties of the peace. Two of these actions had been entered in the Queen's Bench in Easter term preceding, and one in the Common Pleas. In the Queen's Bench suits, Gardiner alleges that on two occasions in the spring, May 21 and May 22, at Croydon, Surrey, Langley publicly and slanderously said of him, "He is a false knave, and a false perjured knave; and I will prove him so". Gardiner asserts that his reputation has been damaged by these remarks to the value of a thousand pounds each.[1] In the suit in the Common Pleas, Langley is alleged to have said of Gardiner, again at Croydon, but on June 1, "He is a false knave; a false, forsworn knave, and a perjured knave". For this Gardiner demands two hundred pounds damages.[2]

Langley's defence to each of the three charges is the same. He maintains, adducing records to prove his statement, that in a suit in the Court of Wards a few years before, Gardiner, in giving false testimony under oath, has committed wilful and corrupt perjury. Consequently it is no slander to call him a false, perjured knave, and Gardiner's action will not lie—that is to say, be valid in a court of judicature. Gardiner in reply insists that Langley's words were not occasioned by this alleged perjury, but by "his own wrong"; and that he should therefore have his action for slander. It is to be noted, however, that none of these three suits was prosecuted to a trial. Evidently Gardiner was 'slandered with matter of truth'. No

[1] K.B. 27/1340/425, 433.　　　　[2] C.P. 40/1578/2638.

SIGNATURES OF WILLIAM GARDINER, WILLIAM WAYTE,
FRANCIS LANGLEY, AND WILLIAM SHAKESPEARE

1. Wÿllÿm̄ Gardyn^r [Wyllyam Gardyner.   1584,
   13 July.   Aged about 53.—State Papers,
   Domestic, Elizabeth, 172, f. 49.]

2. Wÿllÿm̄ Gardyn^r [Wyllyam Gardyner.   ?1584/5,
   27 January.   Aged about 53.—State Papers,
   Domestic, Elizabeth, 176, f. 30.]

3. Wÿllÿ Wayte [Wyllyam Wayte. 1595, 23 August.
   Aged 40.—Star Chamber Proceedings, Elizabeth, G19/28.]

4. Wyllyā Wayte [Wyllyam Wayte. 1602, 26 March.
   Aged 47. — Town Depositions, Chancery,
   Bundle 294 (pt. 1), 5.]

5. ffrç Langlay [Francis Langlay.   1600, 30 April.
   Aged about 50.—Star Chamber Proceedings,
   Elizabeth, S18/8.]

6. Wīllm̄ Shakp [William Shakspere. 1612, 11 May.
   Aged 48.—Court of Requests, Uncalendared
   Proceedings, Belott v. Mountjoy. Discovered
   by Professor C. W. Wallace.]

doubt when Langley brought forward his evidence of Gardiner's perjury on record, his angry opponent felt less confident of the strength of his suits for slander, and did not care to risk a jury trial, with its public airing of the evidence as to his character. He abandoned his claims for £2200 damages.

We are not told what made Langley so incensed with Justice Gardiner in the spring of 1596 as to stigmatize him publicly and repeatedly as a false, perjured knave. But we do know that he successfully roused Gardiner's spleen against him. By the autumn, irritation had mounted to such a pitch, as we have seen by our new documents, that threats of violence were bandied between Gardiner, joined with his henchman Wayte, and Langley and Shakespeare.

Whatever may have started the quarrel, it is fair to infer that, in the autumn of 1596, Gardiner, to get some satisfaction for the vile name he had been given, was doing his best to revenge himself on Langley. The City's attack on the playhouses was at its height. Langley's most vulnerable point was therefore his position as owner of a theatre. Using his power as justice of peace in Southwark, and seconded by the lord mayor and the aldermen, Gardiner could piteously persecute Langley and Shakespeare and his fellow-actors at the Swan. The latter, however, though deprived of their strong support in the Privy Council, had nevertheless a present protector in their new patron, Sir George Carey, now Lord Hunsdon after his father's death. As for the wealthy and energetic Langley, he was far from defenceless. Whenever therefore Justice Gardiner may have descended on them in person, or through the medium of his man Wayte, in an attempt to put the Swan out of business, they were prepared to resist him.

The 'false knave' Justice Gardiner and the 'loose person' William Wayte, by their assault on the embattled Langley and Shakespeare, took on an absorbing interest. I set out eagerly to learn everything I could about these fascinating enemies of our men of the theatre; and with every new-found fact their interest grew.

THE LIFE OF JUSTICE GARDINER

> I know he got his wealth with a hard gripe . . .
> He would eat fools and ignorant heirs clean up—
> And had his drink from many a poor man's brow
> E'en as their labour brewed it.
> He would scrape riches to him most unjustly;
> The very dirt between his nails was ill got,
> And not his own.
>   *The Puritan*, ii, 1.

IT will sufficiently appear that the above description may be not unfairly applied to the Southwark justice who attacked Langley and Shakespeare. His life, as I have woven it together from new documents, will grow before our eyes into a tissue of greed, usury, fraud, cruelty, and perjury: of crime, in short, enough to make him a marked man even in the Elizabethan age. We shall see him lending money at ten in the hundred, defrauding his wife's family, his son-in-law, and his stepson, oppressing his neighbours, and rack-renting his poor tenants. By these and similar means he will amass great wealth, and at the close of the chapter die detested.

By reckoning his years from his funeral certificate we learn that he was born about 1531, the younger son of William Gardiner, a yeoman or gentleman who farmed Bermondsey Grange, on the borders of Southwark. As a youth, the future Surrey justice was most probably sent to one of the Inns of Chancery, the schools of law subsidiary to the great Inns of Court. Some knowledge of the law was considered essential to the education of an Elizabethan gentleman; but Gardiner used his as a foundation for his later mastery of sly law-tricks.

Our first document brings him into view in 1555, on the wrong side of a lawsuit; for he was convicted and heavily fined in that year for breaking a fence and pasturing his cattle on a neighbour's land. In the same year, we find a certain William Gardiner obtaining from Cardinal Pole a dispensation to eat flesh in Lent, on the ground that his ailments made the consumption of fish injurious to his constitution. If this Gardiner be our hero, his health very soon improved on an uninterrupted diet of meat; for in the following year we find our Gardiner of Southwark strong enough to 'make a fray and draw blood upon' another young gentleman, William Beeston, for which feat of arms he paid a fine of three shillings and fourpence. His first recorded misdeeds are, therefore, breaking into a neighbour's pasture with his hungry cows, and a sanguinary brawl with swords. The eluding of fish is doubtful.

But to grow rich rapidly, which was his main concern, the quickest means was to engage in trade in the City; and, like everyone else, Gardiner had to secure the privileges of a citizen of London before he could barter in the metropolis. The necessary step was to become 'free of the city' by gaining admission to one of the livery companies—the Elizabethan successors of the medieval craft gilds. Accordingly in the autumn of 1556 we find him buying himself into the Company of the Grey Tawyers, the dressers or workers of grey skins and leathers. We remember that John Shakespeare, the poet's father, was called a glover or white tawyer (whittawer, whittier), a worker in white leathers. Gardiner, however, did not propose to work, but to lend money, buy, and sell. He had no knowledge of tawing, and did not want to taw. Yet it seems that he got in among the workers in leather by false pretences, for we find a complaint lodged in the Lord Mayor's Court to the effect that Gardiner was 'not skilful in the said art, nor yet [did] practise the same'.

On his brother Richard's death at about this time, William Gardiner succeeded to his father's very substantial estate in Bermondsey, a property which he promptly increased by marriage in 1558.

His wife was Frances, widow of the late Edmund Wayte, a prosperous leatherseller of Bermondsey, and eldest daughter of another rich leatherseller, Robert Luce or Lucy, gentleman, of London. Robert Luce had been Second Warden of the Leathersellers' Company in 1554–1555; and in the following year Edmund Wayte had served as First Warden or Master of the Company. By this marriage it will be seen that Gardiner secured to himself the estates of these two wealthy citizens, for on her mother's death Frances (Luce) Wayte administered her father's property. By her first husband, Edmund Wayte, she had had two sons, the elder of whom in 1558 was fourteen years old and his father's heir. This son must have died, for we learn by a later document that his rights passed to William Wayte (now discovered as Shakespeare's adversary), a younger brother, born about 1555. How shamefully and systematically William Wayte was defrauded by his stepfather Gardiner, and how the latter went further and cheated his wife's brother and sisters of their shares in their father Robert Luce's large estate, we shall see when we come to the appropriate passages in the story of his life.

Meanwhile, following the example of his wife's

and a note on the record shows that Gardiner was very properly obliged to abandon the suit.

The year 1567 furnishes three items revealing various sides of Gardiner's perverse nature. We read that the Leathersellers fined him for failing to pay them certain arrears, and that they had paid sixteen shillings "charges in the law for controversies of William Gardiner". In the Court of Queen's Bench on another occasion we learn that he was fined £10 for making a false claim.

In the next year, 1568, Gardiner appears again in the Court of Queen's Bench, actuated, as we shall see, by vengeful malice. The record shows that he prosecuted an upholsterer, one Thomas Ducke, on a charge of perjury, and demanded the full penalty of the law for that crime—£20 fine (half for himself and half for the Queen, as the law provided)—insisting that if the unfortunate man could not pay, "he should be nailed by the ears to the pillory": thus pressing for the full barbarity of the statute. Luckily for our clearer understanding of the rights of the case, Ducke's own account of the affair, given in another connection some years later, has been preserved. From this it appears that he had stirred up Gardiner's hatred by testifying against him at a trial in which the latter had been convicted of wrongfully selling a certain Humphry Baker's furniture and appropriating the proceeds. For this offence Gardiner had been fined £13 12d. In recalling the details of Gardiner's vengeful prosecution of him for perjury, Ducke says, "the point of the supposed perjury consisted in this: [I] deposed in a suit before the Justices of Assize at Croydon . . . in the suit between [Gardiner] and [one Baker] that certain goods—as a table in a frame, and stools, mattress, and such other things—were lying and standing in [Gardiner's] house . . . and thereupon [Gardiner] endeavoured to prove [me] perjured, because he supposed the said tables and such other things were not standing; and so, having a jury whom he had in some awe, and some his poor neighbours, found this poor deponent guilty of perjury. And afterwards [as I laboured] to attaint the jury (as indeed [I] had done if Mr. Justice Southcote had not taken up the matter), Mr. Gardiner, unexpectedly on [my] part, sought an end and agreement at [my] hand."

Here is revealing testimony. According to Ducke, Gardiner prosecuted him for perjury on a quibbling point before a packed jury, which had reason to be afraid of the rich rascal. Knowing that the jury had been corruptly empanelled, Ducke challenged it; but Mr. Justice Southcote took the affair in hand (perhaps to save appearances) and no doubt advised Gardiner to drop his malicious prosecution. What a picture of Gardiner's unscrupulous use of power and legal corruption for purposes of revenge!

Though he frequently found leisure to indulge his malicious stomach in prosecutions of this sort, Gardiner bent his chief energies on the more gainful activity of scraping riches to himself. The list of his acquisitions of large pieces of landed property, as I find it in the records, grows steadily with the years. And in spite of the obnoxious behaviour already recorded and his detestable disposition, his wealth made him rise in the ranks of the Leathersellers. The Company had four leading officers or wardens, elected annually, ranging from Fourth or Junior Warden to First Warden or Master; and we learn that Gardiner served as Fourth Warden in 1568–1569, and as an auditor in 1570, though in 1573 he was again fined by the Company forty shillings "for words spoken by him".

An interesting link between Gardiner and John Shakespeare, the poet's father, comes to light in the discovery of a suit which the latter prosecuted in the Court of Common Pleas in Easter and Trinity terms 1572, against John Luther, a Banbury glover, for payment of a debt of £50 contracted on June 16, 1571. Shakespeare, we find, received judgment to recover his £50 with 33s. 4d. damages, but we are not told whether he obtained the money.[1]

It is instructive to note that Henry Burr, the London attorney who appeared for John Shakespeare in this suit, was also William Gardiner's lawyer at this period. It is not impossible that John Shakespeare, the ex-bailiff of Stratford, in

[1] C.P. 40/1304/910d. Trinity 14 Eliz.
London. John Luther, late of London, glover, *alias* John Luther of Banbury, Oxon., glover, was summoned to answer John Shaxbere of Stretford on Avon in co. Warwick, yeoman, in a plea that he owed him £50, etc. And John Shaxbere, by Henry Burr his attorney, said that John Luther on 16 June 13 Eliz. at London by a certain writing obligatory had acknowledged himself bound to the same John Shaxbere in the aforesaid £50 to be paid on demand. The said John Shaxbere had been damaged to the value of £10. And he produced there in Court the writing. And John Luther, by Thomas Gardener his attorney, came and defended force and injury, etc. It was considered that John Shaxbere should recover his debt and 33s. 4d. damages. [An earlier reference to the same suit, Easter 14 Eliz., mem. 1410, cannot be traced, as the plea roll on which it is contained is unfit for production. I owe the discovery of this new light on John Shakespeare to the help of my friends Mr. J. H. Morrison and Miss N. McN. O'Farrell.]

his visits to Henry Burr in London, came into contact with another client, the rich swindler and money-lender who was to persecute his son some fifteen years later.

But during these fifteen intervening years Gardiner was busy with nefarious practices, some of which brought him money, and all of which intensified the bad odour of his name. For example, we find him in 1573 playing one of his typical tricks on a fellow-leatherseller, Ralph Walker. Though Walker had paid in full a sum of £50 due on a bill, Gardiner nevertheless kept the bill uncancelled, and put it in suit afterwards to force Walker to pay another £50. Walker complained of Gardiner's dishonest attempt in the Court of Requests; and a witness in this suit on his behalf, one Thomas Kendall, gentleman (who had tried in vain to collect £3 that Gardiner owed *him*), gives us in his deposition a taste of Gardiner's unsavoury character, as follows: ". . . meeting with the said Gardiner in Southwark, [I] demanded the said £3 again of the said Gardiner, who denied the same again; and then [I] asked him again if that he were not paid his said £50 of the said Walker; who said, 'Yes, I am fully satisfied, contented, and paid; but yet I have his bill for the said £50 yet remaining in my hands'. And [I] asked him wherefore he did keep the said bill, being fully satisfied, contented, and paid; and then the said Gardiner answered that in keeping of the said bill he had a meaning which [I] should not know, and then [I] departed." Gardiner's secret meaning became perfectly plain when he used the bill, as we have seen, as the ground for a dishonest prosecution at law. It is to be hoped that he was restrained from robbing Walker.

Gardiner went back and forth between the city and his suburban Bermondsey, and it is clear that to his predatory activity among his business associates he added raids on the pocket-books of his neighbours and tenants in Bermondsey. It appears that in October 1577 some of the latter, driven beyond their endurance, turned on him with threats of violence; for in that month we discover Gardiner begging in the Court of Queen's Bench for sureties of the peace, swearing that two groups of four persons each in Surrey had threatened him with death or mutilation. Two of these persons, John Strangman and his wife Eleanor, I have identified as neighbours of Gardiner's in Bermondsey. With no additional details to help us, we are left to conclude either that his ill-treat-

ment had goaded them into threatening him, or
that his oath against them was false, and his proceeding a malicious and vengeful means of annoy-
ing them. However that may be, Gardiner certainly hounded Strangman in the law. After he
had sworn the peace against him, Gardiner got a
judgment in the Court of Common Pleas against
Strangman on an action of trespass and a writ of
execution to the sheriff to raise £120 on the latter's
goods; and in a further suit we find him alleging
that Strangman had carried off forty cartloads of
his hay.

Execrated though he was, and with reason, in
Bermondsey and among his fellows in the Company of Leathersellers in the City, the records
show that Gardiner nevertheless served as Second
Warden of that Company in 1577–1578. No doubt
the Leathersellers had certain ends to serve in
electing him to office, but such a character as his
could hardly have added to the dignity or pres-
tige of the Company.

We now come to a passage in Gardiner's life by
which he aggravated his already heavy load of ill-
repute. Thomas Radcliffe, third Earl of Sussex,
who was Elizabeth's Lord Chamberlain and a
deadly enemy of her 'gypsy favourite' Leicester,

lived near Gardiner in Bermondsey. The Queen had visited the Earl there twice in 1571, when he lay 'very sick'. At least as early as 1579, Gardiner, though already a rich man, had attached himself to the Earl, entering that great official's 'service' no doubt, as we shall see, for certain advantages and immunities which Sussex's protection might afford him. Associated with him, of course, in the Lord Chamberlain's household was the famous company of players which acted frequently before the Queen at Court. This new light on Gardiner reveals the fact that he had been in touch with actors long before his quarrel with Langley and Shakespeare.

Our first indication that Gardiner gained by sheltering under the protection of the Lord Chamberlain comes from the year 1579, when we find a certain William Stedman complaining to the Privy Council that Gardiner, by altering the terms of an indenture, was trying to cheat him. The Council, which naturally included Gardiner's master Sussex, called Gardiner up and made some effort to put matters right; but later documents show that his crafty crookedness evaded their purpose, and that he made at least £100 clear out of his dealings in Stedman's land.

As a very wealthy citizen, Gardiner was now liable to election as one of the two sheriffs of the City. None but rich men were called to this dignity, for the honour was a burden, and cost its incumbent sometimes as much as £20,000 a year in modern values; for "in London, if anywhere in the world, *honos vere onus est*", as William Smith tells us, in his *Brief Description of the Famous City of London*, adding that "the estate and charge that one sheriff in London keepeth amounteth sometimes to £2500 that year". In the summer of 1579 Gardiner was duly elected to this expensive office of sheriff; but, greedy as ever to get other men's money and determined to hold what he had got, he promptly refused to serve, pretending that his duties as servant to the Lord Chamberlain made it impossible for him to accept the position. He thus incurred the usual fine of £200 imposed on citizens who upon their election refused to serve. This fine he declined to pay. Thereupon the Lord Mayor and the Aldermen took the suit to the Lord Chief Justice, in an effort to enforce payment by law; but to lend a colour to his excuse that he was already occupied on the Lord Chamberlain's affairs of state, Gardiner quickly undertook an errand for the Privy Council into Munster,

Ireland. The City authorities were not, however, to be put off so lightly, and on his return Gardiner was faced with their demand for the unpaid fine. His next shift was to persuade his master Sussex to write a letter to the Lord Mayor's Court in his favour. By this intercession of the Lord Chamberlain's, the fine was reluctantly reduced from £200 to £50. But, true to his miserly nature, Gardiner refused to pay even this small amount.

The Lord Mayor and his colleagues were then obliged to write to the Lord Chamberlain, reminding him that "for your Lordship's sake we remitted unto him £150, and abated his fine to £50 only; wherein we beseech your Lordship to remember that for precedent's sake more we could not do for him, and in that which we have done (the fine being not ours but the Commonalty's) we can hardly defend the favour showed him if it should be known to the body of the City, but we should be enforced either to pay it ourselves or to bear greater blame than we gladly would or can with our good reputation. Now Mr. Gardiner, being called upon for this small sum of £50, doth not only not acknowledge the favour showed him for your sake, but also refuseth to obey our order therein. . . . Because we are loath to take our remedy by law against him (being your servant) without first making you privy of the case, we pray your Lordship to take our doing in good part, and command him quietly to take benefit of our said abatement of his fine and to pay the said sum of £50, that we be not for precedent and for our discharge toward the Commons enforced to seek what we ought and may by law; which being once disclosed cannot be less than the whole sum of £200, unless the Common Council discharge him; which we wish him for his own sake not to essay and put all in peril."

Still Gardiner refused to pay; and it was not until 1582, three years after his first refusal to serve, that the City finally forced him by law to pay the £50 fine. The authorities had good reason to be disgusted with so rich a man's evasion of his duty, and were in no mind to let him escape so easily. They waited, however, until his master Sussex was dead; and in the summer of 1585 again elected Gardiner sheriff. When he again gave "his direct and plain answer . . . that he would not accept and take upon him the execution of the said office", they fined him £200. Yet again he defaulted. The Lord Mayor sued him before Lord Chief Justice Anderson; but perhaps the wily

Gardiner had prudently ingratiated himself with Anderson (who as we know was later his friend). At any rate I can find no record that he ever paid this fine.

Grown rich by money-lending and fraud, though he might repeatedly refuse an expensive honour and evade the consequent fines, Gardiner was nevertheless not averse to seeking dignified position, provided the cost was small. Marston's observations on the typical usurer are very apt for him:

> Yet with good honest cut-throat usury
> I fear he'll mount to reverend dignity.
> O sleight! all-canning sleight! all-damning sleight!
> The only galley-ladder unto might.

A promotion to public office would indeed bring increase of power to Gardiner, but we may agree with Anthony Fletcher that it would be a bad thing for the government of England: "the usurer serveth for nothing but Hell; and howsoever he thriveth here, he shall be surely pinched there. It were well (in my opinion) if usurers were censured now in our days as they were in times past: in those days they were never called to any office in the church nor commonwealth. For what right, justice, or equity could be looked for at their hands which were most unnatural and cruel oppressors of their brethren?"[1]

The money with which Gardiner was gilded covered his glaring vices, and in the summer of 1580 we find that he rose from gentleman to esquire on being included in the royal commission for Surrey as a justice of peace. His district was Brixton Hundred, which comprised Southwark, Paris Garden, Bermondsey, Camberwell, and neighbouring places. The following year saw his name pricked or chosen as one of the *quorum*— the select body of justices "eminent for learning or prudence", the presence of two or more of whom was necessary before felonies and other misdemeanours could be inquired of and determined. From the records we learn that Gardiner continued in the *quorum* until his death in 1597. An examination of the files of the Surrey clerk of the peace reveals him as by far the busiest justice in the county. His total of recorded committals to prison during his years of office is 297, as against the 193 of his nearest competitor on the bench, Edmund Bowyer of Camberwell, over the same period. This great number of committals must be taken as evidence that Gardiner's jurisdiction

[1] *Certaine . . . similes* (1595), 123.

was over the most thickly settled and criminal region of Surrey, namely, Southwark.

From what we have seen and are soon to learn of Justice Gardiner, I can imagine no man fitter to illustrate the words of Lear: "See how yond justice rails upon yon simple thief. Hark in thine ear: change places; and, handy-dandy, which is the justice, which is the thief? . . . The usurer hangs the cozener. Through tatter'd clothes small vices do appear; Robes and furr'd gowns hide all."

Judicial duties were never suffered to stand in the way of our crooked justice's lease-mongering and money-mongering; and exacting the full penalty of bonds if payments were delayed a day beyond their date, he frequently "fatted his fingers with many rich forfeitures". One of his favourite shifts was to pretend friendship only to entrap a victim: in the words of Anthony Fletcher, "under colour of love and friendship to take his neighbour by the hand and lift him up, to the end he might give him a greater fall". One such episode is disclosed in 1582 by Thomas Waade, a gentleman of Gray's Inn, in a complaint in Chancery that his father-in-law was cruelly tricked and robbed of his dwelling-house by Gardiner, who pretended to help him and actually cheated him, "as by his subtle dealing before, and sinister practices after, may probably appear". The contemptible trick, Waade tells us, was turned; and Gardiner, coming to seize the poor man's household goods, "behaved himself with such insolency [that] he gave not only great grief and corresy"—corrosive, mental pain—to the daughter and her old father, but by his actions "brought tears even from his [own] servant or friend whom he set as a watchman in the said house". Not content with this heartless treatment of such defenceless victims, Gardiner was now moving to grind the son-in-law, Thomas Waade, and we find the latter entreating the Lord Chancellor to give relief, "for the repressing of so foul and unchristian [an] enterprise".

Some of Gardiner's most foul and unchristian enterprises were reserved, I have found, for his own relatives. In his cormorant-like fishing for fools, family ties were no obstacle: those nearest without any compunction were expeditiously devoured. Two examples of the predatory justice's preying upon his relatives, which offer interest by their contrast, are his treatment of his stepson William Wayte and of his daughter Katherine's husband, John Stepkin. Wayte was systematically swindled throughout his whole association with Gardiner—almost forty years—and apparently was kept dangling in continued hope of better days; whereas Stepkin's agonies, though sharper, were comparatively brief.

By the death of his elder brother, as we have seen, William Wayte had fallen heir to his father's estate. This occurred not long after his mother's marriage to Gardiner in 1558. It is now clear from later documents that though the father had died wealthy, Gardiner kept young William out of his inheritance, and employed him as a servant to further his own ends. We have already quoted the contemptuous mention of Wayte in 1591 as a "loose person of no reckoning or value, being wholly under the rule and commandment of the said Gardiner". More proof that Gardiner kept him poor is found in the lay subsidy or tax rolls. Here Wayte's name first appears in 1598, the year following Justice Gardiner's death, his goods then being appraised for taxation at less than a tenth of what his father's property had been in 1556. Not only did Gardiner take Wayte's inheritance from him, but he used him as a hook to get more; for we find that the justice married his kinsman to an heiress about the year 1580, only to gull him of the property she brought with her. It is only too plain that the avaricious justice "would eat fools and ignorant heirs clean up".

After such experiences as these at Gardiner's hands, there is something pitiful in Wayte's hanging on in the belief that his stepfather would perhaps keep a promise, or some day do him some sort of right. Gardiner must have assured the long-suffering gull that by his will he would restore something of what he had stolen from him. He even went so far, we find, as to put him into his will for a modest bequest of £66 13s. 4d., together with a lease of some land that should have come to him from his father, adding legacies of £50 apiece for Wayte's young children, payable when they should come of age. Before he died, however, the crafty old churl made a new will which excluded Wayte entirely, and reduced the children's portions to £40 apiece.

To be cut off without a farthing: this was William Wayte's reward after long years spent in subserving the covetous ends of his stepfather, in whose thankless service in 1596, as our newly discovered Shakespeare document shows, he may have earned a blow or two from Francis Langley or William Shakespeare, or both. And yet at

Gardiner's funeral, a fortnight after the will had been proved and he had learned how he had been cheated of every last penny, we meet the disinherited Wayte, walking in solemn black, bearing with pathetic pomp the pennon of Gardiner's arms. No doubt his mind had been so completely subjected to Gardiner's that even if he knew his kinsman for a scamp and a cheat, the justice would always be for his weak stepson a great rich scamp and a worshipful cheat.

After Gardiner had been dead some years, Wayte apparently plucked up sufficient courage to make a fumbling attempt to claim part of the Gardiner property; for we discover him in 1602 bringing suit in Chancery against Gardiner's son William for a half-share in a large estate which it seems the justice had purchased in their joint names. A most futile and foolish attempt, doomed to certain failure; for to this part of the Gardiner estate Wayte had not the shadow of a right. There is a bare possibility, however, that this suit may have been a 'friendly' proceeding which young Gardiner persuaded Wayte to institute in order to clear his (Gardiner's) title. But whichever it was, *bona fide* litigation or 'friendly' suit, Wayte got nothing out of it.

The end of the story of this pitiful dupe and tool of the evil justice is written in the records of 1603, the year of the great plague. The pestilence swept Wayte and his second wife away together; and on August 29, 1603, they were buried in Bermondsey with twenty-nine of their neighbours.

William Wayte has been completely forgotten for more than three centuries. But from now on his place in literary biography is secure. As long as men continue to read the story of Shakespeare's life, Wayte will be recalled as the unfortunate fellow who—doubtless at the putting-on of Justice Gardiner—picked a quarrel with the actor-dramatist, and swore in Court that Shakespeare had menaced him with death and mutilation.

We must leave him to enjoy his belated fame, and proceed to an account of Gardiner's treatment of his son-in-law John Stepkin. This young man was tricked just as cruelly as Wayte, but he showed more spirit when he discovered Gardiner's knavery. A gentleman of a good estate in Whitechapel, we find Stepkin enmeshed in the cunning justice's net in 1581. With fair words Gardiner drew him on to take his daughter Katherine in marriage, promising him a handsome dowry with her hand, and craftily persuading the young man not to take any legal advice in the matter except from him. We learn that after the justice had secured an excellent jointure from Stepkin, the marriage took place. It then became clear that not only would Gardiner keep none of his promises, but that he was setting out to drive his son-in-law to utter ruin with all possible speed by unconscionable use of quirks of the law.

Let us hear Stepkin, after his discovery of the villainous plan, begging Queen Elizabeth through her Court of Star Chamber to give him justice against the swindler. Stigmatizing Gardiner as "a man inclined to strange opinions, and using hard and strait dealing towards some of Your Majesty's subjects", he goes on to say that his unnatural father-in-law "did mean nothing else but fraud towards [me], and to beguile and deceive [me] in those things wherein both honesty and fatherly love should have urged him to have done and dealt plainly. . . . [He] boasteth and greatly glorieth in that he hath so defrauded and deceived [me] in matching his . . . daughter with [me] by such fraud, deceit, and evil dealing." It will appear that what Stepkin meant by his phrase "a man inclined to strange opinions" was to charge Gardiner with atheism, or at the least with irreligious beliefs. This is a new and (to an Elizabethan mind) an abominable side of Gardiner's character.

Later, when Gardiner after long delay has put in an answer to the charges of fraud, Stepkin points out that "he hath not replied in all this time; the which argueth that he is greatly ashamed to proceed, lest his lewd and unhonest dealing should now be manifested unto the world; although he be a man already of whom the world generally speaketh evil . . . and especially all those that have had any dealing with him at all, by reason of his hard conscience and corrupt dealing; but for the opinion of the world [he] little regardeth, as he hath very often in speeches affirmed, saying, he careth not what the world thinketh of him, for he hath money enough".

Stepkin's specific charges against Gardiner in this suit were corroborated by one Thomas Kynge, clerk, aged 70, who had been a witness of their conversations. Kynge further swore he had heard Gardiner voice the damnable opinion "that God hath nothing to do with the world since He created it, and that the world was not governed by Him". It is certainly difficult to see how Gardiner could have squared his conduct with any belief in God's ruling of human affairs.

More evidence on the victimizing of Stepkin was
furnished after the young man's death by his
mother and her second husband, William Chester,
esquire, who informed the Queen in the Court of
Exchequer in 1587 that "Gardiner, having by his
fair promises obtained that thing which he desired [viz. the jointure on Stepkin's marriage with
his daughter], performed nothing which he promised, but endeavoured for his own private lucre
and profit rather to hurt and hinder the said Stepkin than to benefit him".

We find that Stepkin did not long survive his ill-
treatment at Gardiner's hands. A certain Mary
Rowland, who as we are told attended him in his
last illness, deposed (in a suit brought on other
grounds against Gardiner in the Star Chamber)
in February 1588 as follows: "She hath heard the
said Stepkin say that he had preferred a bill into
this honourable Court against [Gardiner] containing such bad matters as be mentioned in this interrogatory [sc. 'for witchcraft, sorcery, keeping of
two toads, holding of irreligious opinions']." As
we have already seen, only the last of these 'bad
matters', namely, the charge of irreligious opinions,
had actually been included by Stepkin in his complaint against Gardiner. No doubt he intended to

56

THE LIFE OF JUSTICE GARDINER

superadd accusations of sorcery and the keeping
of two toads (presumably either as 'familiars' or
to furnish what was believed to be poison); but
these particulars are not to be found in the original
suit. In her deposition, Mary Rowland added
that Stepkin, "in the time of his sickness whereof he died, would exclaim against the said Mr.
Gardiner . . . and seemed to be of opinion and
conceit that the ill-usage and dealings he had
received at [Gardiner's] hands was the very cause
of his sickness; and in the extremity of his sickness, when he could but even stir himself, would
cry out and say 'Oh, that I had him here!'—meaning the said [Gardiner]—'He is the cause of my
sickness!'" Before he died Stepkin nevertheless
"did very Christian-like forgive the said Mr.
Gardiner".

According to Mary Rowland, Stepkin had also
said "that the said Mr. Gardiner was of so devilish
opinion that he thought there was no God; and
that He had no government in the world; and that
no man would care how he lived because he was
predestinated either to salvation or damnation".
The inconsistency of Gardiner's alleged utterances
—a denial of the existence of God side by side
with an admission that God existed but had

nothing to do with the world—did not diminish their devilish character for an Elizabethan mind. The alleged fatalistic rejection of the Christian tenet of justification by faith made manifest by works was equally damnable.

Atheism, witchcraft, sorcery, keeping of two toads—no accusation was too bad to be flung in Gardiner's face by the unfortunate who had suffered by his malice, greed, and lies.

So much, then, for Gardiner's treatment of his stepson and son-in-law. I have found that his brother-in-law John Luce and his sisters-in-law Sara (Luce) Manley and Elizabeth (Luce) Bullard also fell a prey to his rapacity. It will be recalled that the justice's wife was Frances, the daughter of Robert Luce or Lucy, and that on her mother's death she took administration of her father's estate. From the records it is clear that Gardiner persuaded her to attempt to defraud her father's creditors; and it is also evident that Gardiner managed to hold Luce's money even after his wife Frances Gardiner's death in 1576, and thereby to exclude the above-named surviving children of Luce from their rightful inheritance.

Thus shamefully wronged, Luce's heirs made ineffectual efforts to obtain justice, and succeeded only in incurring Gardiner's hate. In 1584 Gardiner caught up John Bullard (Elizabeth Luce's husband) and sued him on a charge of slander for saying, "Master Gardiner's wife was forsworn by the procurement of Master Gardiner". Although Bullard defended the truth of his words with evidence to prove that Frances (Luce) Gardiner had sworn to a lie at her husband's instigation, Gardiner obtained a verdict against him from a jury of Southwark men (among whom he was generally feared), and exacted costs and damages of £17 1s., a sum which John Luce and Martin Manley (Sara Luce's husband) helped the unfortunate Bullard to pay. And not satisfied with having already cheated the Luces of their inheritance, Gardiner brought suit against John Luce (at the same time as the action for slander against Bullard) for a debt of £6 on a recent bond, and made him pay not only the £6 due, but an additional £5 16s. 8d. for damages, costs, and charges. Still not content with the harm he had done his wife's family, the implacable justice, though he had their patrimony in his hands, further vexed Robert Luce's heirs in the Prerogative Court of Canterbury, alleging that they had taken some of their father's estate which should have been administered by Gardiner's deceased wife Frances. They were forced to petition for a court decree which freed them from the charge.

Gardiner further schemed to lure Bullard into denouncing him before witnesses, that he might trap him in words that would bear action for slander. Fortunately we have a circumstantial account of the underhanded plot and of how it was frustrated, given, not without humour, under oath in the Star Chamber, by Henry Davy, a young gentleman of Lincoln's Inn, as follows:

Davy (who is mentioned throughout in the customary third person as 'the deponent') said that he knew one John Bullard, because he was the tenant of his (the deponent's) father; and that William Gardiner came to Lincoln's Inn with the deponent's father's servant William Greene; and Gardiner said to them both that if they "would procure the said Bullard to break his fast with one William Hartford his [Gardiner's?] cousin, he (the said Hartford) should accompany him to the said breakfast; and withal earnestly persuaded this deponent and the said Greene to give out some hard speeches of the said Gardiner, thereby to draw the said Bullard to deliver some hard speeches against him (the said Mr. Gardiner), to the end that, the same speeches being spoken in their hearings and presences, they might be witnesses of the speeches, and so thereby the said Gardiner might take his advantage against the said Bullard. Nevertheless, this deponent and the said Greene (noting a circumventious and ungodly meaning in the said Mr. Gardiner, unduly to draw the said Bullard into danger) did give intelligence thereof unto the said Bullard; and (notwithstanding the same intelligence, had a meaning as well to see the issue of this purpose as also not to lose the breakfast offered as aforesaid) went to breakfast accordingly, giving special advertisement beforehand to the said Bullard to beware he did not exceed himself in speeches, and told him all the matter. [At the breakfast] the said Hartford conversed with the said Bullard touching the said Mr. Gardiner, and proceeded to ask him whether he knew the said Mr. Gardiner; whereunto the said Bullard answered, he knew him too well, saying, he went about to undo him and a great sort of fatherless children; whereunto the said Hartford (to draw him on to some hard speeches, as it seemed according to appointment) replied in this sort to the said Bullard: 'Take heed how you deal with him, for he is the subtlest knave in all the country where he dwelleth'; and the more to draw on the said Bullard to use some hard speeches against him (the said Gardiner), proceeded further to say that he (the said Gardiner) 'little or nothing cared to forge a writing than he did to take the cup and drink'; and such other like training speeches, to work the said Bullard to burst out into the vehemency of speech against him. But the said Bullard, having advertisement and caveat given him beforehand of their traps, not only with temperance moderated his speeches, but also in express words (the more safely to be free from danger of the said [Gardiner]) said to the said Hartford that he would not so say of the said Gardiner. 'But', said he (the said Bullard), 'he hath gone about to undo a sort of fatherless children of us,' as he said before, or words of like effect."

It is instructive to see Gardiner's 'circumventious and ungodly meaning' at work, attempting with subtle malice to entrap and injure a man whom he had already fleeced; and it is amusing to picture Davy, Greene, and the forewarned Bullard relishing the breakfast, provided at Gardiner's expense, which he had intended for Bullard's undoing.

Bullard's statement that Gardiner had robbed

the heirs of Robert Luce is corroborated by a Bermondsey grocer, Richard Ryther, who later deposed in another connection that he had heard by report that Gardiner owed Luce's children "of their own right, three times £1100", and also that Gardiner "by shameful falsehood defeated the said children of great sums of money", and had troubled them "in lands, body, or goods, by one subtle device or another".

The justice's neighbours in Southwark and Bermondsey were frequent witnesses and victims of his tyranny. They give us a very lively account of one of his practices in and after 1584. It appears that William Brooke and Agnes his wife unwarily borrowed £80 of Gardiner, giving for security a mortgage on the rent of some houses of theirs of far greater value. Agnes Brooke deposed in a subsequent suit that though the oral agreement for the lease of mortgage was stipulated for a term of fourteen years, Gardiner, taking advantage of their inability to read, had his scrivener write 'fourscore' in the lease and dishonestly read it aloud to them as 'fourteen'. Soon afterwards, Agnes Brooke relates, "finding themselves thus wronged", she and her husband "complained thereof to him [the scrivener] and to Mr. Gardiner;

but getting no redress, they exhibited a bill into the Star Chamber against him; but for want of ability were driven to leave off the suit, by reason that Mr. Gardiner, being a man of great wealth, overweighed them by delays and devices procured by his money".

Discouraged from seeking justice in the Star Chamber, it seems that Brooke and his wife laboured to expose the fraud to the Lord Chancellor, Sir Thomas Bromley; but when Gardiner saw the danger that justice might actually be done, he used his wealth, position, and friendship with the Lord Chancellor to defeat the complainants, as will appear from the following deposition made some years later by a niece of the Brookes, Helen Medland. She relates that her uncle and aunt got a decree from the Chancellor in their favour; and that "there was . . . a certain day set down when the Lord Chancellor . . . should have done something (this deponent remembreth not well what) for confirmation of the said order or decree, but that very day the said old Gardiner had invited the said Lord Chancellor and divers other great personages home to his house to dinner, so that there could be nothing done therein that day; neither could the said Brooke or his wife after

that bring the said matter to any further per-
fection".

Gardiner meanwhile held the mortgage on their
property, and when they came on the quarterly
days of payment with the instalments of their
debt, we learn that he used every trick in his bag
to trap them into a default on which he might
claim forfeiture. Wayte, having been a servant
in his stepfather's house, reminiscently testified
(after Gardiner was safely dead and he could tell
the truth) to the justice's artful intention of avoiding receipt of the payments. He said he "well
remembreth that he hath seen the said William
Gardiner (or his wife or some of his servants to his
use) at four or five several times or more, receive
the several sums of £5 of the said complainants
upon such tender or offer. . . . But sometimes the
said Mr. Gardiner would absent himself when the
time came that the money was to be paid, because, as it seemed, he would take some advantage
of forfeiture against the complainants."

We learn that Brooke and his wife managed,
however, against a series of discouragements, to
get Gardiner to accept the payments up to the last
£5; but here in the last ditch the cunning fox
tricked them into a forfeiture, thus seizing the

property and keeping the money already paid as well. Helen Medland, the Brookes' niece, tells the story in detail: "The whole money agreed upon as aforesaid to be paid was all paid, saving the last £5 . . . and that £5 was also offered and tendered to be paid after the said forfeiture; but the said William Gardiner would not accept thereof, but took advantage upon his mortgage; and this deponent is induced to believe that it was the said William Gardiner's intention always to take advantage by his said mortgage, for that this deponent hath divers times (and almost every time) seen, when the said money hath been tendered by £5 at a time, [that] the said William Gardiner did sometimes set strangers to receive the same who were unknown to the said Brooke or his wife or any with them, thereby to cause them to detain the said money; and sometimes when the same hath been tendered [that is, offered to be counted and accepted] upon the benches or seats at his door, he would not suffer that, but did sweep it off; insomuch as the said Agnes [Brooke] did sometimes bring a joint-stool with her to tell the money upon; and then . . . the said old Gardiner (or some by his appointment) did sweep the money down into the street; so that the said Brooke's wife was afterwards driven to tender the said money upon a cloak spread upon the ground; [and Gardiner] did sometimes shut the doors, and would suffer none to come in or out whereby he would seem to take notice of any such tender; and sometimes he did use to send some of his servants privily abroad to see how the day passed, that he might take advantage of the last hour of payment of the money." While this last statement is not very clear to me, its drift is plain enough: that Gardiner craftily watched his opportunity to claim forfeiture on any grounds, fair or foul.

Continuing her deposition to speak in general terms of Gardiner, Helen Medland sketches in the figure of a grasping and churlish suburban magnate, a harsh man to be detested by his equals and feared and secretly cursed by those whom he held in his power. She says that he "was a great rich man in his estate, and one who had still money to lay out upon anything whereby he thought to get advantage, and was given to deal hardly with his poor neighbours in dealing and bargaining with them; and he was one who carried himself very sternly amongst his neighbours, and by such his dealing he was very hardly thought of amongst his neighbours".

One such neighbour and fellow-leatherseller, Mr. Ralph Pratt, as we learn, had excellent reason to think hardly of the scoundrelly justice. On some ground of malice or greed, Gardiner had corrupted one of Pratt's tenants, a poor handicraftsman named Welles, to lay a cavilling false claim to a half-acre of Pratt's land, and had prevailed on him to go out and dig a ditch to set up a new boundary. In a set of depositions relating to Gardiner's unjust dealings in another matter, we find Pratt testifying as follows: "[I] came unto him, and asked the said Welles what he meant, to dig [my] ground and to use [me] so badly. Whereunto he answered, 'Mr. Gardiner makes me do it. I cannot choose but do it, or I must run away; I have nothing for my pains but coarse bread'; and withal said, 'I know I wrong you,' and with that threw down his spade, went his way, and said he would meddle no further in it." Poor Welles! He was not villain enough to carry out Gardiner's instructions; but he had involved himself with Gardiner, and if he did not do as he was told, he must run from the petty tyrant's revenge.

Another neighbour, Robert Swanne, testified that Gardiner told Welles, when he saw any of

Mr. Pratt's cattle on the land in question to "kill them or throw them in ditches". Further, that Welles declared that he "would openly confess it in the church, and ask the said Mr. Pratt forgiveness; and that he would point unto the said Gardiner as he was in the church, and say unto him, 'The plague of God fall upon thee! There thou art that hast made me abuse Mr. Pratt!'" Swanne added the information that afterwards Welles begged Mr. Pratt's pardon on his knees, and "therewithal wept very bitterly, protesting that his conscience much moved him that he was so miserable that unjustly he would be misled by the wicked procurement of another man". Welles's poor wife testified that her man had been so utterly undone by Gardiner's means that he was "enforced to fly and depart from [me], leaving [me] and two children in very great want and distress".

For some of the choicest of all our information about Gardiner's character we have to thank his miserly greed; for he refused to pay two reasonably honest scriveners, Thomas Newman and John Thompson, whom he had hired to help conceal his actions and to further his law-tricks. The scrivener Newman testified in court that Gardiner had kept him so busy drafting and engrossing deeds that he "could scarce . . . take rest or eat his meat for [his] importunacy". It is through the scriveners' disgust at Gardiner's shabby treatment of them that we learn how the justice obtained property in Bermondsey under their names on a secret trust for his use, and that we get their opinion that this was "so done of purpose . . . to deprive and defraud his wife [Margaret, his second wife] of dower, if she survived him", and also, letting Newman be cursed as the cruel landlord, to "raise and enhance the rents in most unconscionable sort to satisfy his greedy desire, and avoid the exclamations of the poor tenants . . . being his near neighbours".

Scrivener Newman says he found Gardiner "to be a man of such an evil mind and conversation that with one and the self-same breath he would speak a word and deny it again"; and testifies from his own knowledge that "many times it hath been his [Gardiner's] cunning shifting devices to work upon advantages, and when a poor man is falling, utterly to press him down".

One of Gardiner's transfers of property in the names of Newman and Thompson was the sale of some of his houses in Bermondsey to a certain

Mr. Robert Withens. Withens knew that Gardiner was the real owner of the houses, and evidently dealt with Gardiner against his wife's advice; for Mrs. Withens testified in a subsequent suit that after possession of the houses had been given, and she and her husband, with their son William and the scriveners, were "going homewards by the said Gardiner's house in Bermondsey Street, [we] were all of [us] invited to dinner by Gardiner; and at [my] coming into Gardiner's house, the said Gardiner, welcoming [me] with a kiss, therewith used these or the like words in effect: . . . 'God give you joy of your good bargain! I am sure you are now in possession of it.' 'And so are you of our money,' quoth [I]; 'but,' said [I] to Gardiner, 'if my husband would have been ruled by me, he should not have dealt with you; for,' quoth [I], 'Mr. Gardiner, you have taken all the fines aforehand, and the tenements are a sort of ragged houses little worth.'" Evidently Gardiner had impaired the value of the bargain by making new leases to the tenants shortly before the sale, receiving the 'fines' or fees paid by the tenants for the privilege of a new lease. The tenants being poor, it was impossible for Withens to collect new fines from them; moreover since the houses were in a decayed condition,

Mrs. Withens was sure that Gardiner had got the better of her husband.

All was fish that came to Gardiner's net, from the painful pence wrung from his poorest tenant to the interest charges on hundreds of pounds lent to wealthy borrowers at the high rate of ten per cent. In December 1587, just before the opening of the year of the Armada, we find that he lent £600 to a group composed of Sir Walter Ralegh, Sir Walter's brother Carew Ralegh, and William Saunderson. The loan was secured by a bond of £1000 penalty for the payment of £630 six months after date "at the now dwelling house of the said William Gardiner in Bermondsey". Gardiner apparently found difficulty in collecting his money from the Raleghs. By suit in court, five years after the loan, he obtained an order for an execution against the goods of his wealthy debtors on the bond of £1000; and in 1594 he acknowledged satisfaction of the debt. How much more than his loan of £600 he got does not appear.

It would take far too much space to detail here all the devious dealings of Justice Gardiner's that I have found. And we must remind ourselves that for every one of his rascalities that got into court, there must have been from three to five at least that were never recorded. We must pass over with a word the tale of how he obliged young Nicholas Saunder, esquire, a would-be borrower, to purchase a horse of him for £18 as a part of the loan, which horse, two days after it was delivered and before it had been ridden, died in the stable. But we cannot omit some account of Gardiner's shameless and persistent lies and perjuries in courts of law.

In 1561 a certain Edward Welsh had bound himself to Gardiner in a recognizance or bond of £500. It is certain that in 1564 the debt was paid and that Gardiner gave Welsh a deed of release which discharged the bond aforesaid. But in 1585, after Welsh's death, Gardiner put this old bond in suit, in an attempt to extort money from three of the dead man's heirs and former tenants—Richard Ryther, James Chiball, and Lawrence Browne, neighbours of Gardiner's in Bermondsey. Their defence was, of course, the deed of release, which they showed at the trial in the Queen's Bench. Although Gardiner denied that this document was his signed deed, his claim was dismissed; but not (as Ryther later testified) before he had "without all fear of God very boldly stood up in open court and offered to be deposed that the same release was not his deed; and fain would have had his oath taken in that behalf if it would have been accepted". The jury, however, found that the deed *was* his, "to his great shame and discredit".

Furious at the check he thus received, Gardiner attacked Ryther and two Londoners—Henry Lane and George Spencer, who had testified against him—in the Star Chamber, charging Ryther with forging the release, and Lane and Spencer with perjury. But the defendants were cleared, and Gardiner again discredited.

In spite of the disbelief with which his vehement asseverations had been greeted, Gardiner evidently made a further effort to extort a payment on the ancient bond. His intended victim this time was Thomas Walker, still another heir of the lands which had belonged to Gardiner's long-deceased debtor. We find Walker complaining in the Court of Wards against Gardiner for wrongfully putting the released recognizance of £500 in suit. Gardiner appeared, and under oath again denied that the release was his deed, thus adding perjury to his two previous lies. Walker exhibited the release to the Court, and Gardiner's sworn denial was not believed. Gardiner asked the judge, Lord Treasurer Burghley, for a further trial of the issue (having had one jury trial and two judicial hearings already). Burghley evidently knew his man: he granted Gardiner's request, but, aware of the danger that the unscrupulous Surrey justice might corrupt or intimidate a jury composed of Southwark men, he made a prudent proviso for a jury of Kent, "which jury, for the more indifferency and for avoiding of corrupt dealing in the empanelling thereof, shall be nominated and appointed by the Justices of Assize of that county".

Lane and Ryther, discovering that Gardiner, in the face of Burghley's proviso, was nevertheless using a long delay which intervened to corrupt witnesses and tamper with the empanelling of jurors, complained a year later in Star Chamber. Examined under oath in the latter court, Gardiner denied the charges, and once more swore that the release shown him "was not this deponent's release or acquittance, as he very well knew and was assured in his conscience". Lane complained afresh in Star Chamber against Gardiner for this second palpable perjury; but, protected as the Bermondsey justice was by great wealth and powerful friends, we find him dismissed "by the great favour of the Court". Not yet wearied, in the same year he actually sued Lane once more in

the Queen's Bench on the ancient bond of £500.
Lane pleaded the release, and Gardiner yet again
said that he had not made it. This suit, however,
seems not to have come to trial. The hope of
cheating someone of a large sum of money worked
so powerfully on Gardiner that year after year he
went from court to court with his despicable suit,
piling perjuries upon lies.

In this one matter, over a period of seven or eight
years, we have seen Gardiner making the unenvi-
able record of three direct lies and two perjuries
in courts of law, supported by quantities of false
charges and misrepresentations. He could not
well have done more if he had set out definitely
to establish a reputation as a liar with the great
judicial dignitaries before whom he appeared—
Lord Treasurer Burghley, the Lords of the Privy
Council, and the Judges of the Queen's Bench.

Nevertheless, in 1590, Gardiner furnished an
answer to the rhetorical question put by the
satirist Marston:

> Shall I find trading *Mecho*, never loath
> Frankly to take a damning perjur'd oath?

In that year he added to his notoriety by a perjury
at a trial at the Surrey Assizes. Gardiner's nephew,

Thomas Askew, had brought an action against his stepfather Thomas Sheppard, alleging that a certain John Payne had assigned the lease of a house to him (Askew), but that Sheppard wrongfully kept possession. Gardiner appeared for Askew, and falsely swore that Payne had made the alleged assignment. When Askew, defeated in this trial, at Gardiner's instigation brought suit against Payne in the Court of Chancery, Attorney-General Popham appeared for Payne and informed the Court that, at the trial at the Assizes aforesaid, the jury had disbelieved Gardiner and found for Sheppard. "And yet the said Gardiner," relates the Attorney-General, "finding himself grieved that the said jury gave no more faith to his deposition, hath procured the plaintiff [Askew] to exhibit a bill into this Court [of Chancery] against the defendant for proof of a pretended assignment, contrary to the said verdict [in the trial at the Assizes]; intending thereby either to entrap the defendant upon his oath by his answer, or by some examination of him in this Court, or else to procure some colour of credit to the testimony given by the said Gardiner to the jury."

It is only too evident from this sordid recital that Justice Gardiner had richly earned the reputation of being "the subtlest knave in all the country where he dwelleth", and we may be sure that in 1596, the year of our newly discovered Shakespeare document, the theatre-owner Francis Langley felt himself on firm ground in reiterating these words about old Gardiner: "He is a false knave, a false forsworn knave, and a perjured knave."

In 1594 this faithless malefactor of great wealth was chosen by Queen Elizabeth for the office of High Sheriff of Surrey and Sussex. Such an election must not be held to indicate that the ruling powers were deceived into thinking Gardiner an honest man. Sheriffs were chosen for their wealth, men who could answer with their goods to the Exchequer for any default in collecting money due to the Crown. This time Gardiner dared not refuse the appointment, and we find him serving as sheriff for the customary year's term, from Michaelmas 1594 to Michaelmas 1595. We shall see later how he used this new position to defraud one Richard Leech, a rich Surrey squire who was destined to succeed him as sheriff. It is enough for our present purposes to examine the fines he was ordered to pay for negligence in his year of office. These records are preserved among the documents of the Court of Wards and Liveries:

1596. Sussex. William Gardiner, esquire, late
  sheriff of the said county, for his insufficient
  return of Her Majesty's process   .   . £50
1596. Surrey. The said William Gardiner, esquire,
  [as before] £50

These are large fines. Sheriffs of other counties in
the same list of fines are ordered to pay £10, £15,
£20, and one, £30, for their defaults; but £50 for
each of Gardiner's counties reveals exceptional
negligence in office.[1] As might have been expected
from what we have learned of his character, Gardiner served himself far more diligently than he
served his Queen.

In 1596, the year of his violent quarrel with
Langley and Shakespeare, Gardiner was 65. Remarkable only for the number and variety of his
misdeeds, he was growing old in sin. Yet right up
to his death in the following year, we find him
showing no weariness in ill-doing. Buttressed with
his unchristian belief in predestination, Justice
Gardiner would remain, we may be sure, quite un-
touched by such contemporary warnings as this of
Anthony Fletcher's: "The last day of all days, I

---

[1] According to the usual custom, all these fines were 'miti-
gated' from pounds to shillings, and Gardiner therefore paid
100 shillings.

mean the general judgment day, will be a very gloomy and black sessions day for those men which do now keep close and fast locked up in their chests and coffers their thousands and hundreds of gold and silver, and are so covetous that if they could do it, all things that they look upon should be turned into gold, they are so insatiable; and yet suffer their poor brethren to live in great want and misery. Oh insatiable covetousness, oh ungodly greediness, oh lamentable madness!"[1]

As if to turn a neighbour's acres into gold for his own coffers, Gardiner in the spring of 1597 tried to steal a piece of land from his neighbour and fellow-justice, Edmund Bowyer. Bowyer complains in the Court of Exchequer that Gardiner, "of his covetous and insatiable mind, hath not only defaced the bounds [of the land] by extirping the trees standing and growing there," but also levelled the ditches, "to the procurement of perjury in setting forth the true bounds". This is our last glimpse of Gardiner alive. For the last of all his efforts at cheating, he turned on his neighbour and seventeen-years' companion on the Bench!

On November 26, 1597, to the general relief, Gardiner died, having amassed a hoard sufficient to

[1] *Certaine . . . similes* (1595), 111.

leave his four children, and the grandson who was his heir, wealthy. His will, which I reproduce in full in an appendix, makes extraordinary reading, disposing as it does of the goods "wherewith it has pleased God to bless me". There are pious bequests to the poor of the Southwark parishes, the hospitals, and the prisoners in the Southwark Compter, the White Lion, Marshalsea, and King's Bench prisons. The legacies to his second wife Margaret (whom he had married in 1582, some years after the death of his first wife Frances) are carefully conditioned on her giving up her claims to dower. Gardiner even leaves ten marks to the churchwardens of his parish church, St. Mary Magdalen's, Bermondsey—where poor Welles had intended to curse him in the presence of the congregation with the plague of God—"to buy a communion cup", and the same amount to "John Luce my brother-in-law", whom, with the other children of Robert Luce, he had cheated of hundreds of pounds. Gardiner's eldest surviving son Thomas had evidently displeased his father by getting into debt. Thomas is excluded from the will, and is only to be admitted to his inheritance if "at any time [he] become out of debt, or shall not owe . . . above one hundred pounds". Gardiner's useful friends on the Bench are not forgotten: the Right Honourable Sir John Fortescue, Chancellor of the Exchequer, is to have £20 and "my stoned horse", while Sir Edmund Anderson, Lord Chief Justice of the Common Pleas, is remembered with £20 and "my bay trotting gelding".

Gardiner's body lay in his house from November 26 to December 22, while the pomp of the funeral was being prepared under the direction of Ben Jonson's friend William Camden, Clarenceux King-of-Arms. On the latter date the corpse was borne in solemn procession to Bermondsey Church, where, four years before, Elizabeth's favourite the Earl of Essex had been chief mourner at the funeral of Henry Earl of Sussex, brother of Gardiner's late master. Gardiner's funeral sermon was delivered by Dr. Mountfort. Unfortunately it has not been preserved. We are left to wonder what the learned divine could possibly find to say by way of eulogy. The certificate prepared by Camden gives us the details of the funeral: "The said William Gardiner, being of the age of three score years and six, departed this transitory life at his house at Bermondsey Street in the county of Surrey aforesaid, on Saturday the 26th of November 1597, from whence he was very wor-

shipfully accompanied unto the parish church
of Bermondsey the 22d of December following.
The preacher was Doctor Mountfort. The pennon
of his arms was borne by William Wayte, his
kinsman. The helm and crest, by Thomas Lant,
Windsor Herald. The coat of arms by William
Camden, Clarenceux King-of-Arms, who directed
the said funeral. The body borne by six of his own
servants. The chief mourner, Thomas Gardiner,
his second son. The two assistants, William Gardiner, third son, and Nicholas Smyth."

So passed William Gardiner, esquire, justice of
peace and of the *quorum*, sometime Second Warden of the Company of the Leathersellers, High
Sheriff of Surrey and Sussex, and twice Sheriff-
elect of London; but his execrable memory hung
on in the minds of those whom he had oppressed
and ruined. If we are asked for an epitaph, we
may offer some of the verses, mentioned by Sir
John Harington, on the memory of Bishop Stephen
Gardiner. With very slight modifications, these
will serve admirably for the tyrant of Bermondsey:

> A Gardiner such he was
>   As spoiléd so our plants
> That justice wither'd, mercy died,
>   And we wrung by their wants.

83

A [Will] in name, a Fox in fact,
    A [Justice] but in weeds;
A faithless man full-fraught with frauds,
    As deem him by his deeds.

A heart to harm and not to help,
    His lust was laid far low;
A mind with malice overwhelmed,
    Of God nor man no awe.

A tried untruth in trust,
    As tongues well-tried have told;
A mouth that breathed more odious lies
    Than I t'upbraid am bold.[1]

[1] *Nugae Antiquae*, 1769.

WHITE LUCES

Time will no doubt shed still more light on Justice Gardiner. Enough has already been thrown to show that his neighbours in London, Bermondsey, and Southwark had good reason for considering him a notorious knave. It was this avaricious cheat, liar, and heartless toady who had jurisdiction over the Bankside, and who came, in the autumn of 1596, into violent collision with Francis Langley and William Shakespeare.

Langley, as we have seen, put his opinion of Gardiner into words, and promptly found himself with three suits for slander on his hands. Did Shakespeare perhaps have something less actionable to say of William Gardiner, esquire, in the county of Surrey, justice of peace and *quorum*?

Some scholars have supposed that Shakespeare's figure of Justice Shallow, in the first scene of *The Merry Wives of Windsor*, contains a satirical hit at Sir Thomas Lucy, the dramatist's much respected neighbour in Warwickshire. Accepting the late tradition that Shakespeare as a youth had poached Lucy's deer, and was punished by the knight, they believe that the poet took his revenge in the *Merry Wives*, a dozen years or more after the date of the legendary deer-stealing. Their ground for seeing such a tardy hit at Sir Thomas Lucy is Slender's flattering reference to the 'white luces', or heraldic fishes, blazoned in Justice Shallow's coat of arms. It is common knowledge that Sir Thomas bore as his arms *Gules, semée of crosscrosslets Or, three luces haurient Argent:*[1] in language less technical, "on a red field strewn with small golden crosses, three silver (white) luces— large fish of the pike family—placed perpendicularly". Because of the presence of the luces in the two coats, the identification of Shallow with Lucy has been held to be inevitable. So firmly has this notion been planted in some minds that it has become the central prop of the belief in the deer-stealing tradition.

In his admirable edition of the play (Arden, 1904), H. C. Hart sums up the matter as follows: "The probability of the truth of the tradition appears to me to hinge upon the passages in *Merry Wives*." And although he is loath to swallow the tradition whole, Hart justly observes,

[1] "Description of the Stained Glass in Charlecote House near Stratford-on-Avon, the seat of George Lucy, esquire," in *Collectanea Topographica et Genealogica*, iv. (1837), 346-350.

"If we had no tradition, what should we make of the coat of arms passage? It would be utterly unmeaning."

There is the case in a nutshell. Those of us who reject both the tradition and the Shallow-Lucy equation have never been able to supply a satisfactory meaning for the passage in question.

As I thought the matter over, it suddenly occurred to me that the newly reconstituted life of Shakespeare's enemy Justice Gardiner held the essential clue. Gardiner's first wife, I had found, was Frances, the widow of Edmund Wayte. But we remember that she was born Frances Luce or Lucy, the daughter of Robert Luce or Lucy, gentleman. Lucy! Here was the clue. If Robert Luce had a coat of arms, his daughter would have a right to bear his arms, and her husband could impale them: that is to say, marshal them with his own on one shield. A tremendous possibility opened before me. What if Robert Luce's arms had contained the white luces, and Justice Gardiner perhaps bore them side by side with his own? Could this be the true significance of the coat of arms passage in the *Merry Wives*? Was the Justice Shallow of the play a caricature of Justice Gardiner? No time was to be lost in speculation. The question demanded an answer at once, and I 'made sudden speed' to the Manuscript Room of the British Museum. Once there, I called for the formidable collections of Elizabethan heraldry— the grants, alphabets, trickings, and blazons of arms—a gorgeous gallery, through which I dashed at an undignified rate.

For a long time I met little but disappointment. I ran upon several sketches or trickings of the Gardiner coat—*Azure, a griffin passant Or*—to which was sometimes added his crest, *a lion passant guardant Argent*. It satisfied one's sense of fitness to find the griffin, that twyformed monster in nature, in the armorial bearings of the raptorial Gardiner. Thomas Lodge's description of the character of the griffin is in point: "This bird is like unto an Eagle both in head and wings, and in all other parts of his body he is like unto a Lion. . . . He slayeth and destroyeth all men that dwell about him, neither is his insatiable covetousness ever satisfied."[1] Though very suitable for Gardiner, griffins were not precisely what I was after. I pursued my search.

At last, and suddenly, came the reward. In a

---

[1] *Catharos*, 1591.

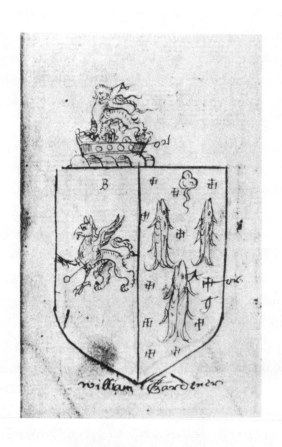

**ARMS OF GARDINER
IMPALING LUCY**
[B. M. Harley MS. 5849, f. 63ᵛ.]

volume of quarterings of arms, Harley Manuscript 5849—for me easily the greatest treasure of the Museum—wild surmise was turned into certainty. Here was the proof before my eyes: *Gardiner impaling Lucy*—a sketch of the golden griffin side by side with the three white luces; and beneath, the legend *William Gardener*.

I drew a long breath. Shakespeare seemed to stand at my very elbow, unlocking the age-old mystery of the scene in the *Merry Wives*. Yet even as I sat in a daze of realization, something told me that I must not rest here. This quarry held out the promise of more corroborative material. Casting about for a fresh scent, I thought of the heraldic notes of funerals of important persons, often kept by the officers of the College of Arms who directed the ceremonies. We had seen that William Camden, Clarenceux King-of-Arms, had been in charge of Gardiner's funeral at Bermondsey. A search under the word *Funerals* in the catalogue of manuscripts guided me to several volumes of such notes; and on the first leaf of one of them— Stowe Manuscript 587—I ran down my quarry: a record of Justice Gardiner's funeral, with the impaled arms in trick as before—the golden griffin beside the three white luces—but with the memorandum *Lucy* written above the impalement of the Lucy coat.[1]

Here was rich finding. Then of a sudden came another thought. I recalled the clause in Gardiner's will by which he left ten marks to the wardens of his parish church, St. Mary Magdalen's, Bermondsey, "to buy a communion cup". What of this cup? Did it still exist? And if it did, might it be ornamented, by any chance, with Gardiner's arms? And would the white luces be there? I found myself forging a chain of shadowy but fascinating possibilities.

Before leaving the Museum, I went to the Reading Room, and taking the Surrey volumes of the *Victoria County History* from the shelf, I opened to the description of the Bermondsey church as

[1] Robert Luce's coat as shown in the accompanying illustration is *Gules, semée of crosscrosslets Or, three luces haurient Argent, in chief a trefoil slipped for difference.* Except for the specified difference, this coat is identical with that of Sir Thomas Lucy of Charlecote. Robert Luce's father was of Kynver, Staffordshire, and I have not succeeded in tracing his grant of arms. Nor can I learn whether there was any connection between the Luces of Staffordshire and London and the Lucys of Charlecote. A note contained in a later pedigree of the Gardiners (Rawlinson MS. B75, f. 116ᵛ) gives Robert Luce's arms as *B[lue] crusilee* 3 *lucies*, instead of *Gules*; but this must be an error. This late note has not the authority of the two manuscripts already mentioned, which emanated from officers of arms contemporary with Justice Gardiner.

ARMS OF GARDINER IMPALING LUCY

[B. M. Stowe MS. 587, f. 1ᵛ.]

"Mʳ William Gardiner esquier of Barmondsey in the Countie of Surrey maried Francis daughter of Mʳ Robert Lucey of London departed this mortall life [blank] and his Fewnerall was solemnized at Barmondsey afore named, the officers [blank]" it stands to-day. My excitement grew, for among the plate of the church I found that there was said to be an ancient cup, given by 'William Gardner', and engraved with his arms. A letter despatched to the Reverend Arthur Sinker, rector of Bermondsey, brought a kind invitation to view the cup. Hastening to the scene of Justice Gardiner's ancient tyrannies, I entered the church; and there in the vestry Mr. Sinker put the silver cup into my trembling hands. He must have wondered at my visible emotion, for on the side of the cup I beheld the engraving of the achievement of Gardiner's arms, quartering the three white luces. Below ran the inscription: *The gifte of William Gardner Esquier*. The coat of arms was blazoned as follows: In two quarters, dexter chief and sinister base, were Gardiner's arms, *a griffin passant*; in the sinister chief quarter were the three luces for *Lucy*, while the fourth quarter seemed to be *three herons' heads erased* (that is, torn off).[1]

---

[1] I have not been able to explain Gardiner's connection with this last coat. One would naturally expect it to be either his mother's or his second wife's. In a late manuscript of doubtful authority (Rawlinson MS. B75, ff. 116-118) Gardiner's mother is said to have come of a Yorkshire Michell family who bore *Azure, a leopard's head Or*; and the arms of his second wife Margaret (born a Lucas of Gloucester) are here given as *a fesse with six crescents*.

From this chalice the parishioners of Bermondsey still take Holy Communion every Sunday. The cup has no doubt been in regular use for more than three centuries. After all these years of service and continual polishings, the coat of arms still stands out distinctly. The Elizabethan engraver did his work well.

The Lucy coat of white luces is honourable and very ancient. We are told that these arms were borne in the eleventh century by a noble Lucy, 'Earl of Anguish', who came over with William the Conqueror. In Gardiner's day the luces appeared on the escutcheons of several great lords, among whom were numbered Edward Earl of Bedford, John Lord Darcy of the North, and Edward Lord Vaux of Harrowden. Gardiner's chief pride, however, in blazoning the Lucy coat doubtless lay in the fact that it was quartered by his master Thomas Radcliffe, Earl of Sussex, Queen Elizabeth's Lord Chamberlain from 1572 to 1583.

JUSTICE SHALLOW & ABRAHAM SLENDER

EQUIPPED as we now are with a knowledge which though common property in Shakespeare's time has lain *perdu* for three hundred years, let us turn to the first scene of *The Merry Wives of Windsor*.

Windsor. Before Page's House.

Enter JUSTICE SHALLOW, SLENDER, *and* SIR HUGH EVANS.

SHALLOW. Sir Hugh, persuade me not; I will make a Star-chamber matter of it: if he were twenty Sir John Falstaffs, he shall not abuse Robert Shallow, esquire.

SLENDER. In the county of Gloucester, justice of peace and 'Coram'.

SHALLOW. Ay, cousin Slender, and 'Custalorum'.

SLENDER. Ay, and 'Ratolorum' too; and a gentleman born, master parson, who writes himself 'Armigero' in any bill, warrant, quittance, or obligation—'Armigero'.

SHALLOW. Ay, that I do, and have done any time these three hundred years.

SLENDER. All his successors gone before him have done 't; and all his ancestors that come after him may: they may give the dozen white luces in their coat.

SHALLOW. It is an old coat.

EVANS. The dozen white louses do become an old coat well; it agrees well, passant; it is a familiar beast to man, and signifies love.

SHALLOW. The luce is the fresh fish; the salt fish is an old coat.

On the assumption that Shakespeare was here

taking enough material from the life about him to make a series of humorous hits at the men who had annoyed him, let us ask what his fellow-actors and the London audience might see in this scene.

Nothing could be closer, to begin with, than the parallel between the description of Robert Shallow and that of William Gardiner, esquire (Latin *armiger*), justice of peace and of the *quorum* for the county of Surrey. The next bit, 'Custalorum, and Ratolorum', with its intentional scrambling of the words *Custos Rotulorum*, is probably satire: the county office of *Custos Rotulorum* or Keeper of the Records was a high one, to which few men of Gardiner's or Shallow's rank could aspire. For Surrey at this period the place, together with that of Lord Lieutenant, was held by one of the greatest nobles in the land—Charles Lord Howard of Effingham, Lord High Admiral of England. His deputy *custos* was Sir William More of Loseley.

Proceeding to boast of his uncle's heraldic honours, Slender avers that Shallow's "ancestors that come after him" may display the luces on their shield. Gardiner had added the luces to his arms by marriage; his descendants by Frances Luce could therefore quarter the Lucy arms. Parson Evans makes the complaisant observation that the 'louses' agree well, *passant*. Now the luces were blazoned *hauri-ent*, that is, perpendicularly, as fishes rising to the surface of water. Yet the 'louses' are said to agree well, *passant*. We must understand Evans to mean "agree well with your other heraldic charge, which is blazoned *passant*". Gardiner's luces were impaled with his family arms, a griffin *passant*; and his crest was a lion *passant*.

Shallow brags of the antiquity of his coat; and after Evans's babble of the nature of the louse, he remarks, "The luce is the fresh fish; the salt fish is an old coat." A reference in heraldry to fresh fish and salt fish would, I am confident, be plain to every Londoner as an allusion to the combined arms of the great Fishmongers' Company. The Fresh or Stockfishmongers' coat displayed luces, and that of the Saltfishmongers bore dolphins. Of the two, the Saltfishmongers' coat was the more ancient. If we picture Gardiner as Shallow, the remark is quite natural. As a former Warden of the Leathersellers' Company, and twice Sheriff-elect of London, the arms of the important livery companies were as familiar to him as his own.

Coincidences can be remarkable; but it seems to me that there are here too many of them to be set down as accidents. Esquire, justice of peace and of the *quorum*, a coat with heraldic luces that agree well, *passant*—it all fits the enemy of Langley and Shakespeare like a glove.

Nor have we yet done with coincidences. Old Shallow is incensed with Falstaff for raiding his park; he remembers the hot anger and cold iron of his youth, with the exclamation, "Ha, o' my life, if I were young again, the sword should end it." Moreover he pretends to have achieved monstrous skill in old-time sword-play: "In these times," he says, "you stand on distance, your passes, stoccadoes, and I know not what: 't is the heart, master Page; 't is here, 't is here. I have seen the time with my long sword, I would have made you four tall fellows skip like rats."

We have seen that as a youth, Gardiner, the future guardian of the peace, had ended at least one personal quarrel with the sword. From the manor court records of Southwark, I had learned that in his early twenties he was fined three shillings and fourpence for shedding another young gentleman's blood in a fight. His adversary was William Beeston, to whom four years afterward he sold some land in Streatham, Surrey. That Gardiner's violent temper had not evaporated with advancing age is shown by the threats he ex-

changed with Langley in 1596, when he was
65.

Justice Shallow greets the entrance of Falstaff
with an accusation of riot, poaching, and bur-
glary: "Knight, you have beaten my men, killed
my deer, and broke open my lodge."

Now Justice Gardiner owned a park; and with
it is connected a pretty tale, as follows. In 1592,
Nicholas Saunder, the spendthrift son of a wealthy
Surrey squire, was rapidly running through his
patrimony. Gardiner had recently cheated the
young man by selling him a dying horse for £18;
but this was a small matter compared to what
followed. He now took the opportunity of buying the young wastrel's largest piece of property,
Lagham Park, in Godstone, Surrey—a manor and
an enclosed park complete with a gate-house.
Saunder, however, had previously granted to
Richard Leech, esquire, for £500 ready money, an
annuity of £50 a year out of the income of Lagham
Park, and had bound himself and his heirs and
assigns in a bond of £1000 to pay the annuity
regularly. On succeeding to the ownership of the
estate, Gardiner purposely let the payments lapse;
and scheming to defraud Leech, he managed to get
a smaller bond of Saunder's made over to his own

son-in-law Nicholas Smith, so that he might use it as a means to defeat claims against Saunder's former property.

The plan, as we shall see, was by hurrying into court with this pretended prior claim (which was really friendly), to block the payment of Leech's large and just claim against the estate; and then by getting a packed jury to set a ridiculously low annual value on the property, to use this impossibly small valuation as a means to delay payment to Leech indefinitely, under the excuse that the estate could satisfy even the pretended prior claim only by slow degrees.

Gardiner accordingly had his son-in-law Smith sue out a writ of extent on this smaller bond, which ordered the sheriff to raise the money on Lagham Park. Gardiner had to act quickly, for Leech had already sued out a writ of extent on his £1000 bond. But Gardiner's trump card in his sharp game was his appointment as Sheriff of Surrey and Sussex: these writs against his own property were, therefore, in his own hands to execute. Craftily delaying Leech's prior writ, he went swiftly ahead with the other; and, as Leech complains, he "hath with all post haste caused an inquiry thereupon to be made by the inhabitants

within the borough of Southwark, neighbours to
the said Gardiner, and such as have no knowledge
of the value of the said lands . . . and hath by indirect means procured the inquirers thereof to extend the said . . . Lagham Park, being worth £100
per annum, at the yearly value but of £10". By
thus cunningly holding Lagham Park in extent on
a pretended prior claim of his own son-in-law's,
and setting so low a value on it that that claim
would be long in the paying, Gardiner planned to
defeat the execution of Leech's £1000 bond, and
to pay him no part of his just debt. The shameless
craftiness of this shift to fob off a creditor must
have lent an added ill-savour to Gardiner's name
in Southwark. Within a couple of years of the
chicanery, any allusion to Gardiner's park would
send a smile round a Bankside audience. Falstaff
indeed advises Shallow not to bring the subject of
his park and the inroad on it to the notice of the
Privy Council. "'T were better for you," he warns
him, "if it were known in counsel: you'll be laughed
at."

So much for the park. Meanwhile the scene in
the *Merry Wives* has continued with Shallow's
plan for marrying kinsman Slender advantage-
ously:

EVANS. ... there is also another device in my prain, which
peradventure prings goot discretions with it:—there is
Anne Page, which is daughter to Master Thomas Page,
which is pretty virginity.

SLENDER. Mistress Anne Page? She has brown hair, and
speaks small like a woman.

EVANS. It is that fery person for all the 'orld, as just as
you will desire, and seven hundred pounds of moneys,
and gold, and silver, is her grandsire, upon his death's
bed—Got deliver to a joyful resurrections!—give, when
she is able to overtake seventeen years old. It were a
goot motion if we leave our pribbles and prabbles, and
desire a marriage between Master Abraham and Mistress Anne Page.

SHALLOW. Did her grandsire leave her seven hundred
pound?

EVANS. Ay, and her father is make her a petter penny.

SHALLOW. I know the young gentlewoman. She has good
gifts.

EVANS. Seven hundred pounds, and possibilities, is goot
gifts.

SHALLOW. Well, let us see honest Master Page.

An important episode in the lives of Justice Gardiner and his stepson Wayte discloses a startling
commentary on this passage. We have it from the
complaint,[1] already mentioned, of Thomas Heron,
an under-marshal of the Court of Exchequer,
which alleges that Gardiner, by means of spurious

[1] Exchequer Bills and Answers, Eliz. and Jas. I, Surrey 40.

bonds, was dishonestly attempting to make him pay money he never owed. In the course of his complaint, Heron informs the judge, Lord Burghley, that in 1574 Robert Mote, a wealthy Southwark gentleman, died, leaving his property to his next-of-kin, a young girl named Joan Tayler. During Joan's minority, the estate was administered by William Wilson, one of the overseers of Mote's will. Having thus control over Joan and her property, Wilson conspired with Justice Gardiner "between them both to enjoy the goods and lands of the said Joan Tayler". And to this end "by compact between them, they married the said Joan to one William Wayte, a certain loose person of no reckoning or value, being wholly under the rule and commandment of the said Gardiner. After which marriage being performed, the said Gardiner (having the said Wayte at his commandment) procured the said William Wayte, and the said Joan his wife by the hard dealing of the said Wayte, for small or no consideration to convey the lands of the said Joan unto the children of the said Gardiner. Whereupon the said Joan Tayler, seeing her goods and lands to be gotten from her, consumed and wasted, not long after died; after whose death the said Gardiner procured a letter of administration of the goods and debts of the said Robert Mote unadministered, to be committed unto the said William Wayte, as an instrument by whom he hoped to make some profit." I have found this letter of administration; it is dated 1590 —six years before Shakespeare's quarrel with Wayte.

When the question of marrying the youthful heiress Anne Page, who will come into her property "when she is able to overtake seventeen years old", is broached to Slender, he exhibits a complete subjection to his uncle Shallow's wishes in the matter.

SHALLOW. Will you, upon good dowry, marry her?

SLENDER. I will do a greater thing than that, upon your request, cousin, in any reason.

SHALLOW. Nay, conceive me, conceive me, sweet coz: what I do is to pleasure you, coz: can you love the maid?

SLENDER. I will marry her, sir, at your request; but if there be no great love in the beginning, yet heaven may decrease it upon better acquaintance, when we are married and have more occasion to know one another; I hope upon familiarity will grow more contempt; but if you say 'marry her' I will marry her—that I am freely dissolved, and dissolutely.

According to Thomas Heron, when Joan Tayler had been married to William Wayte at Gardiner's suggestion, and had more occasion to know him and his rascally stepfather, her love of life decreased so much that she died not many years after.

When confronted, the similarities between the figures of Justice Shallow and his foolish nephew Slender, and those of Shakespeare's adversaries in Southwark, Justice Gardiner and his stepson, the 'loose person' Wayte, are in the last degree striking:

Robert Shallow, esquire, in the county of Gloucester justice of peace and *coram* (*quorum*), bears a coat of arms in which white luces 'agree well, *passant*'. He owns a park with a keeper's lodge. He boasts of his youthful prowess with the sword. He endeavours to marry his nephew Slender to a young heiress, Anne Page.

William Gardiner, esquire, in the county of Surrey justice of peace and *quorum*, bears a coat of arms in which white luces are blazoned beside a griffin *passant*. He owns a park with a gatehouse. In his youth he was fined for drawing blood in a fight. He married his stepson Wayte to a young heiress, Joan Tayler.

In the *Merry Wives*, little is actually made of the character of Justice Shallow. But Shakespeare had already drawn him in delightful detail in *Henry IV. Part Two*. We have there the humorous portrait of a wealthy and niggardly old pagan, sufficiently corrupt in administering his office to countenance the arrant knave Visor against the honest Clement Perkes of the hill. He makes much of Falstaff, hoping to benefit by Sir John's supposed influence with the Prince. The fat knight improves the occasion to extract a loan of a thousand pounds from him. Yet it is almost beyond Falstaff's endurance to listen to the old reprobate's gilded lies of his roistering youth in London as a law-student at Clement's Inn; of what a terror he was with the sword, fighting with Simon Stockfish, a fruiterer, behind Gray's Inn; of the *bona robas* he had at commandment; of his familiarity with such nobles as John of Gaunt.

Sir John however redresses matters in a soliloquy:

"I do see the bottom of Justice Shallow. Lord, Lord! how subject we old men are to this vice of lying. This same starved justice hath done nothing but prate to me of the wildness of his youth and the feats he hath done about Turnbull Street; and every third word a lie, duer paid to the hearer than the Turk's tribute. I do remember him at

Clement's Inn like a man made after supper of a cheese-paring: when a' was naked he was for all the world like a forked radish, with a head fantastically carved upon it with a knife: a' was so forlorn that his dimensions to any thick sight were invincible: a' was the very genius of famine; yet lecherous as a monkey, and the whores called him mandrake: a' came ever in the rearward of the fashion and sung those tunes to the over-scutched huswives that he heard the carmen whistle, and sware they were his fancies or his good-nights. And now is this Vice's dagger become a squire, and talks as familiarly of John a Gaunt as if he had been sworn brother to him; and I'll be sworn a' never saw him but once in the Tiltyard, and than he burst his head for crowding among the marshal's men. I saw it and told John a Gaunt he beat his own name; for you might have thrust him and all his apparel into an eel-skin; the case of a treble hautboy was a mansion for him, a court; and now he has land and beefs."

To Falstaff's mind, it's an outrage; but here's his comfort:

"I will devise matter enough out of this Shallow to keep Prince Harry in continual laughter the

105

wearing out of six fashions—which is four terms, or two actions—and a' shall laugh without inter-vallums. . . . O! you shall see him laugh till his face be like a wet cloak ill laid up!"

Like Shallow, Justice Gardiner spent his youth in London; and we have seen him making a fray and drawing 3s. 4d. worth of blood. His appointment, after but one year as justice of peace, to the Surrey *quorum* is evidence of some knowledge of law; and the sordid list of his subtle chicaneries reveals a thorough mastery of legal tricks, and attests his skill in taking advantage of it. Though I have found no record of his admission to any one of the great Inns of Court, I discover that he sent three of his sons to the Inner Temple. This choice makes it more than possible that he himself had studied at Clement's Inn; for Clement's Inn, a preparatory Inn of Chancery, was annexed to the Inner Temple. Later in life he was in the service of the Earl of Sussex, and, as we have seen, ingratiated himself with important personages, lending £600 to Sir Walter Ralegh, entertaining the Lord Chancellor, Sir Thomas Bromley, and other magnates at dinner, and cultivating the acquaintance of Sir Edmund Anderson, Lord

Chief Justice of the Common Pleas, and Sir John Fortescue, Chancellor of the Exchequer.

Falstaff makes old Shallow's proclivity for lying matter for mirth; but the old man's lies are the harmless prattle of a dotard. Justice Gardiner's notorious and repeated perjuries in courts of law, if soberly taken, were a subject less of laughter than of scandal.

It is to be noticed that when he introduced old Shallow in *Henry IV. Part Two*, Shakespeare went to the length of drawing not only his character, but a picture of his emaciated personal appearance as well. In Falstaff's phrase he is a 'bearded hermit's staff', a 'Vice's dagger'. When his shrunken figure appears in the *Merry Wives* he is, therefore, an old acquaintance, and needs no description. But the weak-headed Slender is a newcomer, and Shakespeare here invites his audience to a special enjoyment of the foolish gentleman's physical peculiarities. In Act I. Scene iv., Dame Quickly questions Peter Simple:

QUICKLY. And Master Slender's your master?
SIMPLE. Ay, forsooth.
QUICKLY. Does he not wear a great round beard, like a glover's paring-knife?
SIMPLE. No, forsooth: he hath but a little whey-face; with a little yellow beard—a cane-coloured beard.

QUICKLY. A softly sprighted man, is he not?

SIMPLE. Ay, forsooth: but he is as tall a man of his hands as any is between this and his head: he hath fought with a warrener!

QUICKLY. How say you?—O, I should remember him: does he not hold up his head, as it were, and strut in his gait?

SIMPLE. Yes, indeed, does he.

The celebrated Will Kemp, who in all probability played Shallow,[1] and the actor who took the part of Slender are thus provided by their fellow Shakespeare with the materials for exact physical caricature. None of the other comic figures in these plays receives this special attention. Though we are unfortunate in having no contemporary descriptions of the appearance of Gardiner and Wayte, it is more than tempting to let Shakespeare supply them.

A loving touch to the delicious sketch of Master

---

[1] See *2 Return from Parnassus*, iv. 3:

KEMP. Now for you [Mr. Philo], methinks you should belong to my tuition; and your face methinks would be good for a foolish Mayor or a foolish justice of peace: mark me.—'Forasmuch as there be two states of a commonwealth' ... Come, let me see how you can do: sit down in the chair.

PHILOMUSUS. 'Forasmuch as there be', etc.

KEMP. Thou wilt do well in time, if thou wilt be ruled by thy betters, that is, by myself and such grave aldermen of the playhouse as I am.

108

Slender is his self-portrait as a hot quarrelsome swashbuckler, desperately bold at the bear-baiting:

SLENDER. I love the sport well; but I shall as soon quarrel at it as any man in England. You are afraid, if you see the bear loose, are you not?
ANNE. Ay, indeed, sir.
SLENDER. That's meat and drink to me, now. I have seen Sackerson loose—twenty times, and have taken him by the chain.

Although the scene is laid at Windsor, and Slender is called a Gloucestershire man, this boast sounds pure Southwark. Sackerson's arena was the Bear-Garden, on the very Bankside where the warlike Wayte had picked a quarrel with Shakespeare, and conceived his physical fear of the poet.

In their cumulative force these parallels are over-whelming. It is impossible to escape the conclusion that in these two final Falstaff plays, Shakespeare drew material from the contemporary scene in Southwark. Justice Gardiner and his inconsider-able stepson had willy-nilly forced themselves on his attention; and as an economical artist he used what he saw. What is more, Gardiner and Wayte had put him to trouble and expense at law. Why not make them pay for themselves with a contribution towards the stuff for a couple of plays? Poetic justice!

It was not very clever of Langley to call the justice a perjured knave, and throw himself open to actions for slander. Shakespeare was wiser. He saw that Gardiner throve on execration: the chorus of curses was a sincere acknowledgment of his successes as a cheat. To beknave him was to compliment him. But to stage the cunning justice as an imbecile fit only for inextinguishable laughter would flick him on the raw. And in safety, too; for to call a man a fool is held no slander, since the term imputes no crime.

In *Henry IV. Part Two* Shakespeare therefore aggravated the old knave's style with the outrageous addition of fool. In the *Merry Wives* he played upon the weaker vessel Wayte. Retaining enough of their peculiar features to give a Southwark audience supreme delight, he led the precious pair gently by the nose to a permanent place on the great stage of fools.

THE DATE OF *THE MERRY WIVES*

THE foregoing discoveries, and the conclusions to which they lead, at once raise the question, when did Shakespeare write the *Merry Wives?* Recent scholarship has offered conjectural dates ranging from 1598 to 1601. The new light now at hand should help us to a delimitation more precise.

If Shakespeare, as we have seen, introduced unmistakable hits at William Gardiner into his plays *Henry IV. Part Two* and the *Merry Wives,* he did it during the justice's lifetime. The cream of the jest would pass with the disappearance of the butt. Now Justice Gardiner died November 26, 1597. This date therefore gives us our later limit for the composition of the *Merry Wives.* For the earlier, we can hardly place it before Shakespeare's removal to Southwark and the quarrel of Gardiner and Wayte with Shakespeare and Langley, in October and November 1596. In the year which lies between these two Novembers, then, Shakespeare wrote the two plays which introduce Justice Shallow, *Henry IV. Part Two* and the *Merry Wives.*

In the case of the latter play, it will be seen from what follows that we may be able to fix limits more narrow still. According to a plausible and well-accepted tradition, Shakespeare wrote the *Merry Wives* in obedience to what amounted to a royal command. Queen Elizabeth, it is said, was so pleased with the fat knight in the two parts of *Henry IV.* that she desired a sequel, to show Falstaff in love. We are further told that the piece was written in a hurry—fourteen days only being allowed for its composition. Whether or not we can believe that the fluent Shakespeare actually finished this jolly farce in a fortnight's time, it is certain that the play bears the earmarks of hasty writing.

For what occasion in 1596–1597, we may now ask, was the *Merry Wives* ordered to be prepared in such post-haste? Let us look to the play for a suggestion. Although Shallow is a Gloucester-shire justice, and Falstaff a denizen of London, we see them both brought by the author to Windsor. Now Windsor was, of course, the headquarters of the Order of the Garter and the scene of the brilliant ceremonies of installing the new Knights of the Garter. In the course of the play Doctor Caius is represented as hastening to *la grande affaire* at Court; and in the last scene of the play a graceful and appropriate compliment is paid to Queen

112

Elizabeth in her quality as Sovereign of the Order. These indications lead us to suspect, with Sir Edmund Chambers and other scholars, that the play was written for some Feast of the Order of the Garter. The natural question, for which particular Feast? has however received no satisfactory answer; and I think I can now point to the very occasion which satisfies all the conditions.

The Garter Feast celebrated at the palace of Westminster on St. George's Day, April 23, 1597, was of exceptional splendour and solemnity. Four years had elapsed since the last election of Knights to the Order; and St. George's Day, 1597, witnessed the creation of five new Knights: Frederick, Duke of Württemberg; Thomas Lord Howard de Walden; George Carey, Lord Hunsdon; Charles Blount, Lord Mountjoy; and Sir Henry Lee.

A well-known and amusing story lies behind the election of Frederick, Duke of Württemberg. Five years earlier, as Count of Mömpelgart, and just before he succeeded to the dukedom, Frederick had come on a visit to England. Elizabeth, who had her political reasons for securing his future support in the German States, made him welcome. He failed, however, to gain the general good-will. For one thing, there is more than a suggestion that he and his followers misused a warrant for taking up post-horses free of charge. And whatever else he may or may not have done to deserve it, there was an unmistakable disposition to laugh at him.

During his stay he nevertheless conceived a great desire to be made a Knight of the Garter, and before leaving England he extracted from Elizabeth an assurance that he might expect the honour. From Stuttgart he wrote at intervals, reminding the Queen of her promise. With characteristic subtlety, in her replies to "Our Cousin Mumpellgart", Elizabeth kept him hoping for several years, and thus cheaply retained his devotion to her interests. By 1597, however, she thought it best to humour his wish, and therefore had him elected to the Order *in absentia*; but she did not inform him of the fact until later, and put off the expense of sending him the insignia to an indefinite future. Elizabeth's methods were well understood by her Court. The German duke was to be used, and not taken too seriously. His election was a necessary nuisance.

"Our Cousin Mumpellgart's" unpopular and somewhat comic character would make a small hit at the absent duke's expense relished at the Garter Feast in 1597. The *Merry Wives* contains

FRIDERICVS ∼ DVX WÜRTEMB. & TECC. &c.

Andr. Matth. Wolffgang Sculps. Augustæ

such a sly reference, detected by Charles Knight in 1840. As part of the plan of Evans and Caius to be revenged on mine Host of the Garter for the scurvy trick he had played them, they encourage some rogues to pose as followers of an imaginary German duke and so make off with three of mine Host's horses. When the horses are gone, Evans ironically warns the unsuspecting victim (according to the Quarto version) to beware of "three sorts of cosen garmombles, is cosen all the Host of Maidenhead and Readings"—a palpable reminiscence of Mömpelgart's visit and the consequent scandal of free post-horses and cheated innkeepers. And further to point up the amusing absence of the German duke—his name Mompelgarbled as 'Garmombles'—from the pomp of the Garter election for which he had laboured and longed, Doctor Caius puts his head in at mine Host's door, with the brisk announcement: ". . . it is tell-a me dat you make grand preparation for a duke de Jarmany: by my trot, dere is no duke, dat de court is know to come: I tell you for good vill: adieu."

The Duke of Württemberg being thus cheerfully allowed to be absent, the four Englishmen remained to be invested with their golden Garters and 'massy gold' collars, or Georges, by their

Sovereign's own hands. Elizabeth's favourite among these gentlemen was of course her cousin George Carey, Lord Hunsdon, Shakespeare's master, whom she had recently appointed Lord Chamberlain. Her affection is apparent in the letters which she later wrote to him when he was taking a water-cure at Bath: "Good George," she writes, "I cannot but wonder, considering the great number of pails of water that I hear have been poured upon you, that you are not rather drowned than otherwise; but I trust that all shall be for your better means to health.—Your most affectionate loving Sovereign, Elizabeth R." And later: "As yet I somewhat still doubt that there hath been too great abundance of the same [*i.e.* water] squashed upon you, which I would have restrained, if myself might have been with you." Still later: "And in what place soever you be, you shall find us a mother and a wife to minister unto you all the best effects of that tender and kind affection which we may possibly extend to one whom for many respects we hold so near and dear unto us."

As we have seen, the election of Lord Hunsdon and the rest took place at the Court at Westminster on St. George's Day, April 23, the Feast of the

Garter. The final ceremony of installing the four new Knights at Windsor was set for a month later, May 24. Following her general custom, Elizabeth did not attend this later ceremony, but appointed the Lord Admiral to act for her. I discover that in the month which intervened Lord Hunsdon's preparations for a brilliant following in the great riding to Windsor were carried forward with the most lavish expenditure, outdoing his fellow Knights in a competition of extravagance. On May 7, I find Francis Bacon writing to Dr. Hawkyns "that the lord Hunsdon, Lord Chamberlain, and Knight of the Garter, flaunted it gallantly". Three days later, as a new document in the Record Office shows, Hunsdon fortified his purse, by his mother's assistance, with a loan of two thousand pounds. And on May 14, Rowland Whyte wrote to Sir Robert Sidney: "Upon Monday come sennight the four new Knights are to be installed. It was agreed upon between themselves that they would have but fifty men apiece; but now I hear that my Lord Chamberlain will have three hundred, and Sir Henry Lee two hundred. The other two hold their first purpose, but they shall be all gentlemen."

No one seems to have recognized the illuminating

fact that Shakespeare and his fellows, as the Lord Chamberlain's servants, were a part of the gallant cavalcade of three hundred that escorted Lord Hunsdon from the Court—which had by this time moved to Greenwich—down to Windsor. I have found a detailed account, written by one of the heralds present, of the impressive entry of the four new Knights and their trains into Windsor on the afternoon of May 23, describing the sumptuous liveries—blue coats in honour of the Garter—in which the Lord Chamberlain's servants were dressed for the occasion:

"On the day before [the ceremony of installation] between 4 and 5 a clock in the afternoon, they entered Windsor in manner following:

"First, Sir Henry Lee with his company came riding through the town from Staines-ward, all his men well mounted, and in blue coats and badges.

"Next after him came riding the Lord Mountjoy, with all his men in blue coats, every one a plume of purple estridge feathers in their hats, and his gentlemen, chains of gold.

"Thirdly, and immediately after him, came my Lord Chamberlain, with a brave company of men and gentlemen, his servants and retainers, in blue coats faced with orange-coloured taffeta, and orange-coloured feathers in their hats, most part having chains of gold; besides a great number of knights and others, that accompanied his Lordship.

"Lastly the Lord Thomas Howard came immediately after, with like troop and blue coats faced with sad sea-colour green taffeta, with feathers of the same colours, and many chains of gold; which made a goodly show, and the more for that they came all four together in order, and not dropping one after another, and out of order, as they did two years after."[1]

We may now picture Shakespeare, who since October 1596 could write himself gentleman, riding into Windsor with his fellows before their lord, very brave in a blue coat lined with orange taffeta, orange plumes in his hat, and a chain of gold on his breast.

If his play of the *Merry Wives* was written to be acted before the Queen, as tradition has it, the question now puts itself: did Lord Hunsdon order

---

[1] Bodleian Ashmole MS. 1112, f. 16ᵛ. 'Transcribed from a 4°
MS belonging to Sir Ed. Walker.' Another transcript is found
in Stowe MS. 595, f. 45ᵛ.

it to be acted on April 23 before the Queen at Westminster, on the occasion of the Garter election and Feast, or at Greenwich just before his cavalcade set off on Monday, May 23, for the installation at Windsor?

The earlier date seems far more probable. Hunsdon must have known well before April 23 that his election was assured, and, being master of the company which played most frequently before Elizabeth, could pass on to his servant Shakespeare the Queen's wishes for a play to make them merry after the feast. Sir Edmund Chambers has noted that Hunsdon's household included a musical establishment, from which he might supply singing boys for the masquerade of fairies, which Shakespeare wrote into the *Merry Wives*. The instructions given by Puck and the Fairy-Queen to these sprites in the fifth act indicate in themselves that the play was written to be acted on the earlier date at Westminster. We know that nearly four years had elapsed since 1593 "when the Court lay at Windsor" last (II. ii. 59). The town would therefore need plenty of time to prepare itself to feed and lodge the Knights and their army of over six hundred mounted retainers and friends. Puck's warning would have been too late to come with any force, if the play were acted only a few days before the installation:

PUCK. Cricket, to Windsor chimneys shalt thou leap;
    Where fires thou find'st unraked and hearths unswept,
    There pinch the maids as blue as bilberry.
    Our radiant queen hates sluts and sluttery.

And the Chapel of St. George in the Castle also must be made ready for the coming ceremony:

FAIRY-QUEEN. About, about;
    Search Windsor Castle, elves, within and out:
    Strew good luck, ouphes, on every sacred room;
    That it may stand till the perpetual doom,
    In state as wholesome as in state 'tis fit,
    Worthy the owner, and the owner it.
    The several chairs of order look you scour
    With juice of balm and every precious flower:
    Each fair instalment, coat, and several crest,
    With loyal blazon, evermore be blest!
    And nightly, meadow-fairies, look you sing,
    Like to the Garter's compass, in a ring:
    Th'expressure that it bears, green let it be,
    More fertile-fresh than all the field to see;
    And *Honi soit qui mal y pense* write
    In emerald tufts, flowers purple, blue, and white;
    Like sapphire, pearl, and rich embroidery,
    Buckled below fair knighthood's bending knee:
    Fairies use flowers for their charactery.

The reasonable conclusion to which these pieces of evidence point is therefore that Lord Hunsdon's servants presented the hastily prepared *Merry Wives* before the Queen at Westminster at the Feast of the Garter on April 23, 1597.[1]

[1] I find it difficult to understand why someone before this (even without the help of the discovery concerning Justice Gardiner, which points to 1597) has not seen the Feast of the Garter on April 23, 1597, as the obvious occasion for the first production of the *Merry Wives*. All the evidence has long been either known or readily accessible: that the play was evidently written for a Garter celebration; that Frederick, the 'duke de Jarmany', was elected to the Order in 1597; that his absence and unpopularity would make this election a juncture most apt for the satirical hits in the play; and that Lord Hunsdon, the master of Shakespeare's company, was also elected on the same occasion. Yet in the presence of all this consenting evidence for the Garter feast of 1597, the keenest and ablest commentators have variously suggested such dates as 1598, 1599, 1600, and 1601. As guides for dating the *Merry Wives*, aesthetic criticism, verbal echoes, bibliographical refinements, and the absence of the play from Francis Meres's list in 1598, have all proved, it seems to me, inadequate or misleading.

In our preoccupation with William Shakespeare and Francis Langley, we have neglected to inquire about the two women who, as Wayte swore in Michaelmas term 1596, joined the actor and the theatre-owner in menacing him with death. Dorothy Soer, wife of John Soer, and Anne Lee are therefore excessively interesting; but I have found them no less tantalizing and elusive. What part could they have played in this quarrel? And who were they? Try as I may, I have not been able to throw any light on their connection with the affair, nor even to establish their probable identity. I shall have to content myself with recording the possibilities that I have traced, leaving it to others to provide the world with a positive identification.

The initial difficulty with Anne Lee is that her name is a fairly common one. Of the possibilities, I may mention first the most unlikely: an Agnes Lee, whom I discover in 1564, living near William Gardiner in Bermondsey. (The name *Agnes* is frequently found in Elizabethan documents used indifferently for *Annis* or *Anne*.) Her name appears in a suit brought by Gardiner against Cuthbert

Beeston[1] in which are mentioned seven small tenements in Bermondsey Street, three of which lay
just to the north of the door of Gardiner's house,
and were occupied in 1564 by William Thomas,
Agnes Lee, and Adam Spencer. In view of the
great length of time—thirty-two years—which
had to elapse before the date of the quarrel, I consider it unlikely that this Agnes Lee can be the
woman who in 1596 was active enough to frighten
William Wayte.

On eliminating this Agnes Lee of Bermondsey, I
am left with two others: a certain Anne Lea, wife
of John Lea of St. Olave's, Southwark, brewer,
and an Agnes Lee whom I find living in Copt Hall,
Paris Garden, in 1606.

Anne Lea, the brewer's wife, had long been connected with the family of Brookes who were persecuted and defrauded by Justice Gardiner, as I
have shown, in the matter of a loan and mortgage
in and about the year 1584. In 1602 I find this
Anne Lea, the brewer's wife, deposing on behalf
of the Brookes (in a suit which they had brought
against a certain Frances Smith, widow, and her
son Robert) that she had formerly lived for nine
years in the Brookes's house. The drift of her

---

[1] Hilary term, 1567/8. K.B. 27/1225/310.

testimony is definitely against the Gardiner family who are implicated. William Wayte is also a deponent in this suit. In 1596, the year of the quarrel, Anne Lea was some 28 years old. She appeared again as a witness in 1605 in a suit between the younger William Gardiner and his brother Thomas. Associated as she was with the victims of Justice Gardiner, it is not impossible that this Anne Lea somehow joined Langley and Shakespeare in threats against Gardiner's serving-man Wayte. With this vague suggestion I shall have to leave her.

The remaining Agnes Lee appears in the token book of St. Saviour's parish for 1606 as an occupant of Copt Hall in Paris Garden—an old building which stood to the south of the Swan Playhouse. Possibly this Agnes Lee is to be identified with a certain widow Lee, who in the years preceding had lived in Moss's Alley on the Bankside. In the Bankside token book for 1596–1597, I find the name of John Lee, with the 'John' stricken out and 'widdo' written beneath, indicating that about 1596 John Lee had died, and that his wife survived. Widow Lee continued to live in Moss's Alley, according to the token books, until 1602. The book for 1603 is missing, and in the list for

1604 she is not to be found. As I say, this Widow Lee may possibly be the Agnes Lee who appears in 1606 as dwelling in Copt Hall, Paris Garden. In the registers of St. Saviour's I find a record of the burial on January 19, 1613/4, of 'Agnes Lee, a woman, in the Church'. There is nothing I have been able to find which will help us further.

The other woman alleged to have menaced Wayte, Dorothy Soer, wife of John Soer, is almost as elusive as Anne Lee, even though we are given the additional clue that she had a husband named John. Her husband's family name, appearing under the various forms Sore, Soer, Soare, Sayer, Sawyer, Sare, Sares, Saires, and Sayers, is a common one in Southwark. There was a large family of Soares in Paris Garden when Langley owned the manor. Edward Soare or Soer, shipwright, was perhaps its most important member. He was the Edward Soer who served as constable of the Liberty of Paris Garden in 1584/5, and reported to Justice Gardiner the result of his search of a house suspected of harbouring papists. Another important Paris Garden Soer at this period was a Thomas, also a shipwright. In 1599 and 1600 the token books mention Thomas Soare as a neighbour of the player John Singer in Austen's Rents at 'the end of the Bankside'. Someone of these Soers owned tenements in Paris Garden Lane in 1593, called 'Sore's rents'. One of the family by 1613 had acquired some tenements in Paris Garden formerly owned by Francis Langley, and let certain of them out to stage-players to live in: for in the Paris Garden token book for 1613 we read, 'Langley's Rents, now Soare's: Thomas Soare, Robert Pallant, John Edmondes'. Pallant and Edmonds were well-known actors. The presence of these Soers in Paris Garden gave me the hope that I might find Dorothy Soer, wife of John Soer, among them; but neither John Soer nor his wife turned up.

For a John Soer in Southwark I find several possibilities. There is John Saires, a baker of Southwark, whose child Anne was christened in St. Saviour's on September 12, 1605. The name of the wife of John Saires, baker, which is what we particularly want, is however not given. Another possibility is a well-to-do John Sayer,[1] gentleman, whom I find in 1593 joined with a Henry Sayer in the sale of a large amount of property in the parishes of St. Saviour, St. George, and St. Mag-

[1] A John Sayer appears in the accounts of the Treasurer of the Chamber in 1589/90, receiving forty shillings 'for bringing

dalen, Southwark. Finally, I discover a teasing entry, in the registers of St. George's, Southwark, of the marriage of John Sayer and Dorithie Collard; but the date is August 19, 1605—ten years too late for the quarrel of 1596.

Shakespeare's associates Anne Lee and Dorothy Soer have given me much labour and precious little pay for it. I am left at the end of the search almost as ignorant as when I began it. For lack of facts, I am tempted to imagine that the clerk in the Queen's Bench perhaps made a mistake, and that we should read 'Thomas' or 'Edward' for 'John' Soer. In that case we might see Dorothy as one of the Soers of Paris Garden, and so a near neighbour of Shakespeare and Langley. I might then give fancy a loose rein and picture Dorothy and Anne respectively as a landlady of Shakespeare's and a servant of Langley's—women who would have a very real interest in protecting the men of the Swan Playhouse, with force and arms in the shape of broomsticks, against the annoyance offered by Justice Gardiner's officious but easily terrified serving-man, William Wayte.

letters in post for Her Majesty's affairs from Dartmouth, and for return with letters of like service'. Possibly he is to be identified with the last named.

CONCLUSION

As a result of the investigations detailed in these pages, a number of interesting additions have been made to the sum of our knowledge of Shakespeare's life, of the dates of his works, and of his dramatic methods.

We learn first that by the end of October or the beginning of November 1596 he had moved across the Thames to Southwark. And finding him in close association with Francis Langley, the owner of the Swan in Paris Garden, we conclude that his company was acting in Langley's playhouse. We see the actor Shakespeare and his associate the theatre-owner seriously annoyed by the notoriously unjust local justice, William Gardiner, and that unconsidered trifle, his stepson Wayte: so seriously annoyed, that Wayte swears the gentle Shakespeare put him in terror of his life.

Next we recognize this pair of vexatious interlopers by a series of unmistakable hits in *Henry IV. Part Two* and *The Merry Wives of Windsor*. This disclosure gives the *coup de grâce* to the moribund notion that Shakespeare, in drawing the figure of Justice Shallow, was thinking of his worthy neighbour in Warwickshire, Sir Thomas Lucy.

By combining our discoveries with the annals of Queen Elizabeth's Court and with the internal evidence of the comedy itself, we have been enabled to fix the date of first production of the *Merry Wives* on April 23, 1597—a date earlier than recent scholarship has suspected. And since it is generally agreed that *Henry IV. Part Two* preceded the *Merry Wives*, the two parts of *Henry IV.* must now be pushed back into the season 1596–1597. It is now clear, therefore, that except for the touching account of Falstaff's death in *Henry V.*, Shakespeare had completed his portraiture of the fat knight by the spring of 1597.

More important, however, than the fresh light on the external life of Shakespeare, more significant than the alteration in the dates of his plays, is the ocular demonstration now given us of his dramatic use of some of the life he knew: unique evidence of his use of persons, to quote Ben Jonson,

> . . . such as Comedy would choose
> When she would show an image of the times. . . .

When we consider the true history of Justice Gardiner, and the local world's opinion of him, the figure of Justice Shallow appears as a new triumph of the dramatist. Shakespeare is here revealed for the first time as a master of personal satire, taking with devastating humour a satisfactory revenge for himself, his associates of the theatre, and Gardiner's victims in Southwark. A few months after the production of the *Merry Wives*, exit Gardiner from the Elizabethan scene into a well-merited oblivion, carrying with him the bitter sting of the contemporary caricature. As children see nothing more in *Gulliver* than the fascinating story, so the playgoing world to-day sees in the Justice Shallow scenes no more than inoffensive folly in a care-free atmosphere of perennial comedy. Shakespeare's magic has transmuted a sordid Southwark into a rural Gloucestershire or an ideal Windsor, set in a pleasant England where knaves are fools, and to live is to laugh them out of countenance. We can forgive Gardiner his crimes; did he not give us Justice Shallow? And as for Wayte, it was an act of sublime inspiration in him to pick the quarrel with Shakespeare; for out of it was born that most exquisite of ninnies, Abraham Slender.

APPENDIX

i.

[1555, Mar. 11. Dispensation from Cardinal Pole to William Gardiner, to eat flesh in Lent. Sloane MS. 3299, f. 65.]

REGINALDUS Miseratione diuina sanctæ Mariæ in Cosmedin sanctæ Romanæ ecclesiæ Diaconus Cardinalis Polus nuncupatus Sanctissimi Domini nostri Papæ et sedis apostolicæ ad serenissimos Philippum et Mariam Angliæ Reges et vniuersum Angliæ Regnum de latere Legatus   Dilecto nobis in Christo Guilielmo Gardinerio salutem in Domino sempiternam. Tibi, cui ob uarios morbos et corporis infirmitates quibus laboras, esus piscium uehementer nocet, ut hoc præsenti quadragesimali tempore exceptis Mercurij Veneris et Sabbati diebus, quibus te ab esu carnium abstinere uolumus, carnibus ouis et lacticinijs de utriusque medici consilio et ea circumspectione adhibita, ut nemini ex hoc offendiculum fiat durantibus tuis infirmitatibus libere et licite uti et uesci possis auctoritate apostolica nobis per litteras Sanctissimi Domini nostri domini Julij Papæ Tertij concessa qua fungimur tenore præsentium concedimus et indulgemus prohibitionibus contrarijs non obstantibus quibuscunque. Datum Lambethi prope Londinum Wintoniensi Diocesi Anno a Nativitate Domini Millesimo quingentesimo quinquagesimo quinto quinto Idus Martij Pontificatus Sanctissimi in Christo patris et domini nostri domini Julij diuina prouidentia Papæ Tertij Anno Sexto:

[*signed*] Reg[inaldus] Car[dinalis] Polus leg[atus].

ii.

[1555, Mich. 2 & 3 Ph. & M.
Queen's Bench. K.B. 27/1176/244*d*.]

Surrey. In Trinity last past Henry Chare, by attorney, came into Court and produced a bill against William Gardyner and

133

Randall Smyth in a plea of trespass that on 16 June 1 & 2
Philip & Mary with force and arms they broke his close at Bermondsey and there depastured their horses, sheep, cows, and
pigs, and consumed his grass to the value of £10 from the 16
till 22 of June.

On the Wednesday after the Octave of Michaelmas, William
Gardyner and Randall Smyth come and say they are not guilty.
(They had made default at the Assizes at Croydon, 1 July.)
The jurors consider that William Gardyner and Randall Smyth
are guilty, &c. Damages, £11.

iii.

[1556, Oct. 14. Guildhall, Southwark Courts Leet, 1539–1564.]

Villa de Southwark. 14 October 3 & 4 Ph. & M. View of frankpledge held before William Garett, knight, and William Harper
and John White, Lord Mayor and Sheriffs of London. Inquest
of fifteen jurors.

Item presentant quod Willelmus Gardener ijsdem die et annis
[xiij die Januarij annis predictis] fecit affraiam et effudit san-
guinem super Willelmum Beston. Ideo ipse in misericordia . . .
iijˢ iiijᵈ

iv.

[1556, Nov. 10. Guildhall, Mayor's Court Repertories, 13/446.
Offley, Mayor.]

Item it was granted and agreed that William Gardyner and
Roger Water, bringing into this Court £20 apiece the next
court day, shall not only be admitted into the liberties of this
City by redemption in the fellowship of the Grey Tawyers, but
also have £10 apiece of their said money to them freely given
back again.

v.

[1556, Dec. 3. *Ibid.*, 13/457. Offley, Mayor.]

At this court it was Ordered that the two persons lately admitted into the liberties of the City by redemption in the Com-

pany of the Greytawyers shall be quietly permitted to enjoy
their said freedom until Candlemas next coming, albeit that
the Court is here informed that they neither are skilful in the
said art nor yet do practise the same, to the intent to try the
truth thereof in the mean season.

vi.

[1558/9, March. Records of the Leathersellers' Company.]

In a list of names with sums noted "delivered unto the Chamber of London for the Queen's use by the way of prest, in
March Anno 1558", the following entry was made and crossed
out: "Paid None   Wylliam gardner   £5   not R[eceived]".

vii.

[1559. Close Roll, 1 Eliz., pt. 5. C54/557/2.]

Indenture made 31 March 1559 between Robert Fulleshurst of
Crewe, Cheshire, esquire, and William Gardener of Bermondsey, Surrey, gent. For £160 Fulleshurst grants to Gardener and
his heirs forever lands, tenements, &c. in Crewe. But if Fulleshurst pays £160 to Gardener at Easter this conveyance shall
be void.

[See below, document xxxii.]

viii.

[1558, Trinity. Queen's Bench. K.B. 27/1187/113d.]

London. Trin. 1 Mary (1554). David Cornewell, gent., and
Elizabeth his wife, executrix of Richard Gardyner, executor
of William Gardyner the elder, late of the parish of St. Mary
Magdalen, Bermondsey, Surrey, yeoman, against Michael
Thrale of Luton, Beds., gent., in a plea that he owed £40. The
plaintiffs said that Michael Thrale on 30 November 33 Hen.
VIII (1541) bound himself to pay William Gardyner the £40 at
Christmas following, but had not done so, though often asked
by the said William and Richard in their lifetimes and by

135

Elizabeth after the death of Richard, and by David and Elizabeth after their marriage. It was considered that the said Michael should pay the £40.

Afterwards on 20 June 4 & 5 Ph. & M. (1558) Michael came and said that in the judgment on record there was a manifest error because no damages were taxed. Therefore it is an error, &c.

ix.

[1559, Oct. 2. Chancery Town Depositions, C24/42.]

David Cornewall and Elizabeth his wife, plaintiffs, against William Gardyner, defendant.

Deposition of John Drewe of the parish of St. Mary Magdalen, Southwark, wire seller, aged 41.

He said that Richard Gardyner was in his lifetime possessed of the third part of Bermondsey Grange by the gift of William Gardyner his father, and that he took the profits thereof for three years before his death. And that Richard by his will left his estate and interest in the property to Elizabeth the plaintiff, then his wife. This deponent was present at the making of the will, with five or six other persons "that is to say, one Lambeth a Butcher, one Keyman or Kemyngham a Brewer that dwelleth at the sign of the Horse Head in Southwark, one other called Gryffyn, and one Fryer that wrote the said will, with others". This deponent was overseer of the said will. And since the said Richard's death about two years before, the said Elizabeth had enjoyed the third part of the said Grange.

x.

[1559, May 2. Patent Roll, 1 Eliz., pt. 1. C66/938/23.]

Licence granted, for £5:4:8, to William Dowes, clerk, to alienate all those lands and tenements, parcel of his Manor of Leygham Court, Surrey, including a close called 'Spawne Meade', two parcels of land called 'Lyttle Balshams', a parcel of land

called 'Rusheden', and another called 'Bushe Leas' and all
those parcels of wood called 'Bushe Leas copies' and 'Bushe
Leas Wood' and 'Legham Wood' (60 acres), 'Frydaye Grove',
'Ballams Copies', etc. held of the Queen in chief, by fine to
William Gardener of Bermondsey, Surrey, gentleman, to have
and to hold to him and his heirs forever.

xi.

[1559, May 31. Close Roll, 1 Eliz., pt. 8. C54/560/8.]

Indenture made 31 May 1 Eliz., between William Dowes, vicar
of All Hallows Barking, and William Gardyner of Bermondsey,
Surrey, gent., recites that William Dowes by an indenture of
25 January 1 Mary (1553/4) demised to William Gardyner all
that close called 'Spanne Meade' and two parcels of ground
called 'Little Ballams' and parcel of the land called 'Russhe-
denne' and parcels called 'Busshelease', 'Busheleas Coppies',
'Busheleas Wood', 'Leighams Wood', 'Frydaye Grove', 'Ballams Coppice', and 'Ballams Grove', all parcel of the manor of
Leigham Court, for 71 years at a rent of £17 4s.

This indenture witnesses that William Dowes, for £120, sold
the same land to the said William Gardyner and his heirs forever, William Gardyner to pay half the rent of 30s. due to the
Queen.

xii.

[1559, Oct. 20. Guildhall, Southwark Courts Leet, 1539–1564.]

Manor of Southwark, view of frankpledge.

Item it is pained that William Gardyner do amend the highway to the middle of the causey as far as his rents goeth by the
same feast [Midsummer next] upon pain   .   .   . 40s.

xiii.

[1559. Records of the Leathersellers' Company.]

William Gardener contributed 40s. to wheat money for the use
of the City.

xiv.

[1560, March 8. Patent Roll, 2 Eliz., pt. 11. C66/958/34.]

Licence granted, for 30s., to William Gardener, gentleman, to alienate by fine all those two parcels of land called 'little Balames', containing 40 acres, extending in length to Clapham Common, 'Bushleas Wood *alias* Bristowe Cawseye Copyes' in the parish of Streatham, Surrey, 'Frydaye Grove', 'Ballames Copyes', and 'Ballames Grove', held in chief, to Richard Bostocke, gentleman, to have and to hold to him and his heirs forever.

xv.

[1560, March 11. Close Roll, 2 Eliz., pt. 2. C54/567/27.]

Indenture made 11 March 1559/60 between William Gardener of Bermondsey, Surrey, gentleman, and Richard Bostocke of Newington, Surrey, gentleman. The said Gardener for £266:13:4 sold to Bostocke 'Little Ballams' (40 acres), one of the said closes extending in length to Clapham Common and the other to 'Ballams Coppice', a little close in the tenure of Thomas Piggett, a coppice called 'Busheleas Woods *alias* Bristowe cawseye coppice' (20 acres), lying in the parish of Streatham: between the highway leading from London to Streatham on the east, and a lane leading from Stockwell Common to Tooting Common on the west, Stockwell Common and Leigham Wood on the north, and 'Bushelease' Field on the south; 'Frydays Grove' (15 1/2 acres), 'Ballams Coppice' (12 acres), 'Ballams Grove' (2 acres). William Gardener to pay half the rent of 30s. due to the Queen.

xvi.

[1560, Easter. Feet of Fines. C.P. 25/Surr. E. 2 Eliz./197.]

Between Richard Bostock, gentleman, querent, and William Gardener and Frances his wife, deforciants, of 20 acres of land,

10 of meadow, 10 of pasture, and 50 of wood, in Streatham. Quitclaimed by William and Frances and the heirs of William to Richard and his heirs for £90.

xvii.
[1560. Repertory of Originalia, 2 Eliz., pt. 1. Index 6959.]

Licence to William Gardener, gentleman, to alienate a parcel of meadow called 'Spannmeade' in Streatham, Surrey, to William Beston and Joan his wife.

xviii.
[1560, March 7. Close Roll, 2 Eliz., pt. 3. C54/568/26.]

Indenture made 7 March 1559/60 between William Gardener of Bermondsey, Surrey, gentleman, and William Beston of Streatham, Surrey, gentleman, and Joan his wife. Recites that William Dowes, vicar of All Hallows Barking, sold some land parcel of Leigham Court [as in No. xi.] to the said William Gardener. Now upon this indenture the said William Gardener, for £200, sold to the said William and Joan all the parcels of land now in the tenure of Joan, widow of Henry Holland, husbandman, viz.: 'Spanne Mead' (24 acres), 'Rushdean', 'Busshelease', 'Bushlease Coppice'. William Gardener undertook to pay half the rent of 30s. due to the Queen.

xix.
[1560, Easter. Feet of Fines. C.P. 25/Surr. E. 2 Eliz./202.]

Between William Beston gentleman and Joan his wife, querents, and William Gardener gentleman and Frances his wife, deforciants, of land in Streatham. Quitclaimed by William and Frances for them and the heirs of William, to William and Joan and the heirs of William, for 220 marks.

139

xx.

[1560, Trinity. Queen's Bench. K.B. 27/1195/46.]

Middlesex. In Mich. last, John Waskett, executor of the will of Margaret Assheton, widow, executrix of the will of Adam Assheton, citizen and 'lanii carnificis' of London, produced in Court his bill against William Gardener of Bermondsey, Surrey, gentleman, executor of the will of William Gardener of the parish of St. Mary Magdalen, Bermondsey, yeoman, in a plea that he owed him £40. Alleged that William Gardener the testator 18 March 33 Henry VIII (1542) at Westminster bound himself to Adam in £40 to be repaid at Easter following: and that the said William the executor, though often asked to pay, after the testator's death, will not pay.

By attorney, Gardener says that he is not the executor of the will of the said William Gardener deceased, and has never administered any of his goods and chattels.

Discontinuance recorded.

xxi.

[1561, March 28. Close Roll, 3 Eliz., pt. 1. C54/583/24.]

Indenture made 28 March 1561 between William Gardener of Bermondsey, gentleman, and John Bowyer of Lincoln's Inn, esquire, and Richard Bostocke of Newington, Surrey, gentleman.

Recites Dowes's grant [No. xi.]. By this indenture, for £100, William Gardener now sold Leigham's Wood (60 acres) to the said John Bowyer and Richard Bostocke. Gardener to pay 5s. yearly as a share of the 30s. rent due to the Queen.

xxii.

[1561, May 12. Common Pleas. C.P. 40/1195/Deeds mem. 11.]

William Gardener of Bermondsey, Surrey, gentleman, came into Court 25 June 3 Eliz., and asked to have this deed enrolled: that William Gardener of Bermondsey, Surrey, gentleman, for £100, had sold to John Bowier of Camberwell, esquire, and Richard Bostocke of Newington, gentleman, all that wood called 'Leighams Wood', containing 60 acres, in the parish of Streatham, Surrey, to have and to hold to the use of them and their heirs forever. Dated 12 May 3 Eliz.

<h2 style="text-align:center">xxiii.</h2>

[1561, Michaelmas. Feet of Fines.

C.P. 25/Surr. M. 3/4 Eliz./548.]

Between John Bowyer, esq., and Richard Bostock, gent., querents, and William Gardiner and Frances his wife, deforciants, of 60 acres of wood in Streatham. Quitclaimed by the deforciants for them and their heirs to the plaintiffs and the heirs of John for £40.

<h2 style="text-align:center">xxiv.</h2>

[1561, Michaelmas. Feet of Fines.

C.P. 25/Surr. M. 3/4 Eliz./554.]

Between William Gardyner, querent, and Owen Clune and Agnes his wife, deforciants, of 11 messuages, 11 gardens, 1 orchard, and 3 acres of meadow in the parish of St. Mary Magdalen, Bermondsey. Quitclaimed by the deforciants and their heirs to William Gardyner and his heirs for 140 marks.

<h2 style="text-align:center">xxv.</h2>

[1561. Chancery Proceedings, Series II. C3/128/65.]

Robert Mote of Lambeth v. William Gardener.

Gardener's Answer. (Undated.)

That William Gardener the elder was possessed of the Grange in Bermondsey, and let some part of it to the plaintiff.

That the plaintiff and defendant were bound in several obligations together, and that the plaintiff was arrested at the defendant's suit, and afterwards agreed to make an acquittance.

The plaintiff was bound to the defendant in an obligation of £100 dated 28 March 1 & 2 Ph. & M., whereby the plaintiff bought from the defendant all his title and interest in the Grange. Certain leases were also made to several persons, among whom were Randall Smyth, Roger Bansted, Frydes-with, daughter of William, and John Askewe her husband, of certain parcels of the Grange; the plaintiff was to allow these persons to have quiet possession. "That after the said Robert Motte did break and tear the said obligation, against the will of the said William Gardener", but promised to make another of like effect; and because he did not do so, the defendant caused him to be arrested.

Yet because the defendant's declaration "did not in every point effectual agree" with the condition of the obligation, the defendant was nonsuited, and paid the costs of the suit.

The defendant then made a complaint of trespass in the same Court [? Sheriffs' Court of London] against the plaintiff, declaring that Mote had torn the deed; and after many delays, commenced other suits.

xxvi.

[1561, Michaelmas. Chancery Decrees and Orders, 1561/16.]

Robert Mote, plaintiff, William Gardiner, defendant.

A writ of *certiorari* awarded to the Lord Mayor and Sheriffs of London to certify into this Court all such matter as before them dependeth between the said parties.

xxvii.

[No date, but after 1560. Chanc. Proc., Ser. II. C3/120/76.]

Elizabeth Martyn, widow of Stephen Martyn of Southwark, butcher, plaintiff, against Thomas Shepperd and Frideswide his wife.

Bill of complaint: Shows that about 26 Hen. VIII (April 1534–

April 1535) Robert, late Abbot of Bermondsey, demised to Ralph Wren and Helen his wife the Grange of Bermondsey for a term of years yet uncompleted. About February, 28 Hen. VIII (1536/7), the said Ralph and Helen conveyed two closes (then in the tenure of the said Stephen Martyn), parcel of the said Grange, to William Gardyner of Southwark, deceased.

Afterwards William Gardyner, son of the said William Gardyner, was possessed of the same, and sold his interest therein to Robert Mote of Lambeth, Surrey, yeoman. About February 1 & 2 Ph. and M. (1554/5) the latter demised the same to Stephen Martyn.

But one Frideswide Askewe, sister of William Gardner the son, by her brother's means pretended to have all her brother's estate and interest in the said two closes, by a grant from her said brother made before his grant of the premises to Robert Mote. Afterwards, "to the end that he would be in quietness", Robert Mote agreed with Frideswide that she should have pasture and feeding for "three kye" for her life thereon; and she in return granted him all her pretended title to the premises. And William Gardner the son gave Mote the counterpart of an indenture with the seals torn off, which he said was the lease made by him to the said Frideswide.

Later the said Frideswide married one Thomas Shepperde, who with the help of the said William Gardner made claim to the said two closes, alleging that the indenture delivered to Mote was unsealed. Thereupon the said Robert Mote, "to avoid all trouble", conveyed to the said Thomas and Frideswide the herbage of a parcel of ground in Surrey called "the driving wall, and the lying of six kine within the Grange yard aforesaid, paying but a red rose, for term of thirty years" if Frideswide should so long live. Whereupon Thomas Shepperde granted the pretended lease to Robert Mote, and promised to cancel the unsealed indenture.

143

Stephen Martyn died, leaving the plaintiff his sole executrix; and now the said Thomas and Frideswide (though still enjoying the said pasturage) claim the two closes, and wrongfully enter them "and daily menace to trouble her more".

Answer. The defendants say that in August 1 & 2 Ph. & M. (1554) William Gardner the son demised the closes for 25 years to John Askewe deceased, late husband of the said Frideswide, and that Robert Mote wrongfully entered into possession of them.

xxviii.

[1562. Chanc. Proc., Ser. II. C3/5/64.]

Henry Lord Audley, plaintiff, against William Gardener, and Henry Dyconson, defendants.

Bill of Complaint.

The complainant stated that he had demised to one Robert Luce . . . Ph. & M., Heleye Castle, Staffordshire, with three messuages, two corn mills, five smithies, 400 acres of land, 100 acres of meadow, 500 acres of pasture, 600 acres of wood, and 400 acres of furze and heath, for a term of 10 years.

The said Robert Luce by his will made his wife Katherine his sole executrix; after the death of the said Robert, Katherine was possessed of the property and died intestate; upon which the administration came into the hands of Frances, wife of Edmond Waight, citizen and leatherseller of London. Afterwards Waight conveyed the property to Robert Lydington; but by a counter-assurance, the former was to occupy the premises.

After Edmond Waight's death, Frances his widow married William Gardener the now defendant, and they occupied the premises. But afterwards, by a new lease made by the old Lord Audley and the complainant to Frances and William Gardener, the complainant and his father were to occupy the premises, paying a yearly rent to the said Frances and William, and the complainant stood bound to the said Gardener and his wife in a recognizance of statute staple.

And since that time, the said Lydington granted his lease and interest in the premises to Henry Dyconson, who now has recovered the same against the complainant, and has taken possession thereof; whereby the complainant could not pay the yearly rent to William Gardener and Frances his wife, and was in danger of forfeiting his bonds.

Answer of William Gardener.

He said that George, late Lord Audley, and the now complainant by their deed of 17 May 1 Eliz. (1559) demised Heley Castle and the lordship and manor of Audley to the defendants from Michaelmas then next following for a term of 11 years, for the performance of which covenant the complainant and his father were bound to the defendant in £500, "which, as this defendant supposeth, is forfeited".

That if an agreement was made between Waight and Lodington that the latter was to occupy the premises, it was not known to the defendant; "and if the said Edmunde Wayght had any such interest at will in the premises, then . . nothing thereof after his death could come unto the said Frances or to the defendant that took her to wife".

By agreement with the late Lord Audley and the complainant, the said defendant William Gardener and Frances surrendered all their interest in the premises, in return for the new lease, as mentioned in the bill of complaint.

Demurrer of Edward [sic] *Dyconson, gentleman.*

Said that in November last past it was decided before the Council in the Star Chamber that the defendant Dyconson should not be disturbed in his occupation of the said premises until he had recovered the same at the common law; therefore he "demurreth in judgement of this Court, if he be vexed or molested".

xxix.

[1587, Jan. and Feb. Chanc. Proc. Eliz. C2 Eliz. A8/31.]

George Lord Audley, plaintiff, against Mary Dickinson, widow, Rowland Lytton, and William Gardener, defendants.

Audley's bill of complaint. Said that plaintiff, wishing to sell Heley Castle and purchase land in Wiltshire, had to acquit and discharge and hold harmless all the persons to whom his father and grandfather had made leases of that property.

That one Edward Diconson, deceased, "being a man well known in his lifetime to be very subtle and crafty", forged a deed dated 11 Nov. 3 & 4 Ph. & M. (1556) by which George Lord Audley and Henry his son demised the Castle of Heley, worth £100 a year, besides the profits of the woods for 99 years, for a yearly rent of £20 to be paid at the will and pleasure of the said Diconson.

Yet the said Diconson made no use of this forged lease in the lifetimes of the plaintiff's father and grandfather, but allowed them to make other leases of the premises.

But after the deaths of the father and grandfather, the plaintiff then being a minor and a ward of the Queen's, the said Diconson in 8 Eliz. (1566), "minding very lewdly and corruptly" to appear more credible, conspired with some of the Chancery clerks and caused this forged lease to be enrolled, and got it passed under the great seal by way of a *vidimus* or *innotescimus*. The said Diconson, "although he was continually a very bare and needy man", never made any open claim to the property: but now that he is deceased, Mary his widow, confederating with a certain Rowland Lytten, finding the forged deed and the *innotescimus*, and knowing the same to be forged, has offered the same to divers persons for sale; "and hath delivered the said *vidimus* or *innotescimus* thereof under the great seal of England unto one William Gardener of Southwark, to be kept, to the great hurt and slander of such interest and title"

146

as the complainant had in the property. And the said plaintiff
was in danger of forfeiting his bonds. He asked for a writ of
subpena to be issued to the defendants, "as also unto the said
William Gardener .. commanding the said William Gardener
thereby to appear in this honorable Court and to bring with
him the said *innotescimus*".

Answer of Mary Dickinson. She confessed that she had heard
of such a lease made to her husband, but stated that she was
not born at the time it was made, and that "she is unlearned
and cannot so well read written hand as to understand what
such a writing meaneth". She thought that her husband had
made no claim to the property because he could not contend
"with such great personages", and that the *innotescimus* was
taken away from her husband.

After her husband's death, the deeds came into her possession
again, "and without that, that she delivered the same *innotescimus* to the said William Gardener to keep .. but only at his
earnest request showed it him to copy out and to redeliver"
to her again [or to] the administrator of the said Edward
Dickinson, "which he swore he would do within some days
after".

xxx.

[1562 & 1563. Records of the Leathersellers' Company.]
1562, Oct. William Gardiner contributed £4 to wheat money.
1562/3, Jan. „   „   „   „   „   „   „

xxxi.

[1562, Nov. 14. Close Roll, 5 Eliz. pt. 11. C54/640/23.]
Indenture made 14 November 1562 between Bartholomew
Lynton of London, gentleman, and William Gardyner, citizen
and leatherseller of London, who paid the said Lynton £50 for
lands and marshes in Romney Marsh in the parishes of New-

church and Bylssyngton, Kent, now in the tenure of William and Richard Hall, and for those lands in the same places whereof Katherine Lynton, widow of Robert Lynton, and mother-in-law of Bartholomew, is seized for life. But if the said Bartholomew should pay the sum of £50 to the said William in the parish church of St. Saviour, Southwark, at several feasts then following, this indenture was to be void.

xxxii.
[1563, June 25. Chanc. Proc., Ser. II. C3/63/28.]

Robert Fullhurst, of Crewe, Cheshire, esquire, plaintiff, against William Gardyner, defendant.

Fullhurst's bill of complaint. "That whereas one William Gardyner, subtly and without just cause, did obtain a judgment before the Justice of the Common Pleas against your said orator as administrator of Thomas Fowlehurst, knight, his father, for the debt of £50 and 40s. over for costs, for satisfaction whereof afterwards your said suppliant (although there were no just cause for the said William Gardener to recover the said debt . . in that your said suppliant had before the suit against him commenced fully administered all the goods and cattle of the said Sir Thomas Fulleshurst) was nevertheless contented, in avoiding of further vexation and trouble, to compound with the said William Gardener for satisfaction of the said debt . . . and of all such other debts as the said William Gardener claimed to be in any wise owing unto him by the said Sir Thomas Fullehurst, and in full recompense and satisfaction thereof concluded and agreed to pay unto the said William Gardener the sum of £80 of lawful money of England at two several days [£40 at St. Thomas the Apostle last past and £40 at St. Thomas the Apostle next following]." Fullhurst bound himself to pay, and Gardener gave him a deed of general release. Before the first day of payment, Fullhurst, by the hands of his servant Thomas Mekyns, paid Gardener the first £40, and asked to give him an acquittance or receipt. This however Gardener, "craftily intending to use some advantage against your said orator, did refuse to perform; and not thus satisfied, minding and intending the utter undoing of your said suppliant, did craftily and very dishonestly prosecute process of outlawry upon the said judgement against your said suppliant, whereby your said suppliant was outlawed and thereby forfeited unto the Queen's Highness not only all the profits and revenues of his lands but also all and singular his goods and chattels, to his loss, damage, and hindrance of £1000 and above".

xxxiii.
[1563, June 6. Close Roll, 5 Eliz. pt. 11. C54/640/46.]

Edward Welshe of Lymesfield, Surrey, esq., acknowledged that he owed £500 to William Gardener, citizen and leatherseller of London, to be paid on the feast of the Nativity of St. John the Baptist. Dated 6 June 3 Eliz. (1561). They were jointly bound to Walter Roberts, of Glassenbury, Cranbrook, Kent, esq., in £300 for the payment of £200 at the fount stone in St. Paul's Cathedral on 2 August 3 Eliz. and £100 on 9 October following, at the same place.
On 6 July 1598 William Gardener and Nicholas Smythe, executors of the will of the said William Gardener, came and acknowledged themselves to be satisfied.

xxxiv.
[1563 & 1564. Records of the Leathersellers' Company.]

1563. William Gardiner contributed 20s. towards the discharge of such debts as the Hall did owe to the Rentor Warden.
1564. William Gardiner assessed for wheat money.

149

xxxv.

[1564, Sept. 4. Common Pleas. C.P. 40/1226/5d.]

Cuthbert Beeston, citizen and girdler of London, came into Court 14 October 6 Eliz. (1564) and asked to have this deed enrolled: an indenture made 4 September 6 Eliz. between William Gardyner, citizen and leatherseller of London, on the one part, and Cuthbert Beeston, citizen and girdler, on the other; by which it was agreed that William should recover against Cuthbert, by common writ of entry in Michaelmas term next, one messuage, 9 cottages, and 10 gardens in the parish of St. Mary Magdalen, Bermondsey, to the use and behoof of William and his heirs forever.

xxxvi.

[1564, Michaelmas. Feet of Fines. C.P. 25/Surr. M. 6/7 Eliz.]

Between William Gardener, querent, and Cuthbert Beeston and Alice his wife, deforciants, of a messuage, 9 cottages, and 10 gardens in the parish of St. Mary Magdalen, Bermondsey, quitclaimed by the deforciants for themselves and their heirs to William and his heirs for 230 marks.

xxxvii.

[1565, Trinity. Queen's Bench. K.B. 27/1215/165.]

Surrey. In Hilary term, William Gardyner, citizen and leatherseller of London, came and produced a bill against Peter Baker for trespass, saying that a certain Cuthbert Beyston was seized of a messuage in Bermondsey Street, in which the said William Gardyner dwelt, and two other tenements adjacent, and seven other messuages in Bermondsey Street, which the said Cuthbert sold to the said William, 18 August 6 Eliz. (1564). On 25 August, Cuthbert gave William a recognizance of £300 for the fulfilling of the terms of this conveyance. William delivered this recognizance to Peter Baker to keep on the condition that

150

if the said Cuthbert Beeston and Alice his wife levied a fine and recovery as was required in the conveyance, that then the said Peter should deliver the recognizance to the said Cuthbert; and if they did not do so, that then the recognizance should be returned to William Gardyner. On 30 August 6 Eliz. the said Peter promised that the said Cuthbert and Alice should levy the fine.

Now Gardyner said that Cuthbert and Alice did not levy the fine on the first Monday in Michaelmas term following as they promised, and Peter refused to return the recognizance to him, so that he could not recover £300.

In Trinity term 7 Eliz., Peter Baker said he received the recognizance from Gardyner on the understanding that when the said Cuthbert and Alice should acknowledge the fine and recovery, then the said recognizance should be void, and should remain in his (Peter's) hands; but that if Cuthbert should die before the said first Monday in Michaelmas term, then Peter should redeliver the said recognizance to Gardyner. And he said that the fine was raised in Michaelmas term 6 Eliz., by which the recognizance became void.

It was considered (after many delays) that Peter should pay Gardyner damages of £8:3:4. And on 1 July 10 Eliz. (1568), William Gardyner came and acknowledged himself to be satisfied.

xxxviii.

[1565. Guildhall, Mayor's Court Repertories, 15/415d, 440d.]

7 Eliz., 25 January. Item William Gardener, leatherseller, for his misdemeanours and contemptuous and unfitting words and language towards his Warden and Company lately had and used, was this day committed to ward in Newgate.

7 Eliz., 17 May. Item it was ordered at the suit of the Company of the Leathersellers, that William Gardener, being one of their company, for his misdemeanours towards them shall be

committed to ward by my Lord Mayor, there to remain till the next court.

xxxix.

[1565. Records of the Leathersellers' Company.]

"Charges paid by William Prestwoode at the mayor's feast, which he paid for William Gardener's part, *somma* 36s. 10d."

xl.

[1566. Records of the Leathersellers' Company.]

The Wardens paid "unto my Lord Mayor's officer for the arresting of William Gardiner, leatherseller, for his disobedience to the Master and Wardens, *somma* 2s."

xli.

[1565, Michaelmas. Queen's Bench. K.B. 27/1216.]

Surrey. In Michaelmas term William Gardyner and Frances his wife came and produced a bill against Richard Pype, saying that on 20 December 4 & 5 Ph. & M. (1557) at the parish of St. George, Southwark, he requested Frances, then *sola*, to give him £287 14s., and faithfully promised to repay it on demand. But the said Richard intended to defraud Frances. And she had asked for the return of the money both before and after her marriage with the said William.

In answer, Richard Pype said that Robert Lucye, father of the said Frances, was in his lifetime indebted to the said Richard in the sum of £181:4:6, and to a certain Arnulf Pellys, merchant of Antwerp, in £106:9:4. And being thus indebted, the said Robert Lucye died intestate at Develyn [Dublin] in Ireland, and Cardinal Reginald Pole, Archbishop of Canterbury, appointed Frances administratrix. She then paid to the said Richard what was owing to the said Arnulf Pelles, but not the money owing to him.

On Wednesday after the Octave of St. Hilary the jurors found that William and Frances should be in mercy for a false claim, and that they should pay £3 to Richard for his costs.

xlii.

[1566, November 10. Chanc. Proc., Ser. II. C3/70/124.]

William and Frances Gardner, plaintiffs, against Richard Pipe, defendant.

Plaintiffs' bill. They show that Edmond Wayte, at the request of Robert Luce, bound himself with Luce in £600 to Richard Pipe by obligation dated 27 August 2 & 3 Ph. & M. (1555) with the condition, that whereas Luce desired Pipe to take up goods for him in his absence up to the value of £500 for purposes of trading, that Pipe should be saved harmless from all actions by creditors or executors. Luce paid some £300 to Pipe, and then died intestate. Administration was committed to Luce's wife Katherine, who accounted with Pipe, paying him the following sums: Robert Egles, £37:7:6; William Jackman, £36:12:0; Thomas Griffith, £41:0:0; Richard Colmer, £21:6:8; goods attached in the hands of William Chelsham, £5:13:0; goods sequestered in a house, £27:15:3; two cloths at Antwerp sold for £28; certain plate to the value of £20; of John Style for the lease of Luce's dwelling house in St. Lawrence Lane, £126:13:4 [sum, £344:7:9]; wherewith Pipe was fully paid for all debts due from Luce. Afterwards Edmond Wayte died also intestate, and administration was committed to Frances, one of the plaintiffs. She asked Pipe to cancel the obligation, which he promised to do. Later she married Gardiner. Now Pipe has begun an action of debt against them on the obligation, although he has been satisfied.

Answer of Richard Pipe. Says that upon very good will and hearty love for Robert Luce, and at his earnest request, to save Luce's credit, he agreed to take up and sell merchandise to the value of £500, taking Luce's and Wayte's bond for £600 to save him harmless. Luce died in debt to him £181:9:6. His widow and administratrix Katherine accounted to him and Arnold Pelles (a merchant stranger and a great friend unto Luce), but on that accounting she paid nothing at all, and immediately after died. After her death Pipe received the following sums on account: Robert Egles, £20:7:6; William Jackman, £26:5:4; Thomas Griffith, £41; Richard Colmer, £20; for four cloths sold at Antwerp, £38:15 Flemish; certain plate to the value of £22:15; for the lease of Luce's house, £126:13:4 [sum, reducing Flemish to English, £287:19:0]. He did not receive any other sums, although the complainants "very unhonestly and as truly" have charged him with doing so. Afterwards Wayte, who was executor or administrator of Katherine, died; and the administration of his estate was committed to Frances (now wife of the complainant Gardiner), "who in her widowhood conferred with this defendant touching his satisfaction for the said debt, and upon account between them it fell out that this defendant was answered and allowed his due debt, though not in time appointed; for which and other causes the said obligation was and stood clearly forfeited; at which time the said Frances desired to have a discharge and declaration of and for the said payments and satisfaction, which this defendant did not deny; and so thereupon for her better speed in the spiritual court, sealed and delivered unto her such acquittance as she therein devised [? desired] though it was not so in all parts as therein was mentioned. After which the said Frances took to husband the said William Gardiner, who now of late very craftily, falsely, and as unconscionably thinking to win back again from this defendant the said sum of £287:19:0 (which before came to his hands in consideration and satisfaction of his own due debt and the debt of the said Arnold Pelles taken up by exchange and disbursed for the said Robert Luce, to his great cost, travel, and charges, and all yet not fully recompensed), commenced one action upon the case against this

154

defendant in the Queen's Bench at Westminster . . . declaring that the said defendant did . . . take upon him to pay unto the said Frances the sum of £287:19:0; whereunto the now defendant was compelled to answer, and the suit proceeded to issue and . . that is to say, in Lent past in this eighth of the reign of the Queen's Majesty that now is, at the Assizes holden at . . . upon Thames before . . [Document torn. *Desunt nonnulla.*]

xliii.

[1557, Easter. Chanc. Decrees and Orders, 1556/119*d*.]

Gardyner v. Pype. "Forasmuch as it appeareth by the answer of the defendant made to the bill of the plaintiff that he confesseth himself to have been satisfied and answered upon account between the said Frauncys, one of the plaintiffs, in her widowhood . . of his due debt, although not in time appointed" and that he had later put in suit at the common law an obligation of £6 acknowledged by Edmond Wayte (whose administratrix the said Frances was), and by one Robert Luce, it was therefore ordered that if the defendant did not show good cause to the contrary by Monday next, an injunction would be awarded against him for stay of his suit at the common law.

Ibidem, 310. Michaelmas 9/10 Eliz. (1567).

A day given till Friday next for the plaintiffs to show cause why the Court should not proceed to give order in the cause.

Ibidem, 359. 27 November 1567.

The matter referred to arbitrators until the Octave of Hilary. If the default be in the plaintiffs, then it is to be dismissed, and if in the defendant, he should be proceeded against.

xliv.

[1567, Easter. Queen's Bench. K.B. 27/1222/261.]

London. Richard Pype, citizen and leatherseller of London, produced a bill against William Gardener and Frances his wife, administratrix of the goods of Edmund Wayte, citizen and leatherseller of London, in a plea that they owed him £600, saying that Edmund Wayte on 27 August 2 & 3 Ph. & M. (1555) by a bond acknowledged himself bound to the said Richard Pype in £600 to be repaid on the feast of the Purification next following. And though he had often asked the said Edmund, Frances while a widow, and William and Frances after their marriage, they had always refused to pay. And now on the Wednesday after the eighteenth of Easter, a deed was produced, with terms as follows: that Robert Luce "hath earnestly required and desired" Richard Pype in his absence to take up for his use "as much ready money, goods, cloths, wares, and merchandises whatsoever" amounting to £500; "and the same to buy, bargain, barter, utter, and sell or otherwise to employ in the feat and trade of merchandise", to " the only use, and most commodity and profit of the same Robert Luce", and the said Richard to be saved harmless.

William and Frances Gardener said that Richard had made no money for Robert Luce.

Then Richard Pype said that between 27 August 1555 and the 2 February following, namely on 24 December, at Lombard Street, he had borrowed of William Chester, now knight, the sum of £130 (to be repaid on 24 January), which he immediately delivered to Francis Robinson of London, merchant, one of the creditors of Robert Luce. To repay William Chester, the said Richard Pype had had to borrow £130 from George Barford of London, leatherseller.

A day was given.

xlv.

[1566, Michaelmas. Queen's Bench. K.B. 27/1220/164.]

Surrey. In Trinity term last, Humphrey Baker produced a bill against William Gardener, alleging that on 22 February 8 Eliz. (1565/6), he was possessed of "a bedstead with a tester of joined wainscot and beech" worth 20s., "a truss bedstead with pillars turned of beech and wainscot" worth 20s., an oak chest worth 10s., two oak tables with beechen frames worth 20s., four joint-stools worth 20s., various pillows, "a cupboard carpet of dornexe" worth 5s. etc., which articles of furniture came into Gardener's hands, and he knew that they were Baker's, but he would not return them. And further that on 20 February Gardener sold them to some person unknown, to Baker's damage of £40.

Now on 18 July 9 Eliz. (1567) at Croydon, Surrey, the parties came and Gardener pleaded not guilty. On Thursday after the Octave of Michaelmas the jurors found William Gardener guilty. Damages assessed at £13 12d.

xlvi.
[1566, Michaelmas. Queen's Bench. K.B. 27/1220/361.]

Surrey. In Easter term, 7 Eliz. (1565), William Gardener, citizen and leatherseller of London, came and produced a bill against Thomas Lodge, knight, in a plea that he owed him £500. Alleged that on 20 April 5 Eliz. (1563) by a bond made in the parish of St. Mary Magdalen, Bermondsey, Lodge acknowledged himself bound in the said £500, but afterwards did not pay. Now on the Wednesday after the Octave of Michaelmas, the bond was read, in which the said Thomas Lodge agreed to pay 400 marks within a certain time.

The said Thomas Lodge declared that he had paid the money to William Gardener at his (Thomas's) house in the parish of St. Peter le Poure in Breadstreet Ward.

Discontinuance recorded.

xlvii.
[1567 and 1568. Records of the Leathersellers' Company.]

Gardiner was fined and paid £4 for certain arrearages, and the Company paid 16s. for charges in the law for the "controversies of William Gardener".

1567. The Wardens stated that they had not received of "William Gardener for his benevolence which he granted to the building of the parlor, 40s." He was in the list of those "of the Livery that gave their benevolence to the building of the new parlor in anno domini 1567 . . . £2". It was reported that there was also to be received of William Gardener, 40s.

1568. 30s. was received of Mr. Gardener "in benevolence to the building of the parlor".

xlviii.

[1567/8, February 1. Chanc. Proc., Ser. II. C3/70/77.]

William Gardiner, plaintiff, against Richard and Margaret Goodwyn, and Anne Humfrey, widow, defendants.

Gardiner's bill of complaint. Says that his late brother John Gardiner held in fee tail a messuage called "Batalyes", with all its appurtenances in the town and fields of Southwold, Suffolk, and died seized of it. Plaintiff as brother and next heir says he ought to have the property, but the deeds and evidences have somehow got into the hands of the defendants, who keep them locked in a chest, and hold the property from him.

xlix.

[1567/8, Hilary, 10 Eliz. Queen's Bench. K.B. 27/1225/301.]

London. William Gardener v. Cuthbert Beeston, for £300 debt. Mich. 8/9 Eliz. (1566). Cuthbert Beeston was summoned to answer William Gardener in a plea that he owed him £300 on a bond acknowledged 18 August 6 Eliz. (1564) at Southwark. Cuthbert said that before the making of this bond there was an indenture of the same date between them, by which he (for £210 paid him by Gardener) sold to William Gardener all that house in which the said William dwelt at the time, and two small tenements adjacent to it on both sides of door of the said house, in the tenure of the said William Gardener and Thomas Pygg. Also seven other small tenements in Bermond-

158

sey Street, of which three were to the north of the door of the house aforesaid, occupied by William Thomas, Agnes Lee, and Adam Spencer, and four on the south of the aforesaid door, in the tenures of Joan Thorpe, widow, Ellen Charter, widow, Jouce Antony, feltmaker, and Alexander Skynner, brewer. He also sold all reversions, etc.

By a lease dated 21 April 30 Hen. VIII (1539), Adam Beeston, citizen and girdler of London, let to Richard Alee of St. Mary Magdalen, Bermondsey, tailor, parcel of the aforesaid premises for 40 years at an annual rent of 24s. By a lease of 20 October 1 & 2 Ph. & M. (1554), Cuthbert Beeston let another parcel to Richard Sympson, labourer, for 21 years at an annual rent of 12s. By another lease, dated 20 October 2 & 3 Ph. & M. (1555) Cuthbert let another parcel to Simon Holmes, citizen and clothworker of London, for 21 years at a rent of 32s. By another lease dated 25 March 2 Eliz. (1560), Cuthbert let to William Gardener a parcel of the premises for 21 years at an annual rent of £4.

All of which leases Cuthbert handed over to the defendant William at the making of the indenture.

Plaintiff protested that the small tenement on the north side of the door of the house in which Gardiner lived was in the tenure of Thomas Cook, and not of Thomas Pygge, and that there were no encumbrances on the aforesaid premises, the leases already recited excepted.

In reply William Gardener said that Cuthbert had fulfilled none of the articles and agreements in the said indenture, and that on 30 September 6 Eliz. (1564), Cuthbert had sold to William Edwardes the tenement occupied by William Pygge, and that Edwardes had entered the same.

On the Quindene of Michaelmas it was considered that William Gardener was in mercy, and that Cuthbert Beeston should recover £10 from him.

159

1.

[1567/8, Hilary. Queen's Bench. K.B. 27/1225/295.]

On Friday after the Octave of Hilary came William Gardener, gentleman, as well for the Queen as for himself, and produced a bill against Thomas Ducke in a plea that contrary to the statute of 12 January 5 Eliz. (1563) he had committed perjury, and was liable to a fine of £20, and if he had no goods to that value, he should be nailed by the ears to the pillory. Alleged that in Trinity term 8 Eliz. (1566) a certain Humphrey Baker produced a bill against the said William Gardyner in a plea that William had sold his goods [see No. xlv.]. And at Croydon on 18 July 9 Eliz. (1567), before John Southcott, the said Thomas Ducke voluntarily and falsely swore that after 23 February 8 Eliz. (1566) he saw Humphrey Baker's bed set up in William Gardyner's house in the parish of St. Mary Magdalen, Bermondsey, and a mattress of his lying on it which was being used by the said William.

At the Assizes held in Southwark 23 February it was considered that Thomas Ducke was guilty of perjury, and that he should forfeit £20, £10 of which should go to the Queen and £10 to William Gardyner; that he should also be imprisoned for six months; and if he could not pay, he was to be nailed to the pillory by his ears.

li.

[1568, Michaelmas. Queen's Bench. K.B. 27/1228/60.]

Surrey. Continuation of the suit against Thomas Ducke for perjury. William Gardener stated that Thomas Ducke would not pay the £20 which he had forfeited by his perjury, and that he (Gardener) wished to ascertain if the said Thomas had sufficient goods and chattels worth £20 at Southwark.

Thomas Ducke pleaded not guilty, saying that the twelve jurors had made false oaths at the trial.

William Gardener, as well as Thomas Byll and Richard Banys-

ter, two of the jurors, said that the twelve jurors were honest
and lawful men.

A jury of 24 knights was impanelled to come on the Morrow
of St. Martin, but they made default.

The parties were given a day until the 16 October; on which
day they came, and Thomas Ducke said that Richard Ode,
one of the jurors of the first inquest, was dead. And all the
jurors did not come.

A writ of exigent was delivered to the deputy sheriff dated 15
November this term.

lii.

[1568–1569. Records of the Leathersellers' Company.]

William Gardiner served the office of Rentor Warden.

liii.

[1569. *Surrey Musters*, pr. Surrey Record Soc., ii, 147.]

Surrey. 1569, May 15. "The book of all s[uch armor] and weapons as haue beane. . . Increased within the Sayd [county].

The Hundreds of Brixstone and Wallington.

[B]armesey strete

William Gardener $\begin{cases} \text{harquebus} & \text{j} \\ \text{murr'} & \text{j} \end{cases}$"

liv.

[1569. Close Roll, 11 Eliz. pt. 17. C54/803.]

Thomas Kendall of London, gentleman, acknowledges that
he owes 200 marks to William Gardyner of the City of London,
leatherseller. But if the conditions in two pairs of indentures
of 21 December 11 Eliz. (1568) be performed, this recognizance is to be void. Dated 12 July 11 Eliz. (1569).

9 February 12 Eliz. (1569/70). William Gardyner acknowledged himself satisfied.

lv.

[1569. Close Roll, 11 Eliz. pt. 17. C54/803.]

Indenture made 20 November 11 Eliz. (1568) between Margaret, widow of Edward Lord North and William Gardener, citizen and leatherseller of London, reciting that Sir Anthony Hungerford enfeoffed Andrew Fraunces and the said Margaret, then his wife, with his manor of Wardelles, with woods called Okefields and a wood in Deptford, Kent, and Surrey, on 10 May 2 Hen. VIII (1540). Now the said Margaret, for £800, sold the same to the said William Gardener.

lvi.

[1569, Easter. Feet of Fines. C.P. 25/Kent and Surr. E. 11 Eliz.]

Between William Gardyner, gentleman, querent, and Margaret North, widow, deforciant, of the manor of Wardellys *alias* Wardalles and 80 acres of land in Deptford, Kent, and 120 acres of land in Deptford and in Peckham, Surrey, quitclaimed by Margaret for herself and her heirs to William and his heirs for £640.

lvii.

[1570. Records of the Leathersellers' Company.]

William Gardiner served as one of the Auditors, and his signature appears at the foot of the Account.

lviii.

[1571. Close Roll, 13 Eliz. pt. 21. C54/858.]

Indenture made 25 July 13 Eliz. (1571) between William Gardyner, citizen and leatherseller of London, son and heir of William Gardyner, late of the Grange near Bermondsey, deceased, and Edmund Dardes of Northmyms, Herts., yeoman. By this indenture, for £100, William sold to Edmund all his messuages, tenements, etc., in Wheleham Grene, Northmyms, between the highway called Hylles Lane on the east and another way leading against Bradmer on the west, etc. [place names], and all the other hereditaments of the said William in Northmyms "late the said Willyam Gardyner his fathers".

lix.
[1572. Close Roll, 14 Eliz. pt. 20. C54/887.]

Indenture made 19 June 14 Eliz. (1572) between William Chowne, citizen and merchant tailor of London, and William Gardner, citizen and leatherseller of London. By this indenture, for £65 10s., the said Chowne sold to Gardner 14 tenements in Bermondsey Street in the parish of St. Mary Magdalen.

lx.
[1572. Feet of Fines. C.P. 25/Surr. M. 14/15 Eliz.]

Between William Gardyner, querent, and William Chowne, deforciant, of 14 messuages, gardens, and orchards in the parish of St. Mary Magdalen, Bermondsey, quitclaimed to William Gardyner and his heirs forever for 130 marks.

lxi.
[1572 and 1573. Court of Requests Proc. Req. 2/73/41.]

John Philpot, complainant, against William Gardener et al., defendants.

Answer of Gardener. He says that his father William Gardener in 1548 made his will and ordained him and his brother Richard (sons of the said William) his executors, and afterwards died. William and Richard Gardener proved the will and took execution of the estate. Afterwards Richard died, and William Gardener was "sole possessed of the said rents and of the residue of the said Grange and demesne lands of Bermondsey by right and title of survivor."

163

lxii.

[1573. Records of the Leathersellers' Company.]

William Gardiner was one of the signatories of a Minute about an act respecting feasts and meetings for dinners.

According to an item which is crossed out, he was fined 40s. "for words spoken" by him.

lxiii.

[1573, Easter. Common Pleas. C.P. 40/1315/1108.]

London. William Gardyner, citizen and leatherseller of London, plaintiff, by his attorney Henry Burr, against Thomas Spencer of Lincoln's Inn, gentleman, late of Wisden, Salop, defendant, in a plea of debt for £10 on a bond dated 13 December 9 Eliz.

lxiv.

[1573, Easter. Common Pleas. C.P. 40/1315/1217.]

London. William Gardyner, citizen and leatherseller of London, plaintiff, by his attorney Henry Burr, against Ralph Higgons of Lincoln's Inn, gentleman, late of Stafford, defendant, in a plea of debt for £10 on a bond dated 13 December 9 Eliz.

lxv.

[1573, Trinity. Queen's Bench. K.B. 27/1246/233d.]

In Easter term last William Gardener, citizen and leatherseller of London, came and produced a bill against Ralph Walker, citizen and leatherseller of London, in a plea that he owed him £50 by a bond of 9 February 12 Eliz. (1570).

On the Friday after the Morrow of Trinity 15 Eliz. (1573) it was considered that Ralph owed William £50 and £1:6:8 damages.

lxvi.

[1573. Court of Requests Proc. Req. 2/36/33.]

Raffe Walker, plaintiff, against William Gardyner, defendant. *Deposition* for plaintiff, 24 July 1573, of Thomas Kendall of Milton *alias* Middleton, Kent, gentleman, aged 24.

He says that Walker owed Gardyner £50 on a bond made "about a sennight after or before Candlemas was three years. . . He well remembreth the same for that the said Gardyner owing unto this deponent £3 for a certain contract beforehand made touching the said sum of £50, and this deponent coming unto him for the said £3, hearing and understanding that the said £50 was paid, and did demand of him the said £3 according to his promise and said, 'Now that Master Walker hath paid you your £50, I pray let me have the £3 which you [owe] unto me', who then said, 'I confess that Mr. Walker hath paid me the said £50, and that I am thereof fully satisfied and paid; but I will not pay you your £3', and then this deponent departed. And about half a year after, this deponent meeting with the said Gardyner in Southwerke demanded the said £3 again of the said Gardyner, who denied the same again; and then this deponent asked him again if that he were not paid his said £50 of the said Walker, who said 'Yes, I am fully satisfied, contented, and paid; but yet I have his bill for the said £50 yet remaining in my hands'; and this deponent asked him wherefore he did keep the said bill, being fully satisfied, contented, and paid, and then the said Gardyner answered that in keeping of the said bill he had a meaning which this deponent should not know, and then this deponent departed."

lxvii.

[1573–1576. Records of the Leathersellers' Company.]

1573. Gardiner was assessed for provision of corn at 40*s.*, and again at £3.

1573/4. The following item is crossed out of the list of payments: "Paid in expenses at the agreement made between Mr. Gardener and Mr. Willis, *somma* 6s."

1575. William Gardener signed a Minute of a Court held 10 August 1575 concerning feasts and dinners, and also Minutes of two Courts held 15 August 1575 concerning leases in reversion and loan money.

In this year Mr. Gardener was one of the Auditors.

1575/6. The Company "received at the burial of Mistress Gardener the 1 of January, *somma* 40s."

lxviii.
[1576. Chancery Proc. Jas. I. C2 Jas. I. P1/18.]

Pratt v. Leedham et al. Mentions William Gardiner, citizen and leatherseller, as a churchwarden of St. Mary Magdalen's, Bermondsey, 18 Eliz. (1576).

lxix.
[1575/6. Patent Roll, 18 Eliz. pt. 13. C66/1149/38, 39.]

A farm for William Gardyner, gentleman. Recites Abbot Robert's grant (21 May 1534) to Ralph Wryne and Helen his wife of the farm of Bermondsey Grange for 60 years from 29 September 1534 at an annual rent of £48.

For a fine of £166:13:4 paid by Gardiner at the Receipt of the Exchequer, the Queen grants to him the reversion of the farm of Bermondsey Grange with all its appurtenances except all great trees, woods, underwoods, wards and marriages, minerals and quarries; after the expiration of the aforesaid term of 60 years, for 21 years at an annual rent of £48; Gardiner and his assigns to keep scoured the ditch which stretches from the bridge of St. Thomas à Waterings to 'le Sluce' on this side of Rederith.

lxx.

[1576. Common Pleas Deeds Enrolled. C.P. 40/Easter 18 Eliz.]

Surrey. William Holstock, esq., grants to William Gardener and William Edwards lands and tenements in St. Mary Magdalen, Bermondsey.

lxxi.

[1576, Hilary. Feet of Fines. C.P. 25/Surr. H.18 Eliz.]

Surrey. Between William Gardiner and William Edwardes, querents, and William Holstocke, esquire, and Agnes his wife, deforciants, of two messuages, three gardens, and two orchards in the parish of St. Mary Magdalen, Bermondsey, quitclaimed by the deforciants for themselves and the heirs of Agnes to the querents and the heirs of William Gardiner for 100 marks.

lxxii.

[1577. Court of Requests Proc. Req. 2/41/99.]

Thomas v. Finch et al. Two depositions by William Gardiner. On 2 May 1577 his age is given as "42 years or thereabouts".

lxxiii.

[1577, Trinity. Queen's Bench. K.B. 29/212/Trin. 19 Eliz.]

England. William Gardner craves sureties of the peace against John Strangman and Eleanor his wife, James Langdall, and James Clyfords, for fear of death, etc. "Att vic Surr r oct mich."

England. William Gardner craves sureties of the peace against Edward Lucas, Charles Shewersby, Robert Pakes, and John Tusson, for fear of death, etc. "Att vic Surr r oct mich".

lxxiv.

[1577, Michaelmas. Common Pleas. C.P. 40/1350/775.]

London. John Strangman of Bermondsey, gentleman, was sued for a debt of £20 owing to Anne Blowite, widow, and was imprisoned in Michaelmas last past.

167

The said John came before the Justices at their chamber in Fleet Street on 16 November; and the Mayor (Thomas Ramsey) declared that the said John, 31 October 19 Eliz. (1577) had been taken by virtue of an original bill in a plea of debt of £100 at the suit of Edward Thruxton, and by virtue of which he was detained in prison. And by virtue of another suit against him 14 November by William Gardyner, leatherseller, in a plea of trespass with damages of £100.

He was released and mainperned by Thomas Andrewes of Lincoln's Inn and Edward Meggs of Gray's Inn in £300 for himself, and 200 marks for the others.

And if he did not pay his debt, £120 should be raised on his goods and chattels to the use of William Gardyner.

lxxv.
[1577/8, Hilary. Common Pleas. C.P. 40/1354/1199.]

Surrey. John Strangman of Bermondsey, gentleman, was attached to answer William Gardener for breaking his close at Bermondsey and taking 40 cartloads of hay worth £40. Henry Burr was Gardener's attorney. A day given.

lxxvi.
[1577, 1578. Records of the Leathersellers' Company.]

1577. There was delivered to Mr. Warden Gardner one key of the hanging lock.

1577–1578. William Gardener was second Warden, and as such joined in an assessment "for provision and setting forth soldiers".

lxxvii.
[1578, Michaelmas. Common Pleas. C.P. 40/1362/1088.]

London. William Gardyner, gentleman, by Henry Burr his attorney, plaintiff, against Nicholas Lestrange of Lynn, Norfolk, knight, in a plea of debt for 200 marks, on a bond dated 6 May

19 Eliz. (1577). Nicholas Lestrange said his son John sold to the said William certain messuages in Blackman Street, Southwark. A day given.

lxxviii.
[1578/9, Hilary. Feet of Fines. C.P. 25/Surr. H. 21 Eliz.]

Between Christopher Gardener, querent, and William Gardener, deforciant, of 18 acres of meadow and 10 acres of pasture in the parish of St. Mary Magdalen, Bermondsey, quitclaimed by William for himself and his heirs to Christopher and his heirs for 100 marks.

lxxix.
[1579. Close Roll, 21 Eliz. C54/1058.]

Indenture dated 25 March 21 Eliz. (1579), whereby William Stedman of Barking, Essex, yeoman, for £600 sells to William Gardiner of Bermondsey, Surrey, gentleman, 62 acres of "meadow, pasture, marsh, or wet ground" in Barking, that is to say: one parcel (24 acres) of meadow or marsh called "the new-inned ground", another parcel adjoining called "the fourteen acres", two other parcels containing together 20 acres, and one parcel of marsh of four acres. Deed enrolled 9 May 1579.

lxxx.
[1579, 14 April.
Dasent, *Acts of the Privy Council, 1579–1580*, p. 101.]

Westminster. This day one William Gardiner was called in before their Lordships upon a complaint made by William Stedman, that whereas there had been some communication between them touching the buying and selling of a certain piece of land belonging to the said Stedman, and whereof the said Gardiner had gotten assurance with some other clauses and conditions (as it was informed) than were meant and agreed on between them at the first; upon their Lordships'

motion, the said Gardiner was content (seeing he acknowledged to have as yet paid no money for the land) to release
the said Stedman of his promise and bargain, and therefore
would restore and cancel such writings and assurances as he
had of the said Stedman, upon condition that Stedman should
pay unto him such costs and charges as he had [been] at for
his learned counsel and passing the books, the rating whereof
was referred by their Lordships to Mr. Solicitor; and this done,
Stedman should be wholly discharged of any encumbrances
to be hereafter made by the said Gardiner, and might seek
the best bargain he could for the selling (if he would) of his
land to others.

lxxxi.

[1579, October 15. Patent Roll, 21 Eliz. pt. 11. C66/1185/18.]

A farm for William Gardyner, gentleman. For a fine of £80,
the Queen grants to William Gardiner, gentleman, all those
two pastures called 'Bruettismershe' and 'Bech field' and all
that pightel land containing one acre called 'Bruettismershe'
adjoining the two pastures together in Rederith, Surrey, between the 'Breche' sometime of the Abbot and Covent late
Monastery of Bermondsey, late in the tenure of William Golde
and Agnes his wife on the north part, and the water of Thames
on the northeast, and 'Prestes marshe' on the southeast, and
the pasture of the same late Abbot and Convent called 'Hors-
leas' and 'Cowleas' on the northwest; also 'Prestes mershe',
lying next the fifteen acres (late ours) on the south, containing
35 acres more or less, all in the parish of Rederith and late in
the tenure of John Martyn; also that cottage and garden, the
'ladye crofte', and the pasture called 'the whiles' in the parish
of St. Mary Magdalen, late in the tenure of Robert Hogan
(all which premises were granted by Abbot Robert 21 May
1534 to Ralph Wryne and Helen his wife for 60 years); to
William Gardyner from Michaelmas 1594 for 21 years at an

annual rent of £20, except royalties. Gardiner and his assigns to keep in repair the Thames wall, the sluice-bars and gates, and the pinfold there.

lxxxii.

[1579. Guildhall, Mayor's Court Repertories.]

14 August. Mr. Gardiner's refusal to take the shrievalty upon him. This day . . . Edwards of Southwark reported here to this court that Mr. William Gardiner, leatherseller, now elected one of the sheriffs of the city of London and county of Middlesex, who was sent for to come before my Lord Mayor and his brethren the Aldermen to take upon him the execution of this office, sent him the said Edwards to signify to my Lord Mayor and Aldermen that he will not take upon him the execution thereof, but will refer himself to this court for his fine to be borne and paid for his refusal. (19/481d.) Richard Pipe, Mayor.

27 August. Recognizance of Mr. Gardiner. Item Willelmus Gardener Letherseller ciuis London' recognovit se debere Johanni Mabbe Camerario Ciuitatis prædictæ CC^{li} . . . soluendas per vnam recognitionis sub conditione etc.

The condition and so forth, that is if the said William Gardiner do on the vigil or even of the feast of St. Michael the Archangel now next ensuing personally appear here in this court ready to make answer unto all such things as shall be objected against him, and do not depart the same without licence thereof. That then, etc., Or else, etc. (19/482d.) Pipe, Mayor.

3 November. Gardyner and Saunderson. At this Court it was ordered that Mr. Gardiner, lately elected sheriff of this city and county of Middlesex, and . . . Saunderson, vintner, shall be warned to appear at the next court here to be holden. (20/2.) Woodroffe, Mayor.

5 November. Mr. Gardyner, late elect sheriff. Item, further day was given by this Court to Mr. Gardiner, lately elected

171

sheriff of this city, to be here again on Thursday next ensuing. And it was ordered that the act of Common Council, made and provided for the payment of the sum of £200 for the refusal of such persons as shall be elected sheriffs of the same city and county of Middlesex, shall in the meantime be considered of. (20/5.) Woodroffe, Mayor.

12 November. Mr. Gardyner. Item Mr. Gardiner, lately elected sheriff of this city and county of Middlesex, present here in this court, had further day given him by the same to be here again upon Thursday next ensuing. (20/9.) Woodroffe, Mayor. No date, but just before 8 December. Suit against Mr. Gardyner. Item it is ordered that the learned counsel of this city shall join with William Dalby, gentleman, for the prosecuting of the suit against . . . Gardiner, leatherseller, lately elect one of the sheriffs of this city. (20/20d.) Woodroffe, Mayor.

14 December. Item Sir Roulande Heywood, Sir Leonell Duckett, Sir John Rivers, Sir Thomas Ramsey, knights, Mr. Recorder, and such of the learned counsel of this city as he shall think good, to wait upon my Lord Chief Justice touching the cause of Mr. Gardiner, late elect one of the sheriffs of London and Middlesex; and Mr. Chamberlain appointed to repair to the Lord Chief Justice and Mr. Justice Southecote to entreat their Lordships to appoint the time that they may trouble his Lordship therein. (20/24d.) Woodroffe, Mayor.

17 December. Mr. Gardyner, lately elect sheriff. At this court it was ordered that Sir Roulande Haywarde, Sir Leonell Duckett, Sir John Rivers, and Sir Thomas Ramsey, knights, and Mr. Recorder shall repair unto the Lord Chamberlain of the Queen's Majesty's Household to treat with his Lordship in the matter touching Mr. Gardiner, lately elect one of the sheriffs of this city and county of Middlesex, for his fine due and payable to the use of the Commonalty of the same city, for that he denied to take upon him the execution of the same office. (20/25.) Woodroffe, Mayor.

172

17 December. Mr. Gardyner. Item Mr. Gardiner, lately elected sheriff of this city and county of Middlesex, who made request to be dispensed withal for his fine in refusing the same office, was by this court willed to be here the next court to be holden after the feast of the birth of our Lord God, then to be heard at full touching his request, and to receive the answer of the same court therein. (20/25d.) Woodroffe, Mayor.

lxxxiii.
[1579/80, Hilary. Feet of Fines. C.P. 25/Surr. H. 22 Eliz.]

Between William Gardner, querent, and William Wayte and Joan his wife, deforciants, of three messuages and gardens, and 20 acres of pasture in the parishes of St. Mary Magdalen, Bermondsey, and St. George, Southwark, quitclaimed by William and Joan for them and the heirs of William to William Gardner and his heirs for £220.

lxxxiv.
[1580. Guildhall, Mayor's Court Repertories.]

21 January. Item this day Mr. William Gardiner, leatherseller, lately elected sheriff of this city and county of Middlesex, personally present in this court, did submit himself to stand to the orders of the said court for the payment of such fine as is due to the Commonality of this city in that he refused to take upon him the execution of the same office. (20/31.) Woodroffe, Mayor.

28 January. Item this day Mr. Wyllyam Gardiner, leatherseller, lately elected sheriff of this city and county of Middlesex, did submit himself to this court touching the payment of his fine for his refusal of the said office; whereupon it was by the same court ordered and decreed that the said John [sic] Gardiner shall forthwith content and pay unto Mr. Chamberlain of this city the sum of 100 marks current money of Eng-

land, and the residue of his said fine of £200 was by the same court, at the request of the right honorable the Lord Chamberlain of Her Majesty's Household, clearly remitted, pardoned, and forgiven. (20/34*d*.) Woodroffe, Mayor.

9 February. Item at the further request of the letters of the right honorable the Lord Chamberlain of the Queen's Majesty's Household, it was ordered and decreed that the fine of Mr. William Gardyner, leatherseller, lately elected sheriff of this city and county of Middlesex, for the year last past, shall be clearly remitted and pardoned unto the sum of £50, so as he do forthwith content and pay the said sum to the Chamberlain of this city to the use of the Commonalty of the same. (20/37*d*.) Woodroffe, Mayor.

lxxxv.

[1580, Feb. 4. Dasent, *Acts of Privy Council, 1579–1580*, 382.]

A Commission for 4 post horses for William Gardiner, gentleman, sent into Ireland for Her Majesty's service.

lxxxvi.

[1580, Feb. 4. Chamber Accounts. A.O. 1/383/18.]

Warrants. To William Gardiner, gentleman, upon a warrant signed by Mr. Secretary Walsingham, dated at Whitehall the 4th of February 1579 [1580], for carrying letters in post for Her Majesty's affairs to the Lord Justice of Ireland, being in Munster, from the Court at Whitehall . . . £12

lxxxvii.

[1579. Brevia Regia. Petty Bag Office. C202/1.]

Oath of a Justice of Peace.

Ye shall swear that as Justice of the Peace in the county of . . in all articles in the Queen's commission to you directed ye shall do equal right to the poor and to the rich after your cun-

ning, wit, and power, and after the laws and customs of the
realm and statutes thereof made; and ye shall not be of counsel
with any person in any quarrel hanging afore you; and that ye
hold your Sessions after the form of statutes thereof made; and
the issues, fines, and amerciaments which shall happen to be
made, and all forfeitures which shall fall before you ye shall truly
cause to be entered without any concealment or embezzling
and truly send them to the Queen's Exchequer; ye shall not
let for gift or for other cause, but well and truly ye shall do
your office of justice of the peace in that behalf; and that ye
take nothing for your office of justice of the peace to be done
but of the Queen and fees accustomed and costs limited by the
statute; and ye shall not direct or cause to be directed any
warrant by you to be made to the parties, but you shall direct
them to the bailiffs of the said county, or other the Queen's
officers or ministers, or other indifferent persons to do execution thereof, so God you help and by the contents of this book.

lxxxviii.
[Temp. Elizabeth. Loseley Park. Loseley MS. 992.]

An order to be taken for government of the Queen's Highness'
County of Surrey, whereby the same may be the better ordered and ready to serve Her Highness.
First, that there be division made of the said county into
eight or twelve parts, more or less, according to the quantity
of the said shire. And as to the justices of peace and gentlemen
of the same [which] shall seem most convenient for the good
stay and quiet thereof.
Item that in every of those divisions so agreed upon, the justices of peace and such other honest gentlemen inhabiting
within the same as be of sober behaviour and well given to live
according to the laws that be appointed, to see vagabonds,
spreaders of false rumours, and other disordered persons pun-

ished and the people kept in due obedience and quiet, according to the laws.

Item that the said justices of peace and gentlemen within every division shall cause the constable of every hundred or such other honest and grave men within their precinct to repair to the parishes within the same hundred, and to take the names of all the able men in every of the said parishes: what armour there is for their furniture, what number of horsemen, how many bills, bows, pikes, and other weapons, and so of the whole to make a perfect book.

Item the said justices of peace and gentlemen in every division shall cause the head men of every parish within their circuits to have all the said able men with their armour, weapons, and horses in a readiness to serve upon an hour's warning under such captains and in such sort as shall be by us or by the justices of peace and gentlemen appointed unto them.

Item if any disorder or open force shall happen to be stived [*i.e.* stewed] in any of the said divisions, the said justices and gentlemen shall with all diligence labour to quiet or resist the same as the case shall require; and if they shall find themselves o'erweak to repress the said disorder or stive [*i.e.* stew], they shall in that case desire the aid of the justices and gentlemen of the divisions next adjoining unto them, who shall assist them to the best of their powers for that purpose.

Item the said justices and gentlemen shall within every of the said divisions cause the divine service to be set forth and duly kept as much as in them lieth, and to see that the people obediently come to the same; wherein they shall, if need require, call for the help of the ordinary.

Item that all particular faults or disorders which cannot well be reformed by the justices and gentlemen in every particular division shall be brought to a greater number of the justices of the said shire, and by them ordered and redressed according to the order of the laws.

Item that the justice of assize in the circuit may be well attended upon by some of the justices of every division, and by them all faults not reformed to be presented and punished according to the law.

Item the said justices and gentlemen shall give order for the watches to be substantially kept throughout their circuit, and the same to be of honest sort of men and in a good and substantial number.

Finally the said justices and gentlemen within every division shall, in all other things that by their discretions may any wise serve for the furtherance of the Queen's service and the good and quiet stay of that shire, take such further order and direction as by their wisdoms shall seem most expedient; and especially that good and substantial regard be had unto the punishment of such as shall spread abroad false and seditious rumours, according to our proclamation set forth for that purpose: amongst whom those that shall by any means publish or talk of any prophecy are chiefly to be searched for and sharply punished, their books and prophecies sought out and burnt, and the people by all ways and means dissuaded from meddling with such ways and seditious fantasies.

lxxxix.

[1580. Assizes 35/22, file 2.]

Three signatures of William Gardiner subscribed to recognizances acknowledged before him as justice of peace in Surrey.

xc.

[1580, Trinity. Feet of Fines. C.P. 25/Surr. T. 22 Eliz.]

Between William Gardiner, esquire, querent, and Lewis Davye and Anne his wife and Henry Worthington, deforciants, of 8 messuages, 2 gardens, 2 orchards, and 4 acres of meadow in the parish of St. Mary Magdalen, Bermondsey, quitclaimed by

177   N

the deforciants for themselves and the heirs of Anne to William
Gardiner and his heirs for £100.

xci.
[1580, June 23. Close Roll, 22 Eliz. C54/1082.]

William Gardiner of Bermondsey, Surrey, esquire, for £700
sells to Roger Wilcox, citizen and clothworker of London, the
62 acres in Barking, Essex, which he bought the year before
from William Stedman, free of all encumbrances except a lease
of the property made by Gardiner to Stedman, 26 March 1579,
for 21 years at the yearly rent of £40. Deed enrolled 8 July
1580.

xcii.
[1580, Michaelmas. Feet of Fines. C.P. 25/Surr. M. 22/23 Eliz.]

Between William Gardyner, esquire, querent, and Richard
Sheparde, deforciant, of 12 acres of meadow in Rederith, quitclaimed by Richard for himself and his heirs to William and
his heirs for £80.

xciii.
[1580, November 8. Guildhall, *Remembrancia* i, 160.]

Our duty humbly done to your Lordship. Where Mr. Gardner,
your Lordship's servant and a citizen of this city, whom God
hath blessed with wealth and other good gifts, was by the free
election of the commons of this city, to whom it belongeth according to our charter, orderly chosen to be sheriff of this city,
in which place he ought to have served her Majesty, notwithstanding his dwelling out of the liberties: in which case very
many dwelling in other places, yea and in far distant cities and
towns of this realm have heretofore been chosen, as Jobson of
Hull and other, and have either served or excused themselves
with the usual fines upon the refusal; Mr. Gardner remaining
to take the advantage of the law in that case provided, that is,
with paying the fine limited by act of Common Council to be

discharged rather than to serve the office, did pretend his necessary attendance in your Lordship's service and other causes, and so refused the office; whereby the said fine was and is due to the Chamber and Commonalty of this city, and not to us the Mayor and Aldermen; nevertheless Mr. Gardner afterward used your Lordship's favourable goodness in request to the then Lord Mayor and the rest of us for moderation of his said fine, whereunto we had such humble and loving regard as for your estate became us and your goodness toward us hath deserved, and for your Lordship's sake we remitted unto him £150, and abated his fine to fifty pounds only; wherein we beseech your Lordship to remember that for precedent's sake more we could not do for him, and in that which we have done (the fine being not ours but the Commonalty's), we can hardly defend the favour shewed him if it should be known to the body of the city, but we should be enforced either to pay it ourselves or to bear greater blame than we gladly would or can with our good reputation. Now Mr. Gardner, being called upon for this small sum of £50, doth not only not acknowledge the favour shewed him for your sake, but also refuseth to obey our order therein, which we promised your Lordship that it should be (and so we have performed) such as your Lordship should have cause to like of. Because we are loath to take our remedy by law against him (being your servant) without first making you privy of the case, we pray your Lordship to take our doing in good part, and command him quietly to take benefit of our said abatement of his fine and to pay the said sum of £50, that we be not for precedent and for our discharge towards the Commons enforced to seek what we ought and may by law; which, being once disclosed, cannot be less than the whole sum of £200 unless the Common Council discharge him, which we wish him for his own sake not to essay, and put all in peril. And so we leave to trouble your Lordship. At London this 8th of November 1580. Your Lordship's to command.

xciv.

[1580, November 8.

Guildhall, Mayor's Court Repertories, 20/139.]

Item this day the matter depending in question in the utter court betwixt Gardner, leatherseller, and Richard Reynolds, draper, is referred to the hearing and examination of Mr. William Danyell and Mr. James Dalton, esquires, and they to end the same if they can before Monday next, or else the said cause to proceed to trial. Braunche, Mayor.

xcv.

[1580/1, Hilary. Common Pleas. C.P. 40/1383/1119d.]

London. Record that in Trinity term, 21 Eliz. (1579), William Gardyner, gentleman, was to recover a debt of 200 marks and £5:10:8 damages from Nicholas Le Strange of Lynn, Norfolk, knight; since which time the said Nicholas had died.

In Hilary term 23 Eliz. (1580/1), the said William, by Henry Burr his attorney, asked that John Lestrange, esquire, and · Katherine Lestrange, widow, executors of Nicholas, should pay the debt.

On the Octave of the Purification John and Katherine did not come. . . And it was considered that William should have execution against them from the goods of the said Nicholas.

xcvi.

[1581, Michaelmas. Feet of Fines. C.P. 25/Surr. M. 23/4 Eliz.]

Between William Gardyner, esquire, querent, and William Leedes and Agnes his wife, deforciants, of 2 messuages, 2 tofts, and 2 gardens in the parish of St. Olave, [Southwark], quit-claimed by the deforciants for themselves and the heirs of Agnes to the said William Gardyner and his heirs for £80.

xcvii.

[1581, November 27. Close Roll, 24 Eliz. C54/1144.]

Titus Norris of Norwich, glover, acknowledged that he owed William Gardyner of the parish of St. Mary Magdalen, Bermondsey, Surrey, esquire, £300 ; but if £142 were paid to William Gardyner at his house in Bermondsey on 25 March next, then this recognizance to be void. Dated 27 November 24 Eliz. (1581).

On 27 May 24 Eliz. (1582) William Gardyner came into the Chancery and acknowledged himself satisfied.

xcviii.

[1581/2, Hilary. Queen's Bench. K.B. 27/1280/789.]

Surrey. William Gardiner against John Cottesforde. Recites that Thomas Holcrofte, esquire, on 17 May 21 Eliz. (1579), demised to Henry Megnys *alias* Pope, citizen and goldsmith of London, a house lying in Water Lane, All Saints Barking, for 41 years, etc. Gardiner claims an interest of £300 in it.

xcix.

[1581/2, January 23. Chanc. Proc., Ser. II. C3/220/75.]

Thomas Waade of Gray's Inn, gentleman, plaintiff, against William Gardenor.

Waade's Bill of Complaint. Alleges that one Henry Mekis about two years past was possessed of a tenement and garden for term of years in the parish of All Hallows [?Barking]. The said Mekis became indebted to John Cottesford of London in the sum of £355. Not being able to pay the money due on the day appointed, the property, as security, was forfeit to the said Cottesford. Mekis appealed to the Earl of Sussex, who offered to redeem the tenement and garden for him until the following Candlemas, so that Mekis could sell it to his greater advantage.

This the said Earl did by means of William Gardener of South-wark, gentleman. Gardener caused the said Mekis to enter into a bond of £300 with the plaintiff, with condition that the said Mekis, by February 2 ensuing, should leave his said house, and give Gardener possession thereof, and within the next three years make further assurance thereof to the said Gardener.

Mekis did not sell the house and garden by the date named, but asked if he might stay there till 25 March ensuing to see if he could conclude the sale; to which Gardener pretended to agree "most willingly". But Mekis could not conclude the sale, "the rather through the means of some lewd disposed persons discrediting the same, and the title thereof . . . amongst whom the said Gardener himself hath given good cause to be suspected for one, as by his subtle dealing before and sinister practices after may probably appear".

Some days after March 25, Gardener persuaded the plaintiff and induced his father [Mekis] to leave the house, promising to help him in every way, "intending (as by speech proceeding from him appeared) to wrangle with the said Cottesford for as much of the said household stuff as was sold to him". And Gardener, knowing that the plaintiff was bound to give the household stuff to Cottesford, "took your orator aside into an entry of the said tenement, and then with friendly speeches told him that he was sorry that he had entered so far" . . . [document faded] . . "as subtle and ill-meaning heads are always suspicious", Gardener put a friend or servant of his into the said house, to see that nothing was taken away; so that Mekis's daughter, wishing "to have out of the said house a chest of her own with her apparel and other own goods being therein contained . . he [Gardener] behaved himself with such insolency whereby he gave not only great grief and corresy to the maid and the said Henry her father, but thereby brought, as your orator is credibly informed, tears even from his said servant or friend whom he set as a watchman in the said house".

A chapman offered to take the house for £30 a year, but Gardener would not allow it, and continued in possession, "whereby he might the better with a show of honesty colour such lewd and unchristian devices as he meant to bring to pass and afterwards hath put in practice; whereupon your orator, having cause to suspect his dealing, and withal counselled by divers friends that had heard of and knew the disposition of the said Gardener," had to deliver the fee simple to Gardener, and pay him £50; and Cottesford had to assure him the goods.

Gardener also commenced a suit in the Queen's Bench against the plaintiff for recovery of the bond of £300, "of his covetous humour and unchristianity". For the "repressing of so foul and ... unchristian an enterprise", the plaintiff asks for a writ of subpena to be directed to the said William Gardener.

c.

[1581/2, Hilary. Chanc. Entry Books of Decrees and Orders, A1581, f. 225, and B1581, f. 233*d*.]

Wade against Gardyner. Ordered, that if the defendant did not answer by the following Friday, or show cause to the contrary, his further proceedings at the common law should be stayed until he should have directly answered the material points of the plaintiff's bill.

ci.

[1581/2, Hilary. Feet of Fines. C.P. 25/Surr. H. 24 Eliz.]

Between William Gardener, esquire, querent, and Anthoney Leper, John Leper and Lucy his wife, Robert Warde and Jenette his wife, and Katherine Baylye, deforciants, of 20 messuages, cottages, tofts, and gardens, and 4 acres of land in the parish of St. George, Southwark, quitclaimed to William and his heirs for £160.

cii.

[1581/2, March 1. Guildhall, Mayor's Court Repertories, 20/297*d.*]

Item it was ordered that the suit shall be forthwith prosecuted by William Dalbye, one of the attorneys in the utter court, against William Gardyner, leatherseller, lately elect one of sheriffs of this city and county of Middlesex, for not taking upon him the execution of the same room and office accordingly. Harvey, Mayor.

ciii.

[1582, July 31. Mayor's Court Reps. 20/352.]

Camerarius et Mr. Dalbye. Item it is ordered that Mr. Chamberlain of this city shall disburse and pay unto William Dalbye, one of the attorneys in the utter court, the sum of 10*s.* for charges at the suit commenced in the said court against Mr. William Gardyner, leatherseller, for not taking upon him the execution of the office of shrievalty of the city of London and county of Middlesex. Harvey, Mayor.

civ.

[1582, July 31. *Ibid.*, 352*d.*]

Gardner of Southwark, £50 for £200. Item whereas Mr. William Gardner, leatherseller, of late elect one of the sheriffs of this city and county of Middlesex, should satisfy and pay unto Mr. Chamberlain of this city to the use of the Commonalty of the same the sum of £200 for not taking upon him the execution of the same office accordingly, all which fine but only the sum of fifty pounds hath at the request of the right honorable the Earl of Sussex and Chamberlain of Her Majesty's Household been before remitted and forgiven him, it is therefore ordered and decreed by this court that if the said William Gardyner do forthwith satisfy and pay the same sum of fifty pounds to

184

Mr. Chamberlain of this city to the use aforesaid, that then
the rest of the same fine shall be clearly remitted and forgiven
unto him; whereupon the said Mr. Gardyner did satisfy and pay
the same sum of £50 to the said Mr. Chamberlain of this city,
whereof he acknowledgeth himself fully satisfied and paid, and
therewith chargeth himself. Harvey, Mayor.

cv.
[1582, Sept. Close Roll, 24 Eliz. C54/1130.]

Samuel Thomas, in part of the performance of an indenture
dated 28 September 24 Eliz. between him and Thomas [*recte*
William] Gardyner of Southwark, Surrey, esquire, made over
to the said William all that water mill called St. John's Mill,
next 'Horsely Downe', and 'Harpe Leyes' and 'Crosse Leyes',
in the parish of St. Olave, Southwark.

cvi.
[1582, June. Star Chamber Proc., Eliz. St. Ch. 5/S34/2.]

John Stepkin, complainant, against William Gardiner, defendant.

Stepkin's Bill of Complaint.

                To the Queen's most excellent Majesty.
In most humble and obedient wise complaining showeth unto
your most excellent Highness your Majesty's faithful and obedient subject Jhon Stepkyn of St. Mary Matfelon alias Whitechapel in your Majesty's county of Middlesex, gentleman, That
whereas your Majesty's said subject was and is seized of a lawful estate of inheritance of and in divers lands, tenements, and
hereditaments in St. Mary Matfelon alias Whitechapel aforesaid and in St. Botolph without Aldgate and in Stepney in the
county of Midd., out of the which, or for or in respect of which
said lands, tenements, and hereditaments there is yearly for a
certain space due and answerable to your Highness the yearly

185

rent or sum of £129:6:8 or thereabouts, and whereas your
Majesty's said subject in respect of his living and otherwise
might heretofore have been greatly to his preferment advanced
in marriage and might have received in marriage sundry times
heretofore great sums of money and other considerations by
means whereof your Majesty's said subject might have been
well able to have discharged and paid to your Highness such
sums of money as your Majesty would have accepted in discharge of the said yearly rent or sum of £129:6:8 so payable as
is aforesaid for or in respect of or out of the said lands, tenements, and hereditaments, or otherwise have purchased or procured to himself things of great yearly value for his better
maintenance and stay of living, But so it is, if it may please
your Highness, that one William Gardyner of Bermondsey in
your Highness' county of Surrey, gentleman, a man inclined
to strange opinions, and using hard and strait dealing towards some of your Majesty's subjects, perceiving that your
Highness' said subject did seek to prefer himself in marriage in
some honest stock, thereby to procure to himself friendship,
aid, and furtherance in his just causes by alliance in marriage,
but also some reasonable portion and stock for the increase of
his living or towards the discharge of the said yearly rent or
sum of money so (as is aforesaid) due and answerable to your
Majesty for or in respect of or out of the premises, did very
craftily and subtly undermine your Majesty's said subject
to understand the estate of the living of your Majesty's said
subject, and into what speeches of marriage he had entered
into with others; whereof when he had had certain intelligence,
he dissuaded your Majesty's said subject from taking any other
course for the advancement of himself in marriage than such
as he the said William Gardyner would direct him unto; and
so professed and showed outwardly by fair words and promises
that he greatly tendered the estate of your Majesty's said subject, and took great care of him for his advancement in mar-

186

riage, as that through his vehement persuasions your Majesty's said subject was contented to rest and stay himself wholly upon the said William Gardyner and his travail in that behalf; and the rather to increase and settle in your Majesty's said subject an opinion that he the said Wylliam Gardyner would deal faithfully and profitably for and in the behalf of your Majesty's said subject in those causes, he offered unto your Highness' said subject one Katheryne Gardyner, his daughter, in marriage, promising that if your Majesty's said subject would take her to wife, he the said William Gardyner would not only discharge your Majesty's said subject and the mother of your Highness' said subject, and all the lands and tenements of your Highness' said subject, of and for the said yearly rent or payment and all such sums of money and charges wherewith the said lands and tenements stood charged to your Highness, or which were any way answerable or payable to your Majesty for or in respect of the same, but also would grant to your Highness' said subject and to the said Katheryn an yearly rent charge of fifty pounds by the year out of the manor of Wardalls in the parish of Deptford in the county of Kent, and out of the lands and tenements belonging to the same manor for and during the life of Alyce Stepkyn, mother of your Majesty's said subject, if your Highness' said subject and the said Katheryn should so long live, in such sort as that if the same yearly rent of fifty pounds so to be granted or any part thereof should be behind or unpaid, that then your Majesty's said subject and the said Katheryn should and might lawfully distrain in the said manor and in all the lands and tenements of the said William Gardyner belonging to the same manor in Deptford aforesaid; and also that he would pay unto your Majesty's said subject the sum of £200 of lawful English money in further consideration of the said marriage, and also would pay and disburse to and for your Highness' said subject divers other sums of money for his benefit and profit; upon which offer so

187

made, your Highness' said subject not then perceiving the
fraudulent and indirect practice wherewith the said William
Gardyner sought by that means to entrap your Majesty's said
subject, but thinking that he the said William Gardyner had
meant as faithfully therein as he professed, and the rather because it seemed to tend to the knitting of a link of amity between him and your Majesty's said subject by such alliance as
he sought to procure, did the more give credit to the fair words
and promises of the said William Gardyner; whereas in very
truth the said William Gardyner, as by the sequel of the matter
may appear, did mean nothing else but fraud towards your
Highness' said subject, and to beguile and deceive him in those
things wherein both honesty and fatherly love should have
urged him to have done and dealt plainly; yea, your Highness'
said subject did repose so great trust and confidence in him
that whereas your Majesty's said subject dealt with learned
counsel for the setting down and finishing in writing of such
agreements and conclusions as were had between him and your
Highness' said subject for such assurances as were to pass concerning the said marriage, he the said William Gardyner utterly
dissuading your Majesty's said subject to use any other counsel
or advice therein, your Majesty's said subject was by him the
said William led, persuaded, and caused to relinquish the advice of all others and to put him the said William Gardyner
only in trust about the said cause and assurance so that the said
William Gardyner had his own will and used his own ways in
all things concerning the said marriage and touching the assurances above specified, and caused your Majesty's said subject
to grant an yearly rent of £100 out of his lands for the behoof
of the said Katheryn after the decease of the mother of your
Highness' said subject, which rent your Highness' said subject
granted, and also took the said Katheryn to wife, upon hope
and trust that he the said William Gardyner had dealt plainly
with him, and that he would have performed his promises made

to your Majesty's said subject, and that he would not so injuriously have deceived him; but the said William Gardyner, to
make some show of performance of the said grant of the said
promised yearly rent of fifty pounds, made a deed to your
Highness' said subject and to the said Katheryn of the grant
of one yearly rent of fifty pounds out of the said manor of
Wardalls and out of the lands and tenements in Deptford aforesaid thereto belonging; notwithstanding he the said William
Gardyner, to defraud and deceive your Majesty's said subject
of the said yearly rent of fifty pounds, and to the intent that
no distress should be lawfully taken or had in the said manor
or in any part of the lands and tenements of the said William
Gardyner in Deptford aforesaid for any arrearages of the said
yearly rent, he the said William Gardyner did before the granting of the said yearly rent of fifty pounds make and convey
sundry secret leases and estates of the said manor and of other
the said lands and tenements which should have been charged
with the said yearly rent unto certain persons; yea and also since
the said grant of the said yearly rent of fifty pounds to your
Majesty's said subject made, the said William Gardyner hath
made a lease by deed of the said manor or of a part thereof
unto certain persons for the term of divers years yet to come,
and hath antedated the same deed with such a date as though
the same deed had been made before the grant of the said
yearly rent of fifty pounds to your Majesty's said subject made,
to the intent that when your Majesty's said subject should distrain and avow for the said yearly rent in such lands and tenements as are so demised, then the same deed so antedated
might be showed forth and given in evidence at the common
law against your Highness' said subject as a deed made before
the grant of the said rent, to exclude him from the said rent
and the arrearages thereof, contrary to right and equity, and
manifestly against the laws of this your Highness' realm; and
also the said William Gardyner, now that he hath married his

said daughter to your Majesty's said subject, hath refused and yet doth refuse to discharge your Highness' said subject and his mother and the said lands and tenements of your Majesty's said subject of and from the said yearly rent or payment of £159:6:8 [sic] or of such charges and payments as are answerable, due, or payable for or in respect of the said lands and tenements of your Majesty's said subject unto your Highness (as is aforesaid), and hath refused and yet doth refuse to pay to your Majesty's said subject 200 marks, parcel of the said sum of £200 which he (as is aforesaid) promised to your Majesty's said subject in further consideration of his marriage with the said Katheryn, and hath refused and doth refuse to pay to your Majesty's said subject the arrearages of the said rent of fifty pounds or to give unto your Majesty's said subject any consideration or recompense for such things as he (as is aforesaid) promised to your Highness' said subject which he hath not performed, but boasteth and greatly glorieth in that he hath so defrauded and deceived your Majesty's said subject in matching his said daughter with the said your Highness' subject by such fraud, deceit, and evil dealing as he the said William Gardiner (as is aforesaid) practised against your Majesty's said subject. In consideration whereof, and to the intent that such fraud, deceit, and evil dealing above specified may not remain unpunished nor such like offenders encouraged to commit such ungodly practices, may it therefore please your Highness of your accustomed clemency to grant to your Highness' said subject your Majesty's most gracious writ of Subpena to be directed to the said William Gardyner, commanding him thereby at a certain day and under a certain pain therein to be limited, to appear before your Majesty's Council in the High Court of Star Chamber, then and there to answer to the premises and further to stand to and abide such further order therein as to your Majesty's said Council shall seem meet and convenient; and your Majesty's said subject shall daily pray for your Majesty's most happy and prosperous reign long to continue.

Lewys Reade

Gardiner's Answer. Sworn 21 June 1582.

The answer of William Gardner defendant to the Bill of Complaint of John Stipkin Complainant.

The said defendant saith that the said bill of complaint against him in this honorable Court exhibited is uncertain and insufficient and only forged and set forth by the said complainant against this defendant to the intent to vex and molest him without any just matter or cause reasonable, the advantages of all exceptions to the insufficiency of the said bill now and at all times hereafter to this defendant saved, the said defendant for answer saith that true it is that the said complainant is seized of and in divers lands, tenements, and hereditaments in the said several parishes of St. Mary Matfelon alias Whitechapel and in St. Botolph without Aldgate and Stepney in the said county of Middlesex, which are extended and chargeable to pay unto your Majesty for divers years yet enduring the sum of £129:6:8 (to the full value of the land, as this defendant thinketh). And this defendant doth not know nor ever heard that the livelihood of this complainant was or is such that thereby he might have procured any great marriage, or purchased to himself (his and the charges to your Majesty defrayed) things of any value as in the bill with frivolous allegations vainly is surmised; but this complainant, being an earnest suitor to the said Katherin, daughter unto this defendant, and making great means to this defendant for his good will therein, did in the end, upon the faithful promise of this complainant to assure unto the said Katherin for her jointure the yearly rent of £100 for term of her life, that is to say, after the death of this complainant fifty pounds, and after the death of the mother of the said complainant other fifty pounds or the like in effect, and that the land out of which the said rent should

191

be issuing should be of the clear yearly value of £100 *ultra reprisas*. In consideration of which yearly rent as aforesaid to be
made, he this defendant did assent to the said marriage to be
had between the said complainant and the said Katherin, and,
in consideration thereof, did grant unto the said complainant
and to the said Katherin in consideration of the said marriage
one rent charge of fifty pounds out of his said manor of Wardalls for and during the life of the said Alice Stipkin, mother of
the said complainant, in such manner and form as in the bill is
alleged, and promised further to give £200 more in marriage
with her; he this defendant having already paid the sum of 100
marks and having assured the said rent of fifty pounds as
aforesaid; but this said complainant, fraudulently intending to
defraud the said Katherin of the said jointure of £100, (promised as aforesaid to be assured unto her), hath made a grant
of one rent of £100 unto the said Katherin out of certain lands
chargeable with the payment of the said £129:6:8 to your
Majesty, with as much or greater charge than the said land
is worth, as this defendant thinketh, for which fraud, and for
further and better assurance to be made in accomplishment of
his promise to the use of the said Katherin, this defendant
hath exhibited his bill in your Majesty's high court of Chancery, which dependeth as yet undetermined; and now to weary
this defendant this complainant hath exhibited his bill in this
court, containing in effect the matter depending there; without
that, that the said defendant, in respect of the marriage to be
had between the said complainant and the said defendant's
daughter, did promise to the said complainant and mother of
the said complainant mentioned in the said bill or one of them
as well to discharge the said complainant and his said mother
and all the lands and tenements of the said complainant of and
for the said yearly rent and payment of all such sums of money
and charges wherewith the said lands and tenements stood
charged to her Majesty, or which were any way answerable or

payable to your Majesty, or to pay divers other sums of money for the benefit and profit of this complainant; without that the said defendant did subtly and craftily beguile and deceive the said complainant touching any promise in and about the said marriage had between the said complainant and the said defendant's daughter, or dissuaded him from taking any other course for his advancement in marriage than this defendant would persuade him unto, for this defendant believeth, how vainly and foolishly soever this complainant persuadeth himself, that he might have bestowed his daughter upon a person of more livelihood, discretion, and government; and without that this defendant sought by indirect means to entrap this complainant; and without that for the assurance making of the said annuity of fifty pounds this defendant dissuaded this complainant to use any other advice than his; and without that the said defendant, before the granting of the said annuity of fifty pounds, did make any secret and fraudulent leases or estates of the said lands and tenements in Detford aforesaid, and out of which he had granted the said annuity or yearly rent of fifty pounds to the said John and Katherin; or that since the said grant of the said annuity, that this defendant hath made any lease by deed of the said lands or any part thereof for divers years yet to come; and hath antedated the same lease, or hath made any fraudulent conveyance to defeat the said rent charge, as in the said bill is most slanderously set down and alleged; and without that the said defendant did glory and vaunt that he hath defrauded and deceived the said complainant in matching his daughter with the said complainant by such fraud, deceit, and evil dealing as in the said bill most untruly is alleged; and without that any other matter or thing material in the said bill to be answered unto and in this answer not sufficiently answered unto, traversed, denied, or avoided, is true.

Boys   Lock

193   o

SHAKESPEARE VERSUS SHALLOW

Stepkin's Replication. Trinity term, 1582.

> The Replication of Jhon Stepkyne, gentleman, complainant, to the Answer of William Gardiner, gentleman, defendant.

The said complainant doth maintain and aver his said bill of complaint, and all and every thing therein contained, to be good, just, and true in such sort as in the same is set forth and declared: and also saith that the said answer is very uncertain and untrue, and containeth no matter of substance or sufficiency in it at all; the advantage of exception to the uncertainty and insufficiency whereof to this complainant at all times hereafter saved, the said complainant saith as he before in his said bill of complaint hath said, and doth and will maintain, aver, and prove the same to be good and true in such sort as the same by him in his said bill of complaint is most truly set forth and alleged; and for replication saith that well and true it is, that the defendant, about a year now last past, did exhibit a bill into her Majesty's high court of Chancery at Westminster against the now complainant, praying by the said bill that the defendant might detain in his hands 200 marks, parcel of the said sum of £200 promised with his daughter in marriage, for the livelihood of his daughter, surmising that the lands out of which the complainant hath granted one yearly rent of £100 unto Katherine, the wife of the complainant, for term of the natural life of the said Katherine, are not of the yearly value of £100 by the year *ultra reprisas*; where in very truth the said lands are fully of that value; the which suit in the Chancery is rather commenced by the now defendant for to vex, molest, and disquiet the now complainant and his old mother, knowing that if the defendant could, by such vexation of suit, bring the said Alyce Stepkyne, the complainant's mother, unto her grave by taking of great care and thought, by reason of the fraudulent, deceitful, and lewd dealing of the said defendant, that then the rent charge granted by the said defendant unto

194

the complainant and Katheryne his wife were then determined; and also saith that the now defendant proceedeth very slowly in the Chancery in the said suit, for his bill being answered a twelvemonth ago, he hath not replied in all this time; the which argueth that he is greatly ashamed to proceed, lest his lewd and unhonest dealing should be now manifested unto the world; although he be a man already of whom the world generally speaketh evil of, and especially all those that have had any dealing with him at all, by reason of his hard conscience and corrupt dealing; but for the opinion of the world the defendant little regardeth, as he hath very often in speeches affirmed, saying, he careth not what the world thinketh of him, for he hath money enough; resting himself more upon his substance than upon his honesty and good dealing; without that, that the said lands of the complainant in the bill and answer mentioned are extended unto her Majesty for the full value, as is most untruly in the said answer alleged, the which the defendant knoweth very well, although he go about to estrange himself from the knowledge thereof, or that the complainant made great means unto the defendant for his good will to marry his daughter, as is most untruly alleged. And without that, that the defendant hath assured unto the complainant and Katheryne his wife one rent charge of fifty pounds by the year forth of his manor of Wardalles in the county of Kent in such manner and form that the complainant may now lawfully distrain in the said manor according unto the purpose of the deed thereof made, and true meaning of the agreement between the complainant and defendant. And without that, that the complainant did intend to defraud the said Katherine of the said jointure of £100 promised, or that the lands charged with the said jointure of £100 by the year are not of greater value than the yearly rent with the which they are charged unto your Majesty: for the said lands are worth £100 by the year over and above the said yearly rent of £129:6:8 payable unto your

Majesty. And without that, that any other matter or thing mentioned or contained in the said answer material or effectual to be replied unto by the complainant, and not herein sufficiently confessed or avoided, traversed, or denied, is true: all which matters the said complainant is ready to aver and prove as this honourable Court shall award, and prayeth as before in his said bill he hath prayed.

Hen: Vernon

cvii.

[1582, November. Star Chamber Proceedings,
Eliz. St. Ch. 5/S40/30.]

Stepkin against Gardiner.

Interrogatories to be ministered unto witnesses to be produced on the part and behalf of Jhon Stepkine, gentleman, complainant, against William Gardiner, gentleman, defendant.

Inprimis whether do you know that the complainant did make great means unto William Gardiner the defendant for his good will, that he might marry Katherine his daughter, and by whom did he make means unto him, and whether did not the defendant first make means unto the complainant to come home to his house afore he came, yea or no.

2. *Item* whether did not the defendant, after that the complainant had let him understand his estate and living, promise unto the complainant that if he did happen to join in marriage with Katheryne his daughter, that he would either discharge the complainant's lands of one rent charge wherewith it was charged with his money or friendship, or else disburse a great sum of money for the mitigating of the said yearly rent, being £129:6:8 by the year; and whether do not you know of your own knowledge that that was the chief and greatest benefit that the complain-

196

ant made reckoning to receive at the hands of the defendant, yea or no.

3. *Item* was not the complainant, through the defendant's
   vehement persuasions and great offers, content to rest
   and stay himself wholly upon the defendant, yea or no.

4. *Item* whether did not the defendant also likewise promise
   unto the complainant that if he would take his daughter
   Katherine to wife, that then he would grant unto the
   complainant and unto the said Katherine one yearly rent
   of £50 by the year out of the manor of Wardalles in the
   parish of Deptford in the county of Kent, and out of the
   lands and tenements belonging to the same manor, for and
   during the life of Alyce Stepkine, mother of the complainant, if the complainant and Katherine his wife should so
   long live, in such sort that if the said yearly rent of £50 so
   to be granted or any part thereof should be behind and
   unpaid, that then the complainant and Katherine his wife
   might lawfully distrain in the said manor and in all the
   lands and tenements belonging to the said manor in Dept-
   forde, yea or no.

5. *Item* whether did not the defendant promise that he would
   pay unto the complainant £200 in further consideration
   of the said marriage, and how much thereof hath he paid
   unto the complainant, yea or no.

6. *Item* whether did not the defendant (whereas the complainant used the advice of learned counsel for the setting down
   and finishing in writing of such agreements and conclusions as were had between him and the complainant for
   such assurances as were to pass concerning the said marriage) dissuade the complainant for [*sic*] dealing any
   further with his counsel, or to use any other advice and
   counsel therein, but wholly to rest upon him and his
   counsel and his scrivener, yea or no.

7. *Item* whether did not the complainant, by the defendant's

persuasion, relinquish the advice of all other, and put the defendant only in trust about the said cause and assurances, so that the defendant had his own will and used his own ways in all things concerning the said assurances and marriage, yea or no.

8. *Item* whether hath not the complainant granted one yearly rent charge of £100 by the year out of all his lands unto the said Katherine for term of her life for her jointure, yea or no.

9. *Item* whether hath the defendant granted one yearly rent charge of £50 by the year unto the complainant and unto Katherine his wife, yea or no.

10. *Item* whether do you not know of your own knowledge or have heard of others that the defendant, afore the grant of the said rent charge of £50 by the year, did make a lease of the said manor and of the said lands and tenements which should have been charged with the said yearly rent, yea or no.

11. *Item* whether did not the defendant know that the grantees of the said rent charge of £50 by the year could not distrain for the said rent or for the arrearages thereof during the continuance of the said lease, yea or no.

12. *Item* whether have you not heard the defendant say these words (or words to the same effect): 'that God hath nothing to do with the world since he created it, and that the world was not governed by him', yea or no.

13. *Item* whether do you know or have heard that the defendant threatened and menaced the complainant and his mother that he would so use the matter that neither the complainant nor his mother should rest in their beds, yea or no.

14. *Item* whether do you know or have heard that the defendant hath passed a secret estate of his lands and goods before his last marriage, yea or no.

15. *Item* whether did you hear the defendant say unto the now complainant these words, or the like in effect: 'that if he would not rest in hope and expectation of a greater portion hereafter to come unto the complainant by reason of the marriage of his daughter, that for every hundred pounds he would give the complainant three', yea or no.

16. *Item* whether did not the defendant promise unto the complainant that during the life of the mother of the complainant or the life of the defendant that the complainant and his wife should be at no charges for their diet, for that the complainant should be welcome unto the defendant for his daughter's sake, and the complainant's wife should be welcome unto the complainant's mother for the complainant's sake, or words to the same effect, and during that time the complainant should be at no charges, yea or no.

17. *Item* whether hath the defendant performed all his promises, yea or no; and how many of them hath he performed.

. . ex parte John [Stepkin]

Examination taken 13 November 24 Eliz. [1582].

Thomas K[inge] clerk . . . [in the county] of Surrey, aged 70 years, sworn &c.

To the first, he saith he knoweth nothing of any means that the plaintiff made to the said William Gardener for his good will that he might marry Katheryn the daughter of the said Gardener, but he hath heard one Mrs. Shepperd, a sister of the said Gardener's, say to some friends of the said Stypkyn's that if the said Stypkyns would come to her brother Gardener's house he should be welcome; and, as this examinate thinketh, the same Gardener made means unto the plaintiff to come to his house before the plaintiff came thither.

To the second, he saith that the complainant, having given the

199

said Mr. Gardener to understand the state of his living, this deponent heard the said Gardener promise the said complainant that if the same plaintiff did happen to marry with Katheryn daughter [of] the said Gardener, that then he the same Gardener of mere friendship would discharge or mitigate the rent charge of £129:6:8 by the year . . out of the said plaintiff's lands; that he the said Gardener would discharge the same and though it cost him a thousand pounds; and he also saith that the said promise was the chief and greatest benefit the said plaintiff made reckoning of to receive at the said Gardener's hands, for he hath heard the said plaintiff so say.

To the third, he saith that the said complainant of this deponent's knowledge was through the [said] Gardener's vehement persuasions and great offers of the said Gardener contented to rest himself wholly upon the said Gardener; for he hath heard the said Gardener say to the said complainant (the complainant being about to have some books drawn) that the same complainant for the sparing of money should not need to go to any other for advice of counsel but to his the same Gardener's own counsel.

To the fourth, he saith he heard the said Gardener also promise the said complainant that if the said complainant would take his daughter . . . to wife, that then he the [said] Gardener would grant to the . . complainant and to the said Katheryn the yearly rent of £50 by the year out of the manor of Wardalls in Dartforde [*sic*] and out of the lands belonging to the said manor, during the life of Alice Stypkyn, mother to the said plaintiff, if the said plaintiff and Katheryn his wife should so long live, in such sort that if the said rent of £50 so to be granted, or any part thereof, should be behind or unpaid, that then the said plaintiff and Katheryn his wife might distrain in the said manor and all the lands thereunto belonging in Dartforde.

To the fifth, he saith he heard the said Gardener in further consideration of the said marriage promise to give and pay the same plaintiff the sum of £200; and that the same Gardener of that sum hath as yet paid the same complainant but the sum of 100 marks.

To the sixth, he saith that the said complainant using, or being about to use, the [advice] of learned counsel for the setting out and finishing concerning of [*sic*] such agreements and conclusions as are had . . and agreed on between the said plaintiff and the said Gardener, the deponent heard the said Gardener dissuade the complainant from dealing any further therein with his counsel; the said Gardener then saying to the said plaintiff that he would have the same complainant wholly to rest upon him the same Gardener and his counsel and scrivener as well for the sparing of money as otherwise.

To the seventh, he saith that the said complainant did, by means of the said Gardener's persuasions, relinquish the advice of all other, and put only the said Gardener in trust about the same cause and assurance; by means whereof the said Gardener had his own will and used his own ways in all things touching the said assurance and marriage; and he knoweth that to be true by means he was a great deal with both the said parties in the said cause.

To the eighth, he saith that . . . complainant hath granted and . . . rent charge of £100 by the year . . . out of all his lands to the said Katheryn for the term of her life for her jointure.

To the ninth, he saith that the said Gardener hath granted to the said complainant and Katheryn his wife the yearly rent charge of £50 by the year.

To the tenth, he saith that the said Gardener had, before the grant of the said rent charge of £50 by the year, made a lease of the said manor and of the said lands and tenements which should have been charged with the same yearly rent to one Mr. [?] Foule; and he knoweth this to be true by

means he hath heard the said [?] Foule affirm the having of
the same lease.

To the eleventh, he can say nothing.

To the twelfth, he saith he hath heard the said Gardener use
the words and speeches mentioned in the article, or words to
that effect.

To the thirteenth, he can say nothing.

To the fourteenth, he can say nothing.

To the fifteenth, he saith he hath heard the said Gardener use
the words and speeches mentioned in the article to the said
complainant, or words to that effect.

To the sixteenth, he saith he heard the said Gardener make
such promise and use such speech to the said complainant
as is mentioned in the article, or words to that effect.

To the seventeenth, he saith to his remembrance the said Gardener hath not as yet performed any one of his promises
made to the said complainant, the payment of the 100 marks
before mentioned excepted.

> [*signed*] per me Thom Kynge

cviii.
[1583. (25 Eliz.) Star Chamber Proceedings, Eliz.
St. Ch. 5G37/5.]

Gardiner against Stepkin.

Gardiner's Bill of Complaint.

To the Queen's most excellent Majesty.
In most humble wise showeth unto your most excellent Majesty your Majesty's faithful and obedient subject William
Gardner of Baronsey [*sic*] in your Highness' county of Surrey,
gentleman. That whereas one John Stepkyn of St. Mary Matfelon alias Whitechapel in your Majesty's county of [*blank*], a
man fraught with fraud and subtlety, seeking to marry Katherin, your Majesty's said subject's daughter, the whereto to ob-

tain his purpose, affirmed unto your said subject that he might dispend in lands to the clear yearly value of £200 by the year, above all reprises, and that he would assure unto your Majesty's said subject's daughter for her jointure towards her livelihood during her life £100 yearly over and above all charges and reprises, unto which faithful promise your Majesty's said subject giving credit, did condescend and agree; and in advancement with his said daughter did grant unto his said daughter one rent charge of £50 by the year to be taken out of his manor of Wardals in the parish of Detford in your Majesty's county of Kent and out of all the lands belonging unto the same during the life of Alice Stipkyn, mother of the same John, for the better maintenance of the said John and Katherin (for that the said John affirmed unto your said subject that the said Alice had a portion or dowry to that value), and further gave unto the said John in marriage with the said Katherin 100 marks, and promised, upon sufficient assurance of the said £100 in lands by the year to be made unto the said Katheryn for term of her life, discharged of all charges and encumbrances, to give unto him 200 marks more; and after marriage willed the said John Stepkin to cause indentures to be drawn accordingly; but the said John, intending to defraud your said subject, being confederated with the said Alice Stipkyn his mother, he being indebted to the Queen's Majesty, procured all his lands to be seized into her Majesty's hands, and caused the same Alice his mother to take the same in extent from her Majesty for many years yet to come; and after caused indentures of assurance to be made of certain lands to the use of himself for life, remainder to the said Katherin for her life, the remainder thereof to his own right heirs, with covenants therein contained that the same was discharged, or should be by him saved harmless of all payments to her Majesty, and of all other charges and encumbrances, and sealed the same accordingly; the said John and Alice knowing that the same lands were extended to her Majesty for as much as they were worth, intending this fraud, that the lands should not be liable unto any damages to be recovered by that covenant and agreement after the death of the said John Stipkin by reason of the extent to her Majesty, and that during the life of the said John no action of covenant or other remedy could be had, for that the same was not to take effect before the death of the said John; and yet not thus contented, but utterly to defraud your said subject and his said daughter of her livelihood, they have made, forged, and contrived divers false and secret leases and other estates of the said lands assured unto your Majesty's said subject's daughter (as aforesaid) for many years and long time to endure after the said extent, and hath antedated the same with such a date as though the same had been made before the assurance made as aforesaid to your said subject's daughter; where in truth it was made long since; intending thereby to defraud your Majesty's said subject's daughter of her jointure if she survive him; and also hath granted divers rent charges out of the same, with antedates; and in truth all the lands of the said John were not nor yet are of the clear yearly value of £50 above all charges; by which fraud and conspiracy between him the said John and Alice his mother, your Majesty's said subject's daughter shall be defrauded if remedy be not herein by your Majesty provided; may it therefore please your most excellent Majesty, the premises duly considered, to grant unto your said subject your Majesty's most gracious writ of subpena to be directed unto the said John and Alice Stipkyn, commanding them and either of them thereby at a certain day and under a certain pain therein to be limited, personally to appear before your most excellent Majesty in your Majesty's most high court of Star Chamber, then and there to answer to the premises, and to abide such order and direction therein as to your most excellent Majesty shall seem most convenient; and your

Majesty's said subject shall daily pray for your Highness'
most prosperous reign long to continue.

Boys

The Stepkins' Demurrer.

> The demurrer of John Stepken and Alice Stepken
> defendants upon the bill of complaint of William
> Gardner complainant.

The said defendants say that the said bill of complaint against
them exhibited into this most honourable court is very uncertain and insufficient in law to be answered unto by these defendants for divers and sundry very apparent causes in the
same contained; forasmuch therefore as by the discourse of the
said bill of complaint it manifestly appeareth that the said
complainant in consideration that this defendant John Stepken
should marry with Katherin, daughter of the said complainant,
and that the said John Stepken should assure unto the said
Katheryn for term of her life lands and tenements to the clear
yearly value of £100 by the year, he the said complainant
granted unto the said Katherin one rent charge of £50 by the
year to be taken out of his manor of Wardels in the parish of
Detford during the life of the said Alice Stepken, mother of
the said John, and further that he gave unto the said John in
marriage with his said daughter 100 marks, and that he promised upon sufficient assurance of the said £100 in land by the
year to be made to the said Katherin for term of her life discharged of all charges and encumbrances, to give unto the said
John 200 marks more, and that after he willed the said John
to cause indentures to be drawn accordingly, and allegeth that
the said John, intending to defraud him, being confederated
with the said Alice Stepken his mother, he being indebted unto
the Queen's Majesty, procured all his lands to be seized into
her Majesty's hands, and caused the said Alice his mother to
take the same in extent from her Majesty for many years yet
to come, and that after he caused indentures of assurance to

205

be made of certain lands to the use of himself for life, the remainder to the said Katheryn, the remainder thereof to his own right heirs, with covenants therein contained that the same was discharged or should be saved harmless of all payments to her Majesty, charges, and encumbrances, and sealed the same; in which allegation the said complainant hath not limited any time when the said confederacy was committed or practised, so that if the same be any offence worth examination in this most honourable court it doth not appear whether it were committed before or since her Majesty's general pardon, and therefore this most honorable court cannot proceed to punishment of the same; and also doth allege that these defendants, to defraud the said complainant and his said daughter of her livelihood, they have made, forged, and contrived divers false and secret leases and other estates of the said lands so assured unto the complainant's daughter for many years and long time to endure after the said extent, and have antedated the same with such a date as though the same had been made before the assurance made to the complainant's daughter, intending to defraud her of her jointure if she survive them; in which allegation the said complainant hath not set forth neither any time certain when the said supposed forgery should have been committed, nor what lands or tenements the said supposed forged leases do comprehend, nor what lands or tenements they be which be so assured to the complainant's daughter, nor how long the said supposed forged leases are to endure, nor when to begin, nor when the said extent is to end; and also doth allege that the said John hath granted divers rent charges out of the same with antedates, not expressing what such rent charges be, nor to whom they be granted, nor out of what lands or tenements they be issuing, nor when they were granted; the said defendants therefore, for the causes before alleged, and for other uncertainties and insufficiencies in the said bill contained, and for that also the said complainant hath not alleged any other good matter to give jurisdiction to this most honourable court to hold plea of the same, do demur in law upon the said bill of complaint, and demand judgment of this most honourable court if they shall be enforced to make any other or better answer unto the same bill of complaint; and pray to be dismissed out of the same with their reasonable costs, charges, and expenses in the law in this behalf by them most wrongfully sustained.

Yelverton

cix.

[1582, November 10. Court of Requests Proceedings.
Req. 2/109/50.]

John Hunter of London, ironmonger, against William Gardiner and Margaret his wife.

Hunter's Bill of Complaint. Alleges that he borrowed of Edward Hynde of London, gentleman, £50 for one year at ten per cent interest, payable 16 September 1579, and was bound to Frement Abraham, merchant tailor, and Thomas Cartwright, draper, in £100 for that payment. Now "one William Gardener, who hath married the wife and executrix of the said Frement Abraham, having the said bonds in his hands, hath upon displeasure taken because he cannot enjoy a shop which his predecessor Frement Abraham had, being tenant at will many years, hath and doth prosecute with all severity the said bond of £200, saying that he will break the back of the said complainant, meaning by the suit now in variance; notwithstanding neither he nor his predecessor Frement Abraham were ever indemnified [i.e. damnified] in any respect."

cx.

[1582/3, February 9. Court of Requests Proc. Req. 2/119/45.]

William Gardiner, esquire, and Margaret his wife and John Wigenton, complainants, against John Hunter and John Redman, defendants.

207

Bill of Complaint. Gardiner says he let the shop (late of Fre-ment Abraham's) in Christ Church, Newgate, last August to John Wygenton until Annunciation following, entering a bond of £20 to Wygenton, and the latter enjoys the premises. ". . . until now of late . . . John Hunter, having conceived some dis-pleasure against your said subjects by reason of some suits that of late have happened betwixt the said John Hunter and the said William Gardyner and Margaret his wife, who being in great malice with the said William Gardyner, and desirous to bring the said William Gardyner within the forfeiture of his bond, hath of late very uncharitably made a lease of the said shop unto one John Redman for a four years or thereabouts, which John Redman, by colour and virtue thereof, have entered and expelled the said John Wygenton being a very poor man; and the said John Redman getting and continuing the posses-sion of the shop . . . doth sue the said John Wygenton in the King's Bench by action *de eieccione firme.*"

cxi.

[1583, Easter. Court of Requests Order Book.
Easter 25 Eliz.]

April 24. William Gardyner, esquire, and Margaret his wife and John Wigenton against John Redman and John Hunter. Ordered, that John Redman should not proceed or bring action in any other court against John Wigenton concerning a shop in Newgate Market.

cxii.

[1582/3, Hilary. Feet of Fines. C.P. 25/Surr. H. 25 Eliz.]

Between William Gardyner, esquire, querent, and William Broke and Agnes his wife, deforciants, of 4 parts of 16 messu-ages, 4 cottages and 4 gardens, in the parish of St. Olave, Southwark, in 5 parts divided, quitclaimed to the said William Gardyner for £80.

cxiii.

[1583, Michaelmas. Queen's Bench. K.B. 27/1287/271.]

William Gardener, citizen and leatherseller of London, against Richard Johnson, of the Inner Temple, gentleman. That George Clyffe, Thomas Offley, and Richard Johnson on September 19, 1578, entered into a bond to Gardener of £150, with condition to be void if they paid Gardener £110 on the 28th of August following. Johnson pleads the statute of 2 April 13 Eliz. against usury, alleging that Clyffe was indebted only £100 and that the £10 more was interest. Gardener nevertheless got judgment for £156:0:1 debt and damages.

cxiv.

[1583. *Surrey Muster Rolls* (pr. Surrey Record Soc.), ii, 185.]

[Surrey. T]he Booke [of Must]ers for horsemen . . . [at Cobham, 20 September 1583.]

Bryxstone and Wallington.

Light horses

William Gardner esquier . . . . j

Defectes

Launces

a- William Gardner esquier   j   the horse insufficient.

cxv.

[1583/4, Hilary. Common Pleas. C.P. 40/1423/1942.]

London. William Gardyner, esquire, and Margaret his wife, executrix of Frement Abraham, citizen and merchant tailor of London, by Henry Burr their attorney, against Robert Fulkeshurste, of Crewe, Cheshire, esquire, late of London, servant of Sir Christopher Hatton, knight, in a plea of debt of £8 owing on a bond dated 20 May 23 Eliz. (1581).

Considered that debt is to be paid with 26*s*. 8*d*. damages.

cxvi.

[1584, May. Court of Requests Proc. Req. 2/213/2.]

William Gardiner of St. Mary Magdalen, Bermondsey, esquire, against William Brooke, citizen and freemason of London, and Agnes his wife. Certain messuages in Southwark. Bill, answer, and replication.

cxvii.

[1584, June 26. Court of Requests Proc. Req. 2/133/2.]

Depositions in the foregoing suit, on the behalf of Gardiner. Henry Alyson (Gardiner's scrivener) and his servant George Martin depose that Brooke bargained to sell to Gardiner 4 parts in 5 of two messuages in Bermondsey Street, in the occupation of Christopher Fletcher and Esau Fee; that Gardiner agreed to pay £75 and to discharge the said Brooke and his wife of £70 mortgage of the said houses with others: that Gardiner paid Brooke's wife 40s. "and tendered in this said deponent's shop £3 unto the said Brooke".

cxviii.

[1584, July. Star Chamber Proc. St. Ch. 5/ B8/24; B66/26.]

William Brooke and Agnes his wife against William Gardiner and Henry Alyson. Fraud. Bill, answer, and depositions.

cxix.

[1584, June 20. Chanc. Decrees and Orders. B1583/598d.]

William Brooke, plaintiff, William Gardyner, esquire, and Henry Allyson, defendants.

The plaintiff is adjudged to pay to the defendants 10s. costs for want of a bill.

cxx.

[1584/5, Hilary. Queen's Bench. K.B. 27/1292/212.]

William Gardiner, esquire, against William Brooke, citizen and freemason of London. In a plea of debt for £3 7s. Gardiner got a judgment for debt, costs, and damages of £8 12s.

cxxi.

[1584, Easter. Feet of Fines. C.P. 25/Surr. E. 26 Eliz.]

Between William Gardener, querent, and John Chester and Elizabeth his wife, deforciants, of three messuages, one curtilage, and one wharf in the parish of St. Olave, Southwark, warranted against the said John and Elizabeth and their heirs and against Stephen Marten and Elizabeth his wife and their heirs, for 200 marks.

cxxii.

[1584. Records of the Leathersellers' Company.]

In an assessment, Gardiner's name was included for £3.

cxxiii.

[1584. State Papers, Dom., Eliz., 172, f. 49.]

"Memorandum that the 13th of July 1584, one Mr. Edwardes, dwelling in Barmondseye, did say to me and others that he was in London and there did hear spoken by one Lee and other in the company in talking of the death of the Prince of Orange, the said Lee did say that there was or should come two from beyond the sea who should do the like practice towards Her Majesty, who God long preserve.

[*signed*] Wyllyam Gardyner"

cxxiv.

[1584, Trinity. Common Pleas. C.P. 40/1431/2141.]

London. William Gardyner, esquire, and Margaret his wife, executrix of the will of Frement Abraham, against William Skete of London, gentleman.

The plaintiffs said by Henry Burr their attorney that between 28 July 1572 and 5 April 1577 William Skete bought of the said Abraham black kersey, black cotton, linen called 'double Harford', white fustian, brown canvas, russet fustian, double

211

mockado, a pair of purple stockings, black double baize, two white canvas doublets, black mockado, two 'pair of paned hose', a pair of stockings, a brown canvas doublet, and a pair of black kersey hose, to the total value of £14 9s. He was asked to pay by Abraham, by the said Margaret while she was a widow, and by William Gardyner and the said Margaret after her marriage with him, but has never discharged the debt. It was considered that the plaintiffs should recover the debt with 40s. damages.

cxxv.

[1584, Easter. Queen's Bench. K.B. 27/1289/452.]

William Gardiner, gentleman, against John Luce, citizen and draper of London. Plea of debt of £6 on a bond dated 11 December 1567, payable on demand. A day given.

cxxvi.

[1584, Michaelmas. Queen's Bench. K.B. 27/1291/51.]

Middlesex. In Trinity term last, William Gardiner (by Thomas Good his attorney) brought a bill against John Luce, saying that on 9 October 1583, in consideration that William, at the special instance and request of John, had delivered £6 to John for his special use, John agreed and promised to pay £6 to William on demand. But John, seeking to defraud him, on 1 November 1583, did not pay it or any part of it on demand, whereby William has lost much money and profit that he might have made in trade. William Gardiner asks 20 marks damages. On 9 October of this term, John Luce appeared by Edmond Thurston his attorney and denied the charge.

At the trial on 10 May 1585, the jury found that Luce agreed as Gardiner had charged, and assessed Gardiner's damages at £6:6:8, his costs and charges at £5:10:0: in all, £11:16:8.

On 16 May 1586, Gardiner acknowledged payment of his damages.

212

cxxvii.

[1584, Michaelmas. Queen's Bench. K.B. 27/1291/49.]

Surrey. In Easter term last William Gardiner, esquire (by his attorney Thomas Good) brought a bill against John Bullarde *alias* Bulwarde of trespass on the case as follows: Whereas William Gardiner has always been a faithful and honest subject of the Queen, who because of his good name and estimation appointed him justice of peace and of the quorum in Surrey, yet the aforesaid John, to injure him in goods and reputation, on 2 February 1583/4 at Southwark, falsely taxed him with subornation of perjury in these words: 'That Master Gardener's wife (meaning Frances Gardener, late wife of the aforesaid William Gardener) was forsworn by the procurement of Master Gardener, and that I would prove to be true.' Gardiner demanded £500 damages.

On 9 October of this term, Bullarde appeared by his attorney Edmund Thurston, and defended force and injury, and said that Gardiner should not have his action, on the ground that before the date of the alleged words, to wit, on 18 April 1564 before Dr. Walter Haddon, *Custos* of the Prerogative Court of Canterbury, sitting as a judge in St. Paul's Church, the aforesaid Frances (wife of William) swore upon her oath, by the procurement of William, that she paid one Richard Pype, then citizen and leatherseller of London £108 owing to Pype by one Robert Luce; whereas in truth she did not pay Pype the said sum. Bullarde was ready to verify this, and asked judgment against Gardiner.

Gardiner said that Bullarde said the words as above of his own wrong, and without such cause as is alleged.

Jury trial at Westminster, 12 November 1585. The jury (of Southwark and Bermondsey men) found that Bullarde said the words of his own wrong; they assessed Gardiner's damages at £10, his costs and charges at £7 1s. Bullarde in mercy for £17 1s.

cxxviii.

[1584, October 26. Close Roll, 26 Eliz. C54/1182.]

William Gardyner of the parish of St. Mary Magdalen, Ber-
mondsey, esquire, for certain consideration sold to Samuel
Thomas, his heirs and assigns, all that water mill called St.
John's Mill, lying next 'Horseydowne' in the parish of St.
Olave, Southwark, together with a pightel called 'Harpe Leys'
and another parcel of land called 'Crosse Leyes', both in the
same parish, late parcel of the possessions of the Hospital of
St. John of Jerusalem.

cxxix.

[1584, November 9. Close Roll, 26 Eliz. C54/1181.]
Similar to preceding.

cxxx.

[1584/5 ?January 27. State Papers, Dom., Eliz., 176, f. 30.]

The report of Edwarde Soer, constable of Parrishe
Garden, and one John Bartlem, bailiff there. Taken
before William Gardiner, esquire, the 27th: Anno 1584.
Inprimis they say that about Christmas last they came to the
house of one Hewghe Katlyne, there to search for a papist, and
there they found certain suspected persons within the house.
The which Hewghe Katlyne would not suffer them to come in,
neither to search his house, but kept the door having his
weapon in his hand; and afterward they went to Sar! Vener
for a warrant, and so went to the house again, and afterward
they watched the house with a strong watch, and after that,
upon a new search, they came into the house, and there they
found one John Worrall, a notorious person of papistry, and
two other of his acquaintance within. And afterward, about
the 9th of January, after the death of one Carter, there was
burned in Carter's house certain books of papistry for fear that
they should be seen, and afterward they found divers other

214

books of papistry, upon which they suspected Catline's house for; and so they went thither again to search, and found not Katlyn at home, and in searching the house they found divers suspected persons; and after that they found 8 papists' books hid in sundry places in the house; and never since the aforesaid Katlyn came to his house, but stale away in the night for fear he should be taken; and the next day following there was certain pictures found in his house, and one crucifix; the which books and pictures remains in Mr. Recorder's hand.

[*signed*] Wyllyam Gardyner

cxxxi.
[1585, April 9. Close Roll, 27 Eliz. C54/1206.]

Edward Jobson of West Donyland *alias* Monkwick near Colchester, Essex, esquire, for £330 sold to William Gardiner of Bermondsey, Surrey, esquire, all that marsh and marsh house called Acres Fleete in the Isle of Wallettes in the parish of Canydon, Essex. This conveyance was in the nature of a mortgage, and was cancelled after Gardiner was paid his money.

cxxxii.
[1585, May 22. Somerset House. P.C.C. Brudenell 26.]

Dispute between John Luce and Frances Gardner *alias* Wayte, administratrix of the goods of Robert Luce, citizen and leatherseller of London, not administered by Katherine Luce, Sara Luce *alias* Manley, and Elizabeth Luce *alias* Bullward.

". . . invenimus prefatam Franciscam Gardiner alias Wayte defunctam dum in humanis agebat pro se et suos ex bonis, juribus, ac creditis prefate Roberti Luce patris sui defuncti non administratis per Katherinam Luce relictam et administratricem bonorum ejusdem Roberti similiter defunctam non administratorum usque ad summam £1379:0:10 legalis monete Anglie recepisse et habuisse seu saltem per eandem Franciscam

215

Gardiner alias Wayte vel suos stetisse quominus reciperet seu haberet ceteraque bona jura et credita dicti Roberti per prefatam Katherinam relictam non administrata indisposita et non administrata reliquisse, eandemque insuper Franciscam Gardner alias Waite per se et suos in ac citra solucionem debitorum dicti Roberti Luce defuncti ac in necessarios usus et expensas citra administracionem bonorum ejusdem prefatam summam £1379:0:10 exposuisse et erogasse eaque racione antedictam Franciscam Gardiner alias Wayte bona jura et credita dicti defuncti que (in quantum nobis constare potest) ad manus suas ex administracione predicta pervenerunt sufficienter et ad plenum administrasse pronunciamus decernimus et declaramus partem igitur dicte Francisce Gardiner alias Luce ad instanciam et impetitione prefate Johanni Luce, Sare Luce alias Manley, et Elizabethe Luce alias Bullward quoad dictam summam £1379:0:10 absolvimus et finaliter dimittimus per hanc nostrum finale decretum quam sive quod facimus et promulgamus in hiis scriptis.

cxxxiii.

[1585, June 24. Guildhall, Journals of the Court of Common Council, 21/457.]

In congregacione Maioris Aldermannorum ac Communitatum ciuitatis London'.

Vicecomites pro Anno proximo sequente. Anthonius Radclif merchant electus per Maiorem iuxta prerogativam vt alius associetur sibi per Communitates qui eligerunt Willelmum Gardner leatherseller qui proclamacione facta secundum formam actus Communis Consilij nuper inde edita in propria persona sua venit coram Maiore Aldermannis et Communitatibus predictis in plena hustingo sedentibus et recusavit directe ad super ipsum assumendum officium vicecomitis predictum et super se assumit in presentia predicta ad solvendum finem suam CC secundum formam eiusdem actus Communis Consilij.

cxxxiv.

[1585, June 25. Mayor's Court Repertories, 21/184.]

Curia specialis. This day Mr. William Gardener, leatherseller, who being yesterday last past elected by the right honorable the Lord Mayor, Commonalty, and Citizens of this City, and county of Middlesex for the year ensuing, and thereupon open proclamation being presently made in the Queen's Majesty's Court of the Hustings in the presence of the said Lord Mayor, the whole Court of Aldermen, and Commons of this City, according to the late act of Common Council, came into this Court, and being required by the same to declare his consent whether he will take upon him the execution of the same office accordingly, he gave his direct and plain answer to the same Court that he would not accept and take upon him the execution of the said office; and thereupon it is ordered that the Commons shall be again warned to proceed to a new election. Pullison, Mayor.

cxxxv.

[1585, Sept. *Surrey Muster Rolls*, pr. Surrey Record Soc., ii, 210, 215.]

Surrey. The booke of Musters of horsemen. . . [Croydon, 20 Sept. 1585.]

The Hundred of Brixton and Wallington

	Launces	Light horses
. William Gardenour esquiour *Defalt*	j	j

The horses of the Iustices of peace furnished with Petronells mustred before his Lordshippe the said daye.

.William Gardenor esquiour . . . j

cxxxvi.

[1585/6, Hilary. Queen's Bench. K.B. 27/1296/289*d*.]

Gardiner says that he recently recovered by judgment £17:1s. against John Bullard *alias* Bullward, but that execution re-

217

mains to be done. And since Martin Manley of Bermondsey, leatherseller, and John Luce of Newington, gentleman, in Easter term, 26 Eliz. (1584), came into this Court and became pledges for Bullard, and Bullard neither paid nor went to prison, Gardiner seeks execution against the pledges. Execution adjudged.

cxxxvii.

[1585/6, March 7. Loseley MSS. *Hist. MSS. Comm. 7th Rep.*, App., p. 640.]

Return made by William Gardyner of all the Recusantes now prisoners in the Kinges Benche the vij[th] daie of March 1585. The number of such prisoners being 40, of whom 16 are priests.

cxxxviii.

[1586, May 4. Dasent, *Acts of Privy Council, 1586–1587*, p. 90.]

A letter for a privy search to be made within the county of Surrey, directed to Mr. Bellingham, —— Gardyner, —— Cosyn, Parker, and Robert Leveley [Levesey].

cxxxix.

[1586, May 14. Close Roll, 28 Eliz. C54/1247.]

Thomas Bowes, son and heir of Martin Bowes, knight, deceased, acknowledged that he owed £200 to William Gardener of Bermondsey, Surrey, esquire.

cxl.

[1586, May 17. Guildhall, Mayor's Court Repertories, 21/296.]

Item it is ordered that Sir Rowland Haywarde, knight, Mr. Bond, and Mr. Martyn, Aldermen, or any two of them, shall attend upon the right honorable Sir Edmunde Anderson, knight, Lord Chief Justice of the Court of Common Pleas, for the ending of the cause betwixt this City and Mr. William Gardyner, leatherseller, lately elect Sheriff of the same City;

and Robert Smythe to warn them to meet together and to attend on them. Dixie, Mayor.

cxli.

[1586, May 24. Dasent, *Acts of Privy Council, 1586–1587*, p. 122.]

A letter to John Couper, William Gardiner, and Richard Yong, esquires, to examine Robert Rive of Hollingeborne, Kent, yeoman, an utterer of counterfeit coin.

cxlii.

[1586, Michaelmas. Queen's Bench. K.B. 27/1299/147.]

England. Thomas Bromley, knight, Lord Chancellor of England, in his proper person came to Westminster on the Monday next after the Octave of St. Michael, and produced here in Court a certain record had before the Queen in Chancery in these words: a plea before the Queen in Chancery, etc. Michaelmas 27/28 Eliz. (1585). The lady the Queen by her close writ to the sheriffs of Middlesex orders that, since on 6 June 3 Eliz. (1561), Edward Welshe of Lymesfeld, Surrey, esquire, came into the Chancery and acknowledged that he owed £500 to William Gardener, citizen and leatherseller of London, to be paid at the feast of the Nativity of St. John the Baptist next, and he did not pay, the sheriffs are to produce the said Edward in the said Chancery on the Quindene of St. Michael next, to say why the money had not be raised on his lands and goods according to the form and effect of the recognizance.

On which Quindene of St. Michael the sheriffs of Middlesex returned the writ saying that the aforesaid Edward was dead. Whereupon another writ was directed to the sheriff of Surrey to bring the heirs and tenants of the said Edward into the Chancery on the Octave of St. Martin next.

The sheriff of Surrey returned that by virtue of the said writ, on 26 November 27 Eliz. (1585) he had made known to Richard

219

Ryther, James Chiwall and Lawrence Browne, the tenants of the said Edward, that they should be at Westminster on the day, etc., and that none of them was an heir of the said Edward.

On the Octave of St. Hilary 28 Eliz. (1585/6) the said William, Richard, James, and Lawrence came by their attorneys, etc. On the Quindene of Easter they came again, etc.

On the Morrow of Holy Trinity, the said James, Richard, and Lawrence asked to have the recognizance read. It was mentioned therein that the money might be raised on the lands, etc. It was dated 6 June 3 Eliz. (1561). They also asked to hear the conditions, which were that whereas William Gardener and Edward Welshe, by their recognizance taken 20 May 3 Eliz., were jointly and severally bound to Walter Robertes of Glassenbury in the parish of Cranbrook, Kent, esquire, in the sum of £300 for the payment of £200—£100 to be paid in St. Paul's Church on 2 August next ensuing, and £100 at the same place on 9 October following—the said Edward Welshe held William Gardener harmless, and was to pay William Gardener £100: on 24 August next £50, and on 29 September the remaining £50.

The said Richard, James, and Lawrence said that on 28 June 6 Eliz. (1564) William Gardener remised and relaxed to the aforesaid Edward the sum of £500 aforesaid. William said he had not done so. A day was given.

On the Octave of the Purification it was found that William Gardener could recover nothing because he had given a deed of release; therefore Richard, James, and Lawrence should be without a day.

cxliii.

[1586/7, February 15. Dasent, *Acts of Privy Council, 1586–1587*, p. 328.]

A letter to the Lord Mayor, Recorder and Sheriffs of the City of London, the Deans of Paul's and Westminster, Mr. Ran-

220

dolph the Postmaster, William Gardyner, esquire, and Edward Anlaby, gentleman. Whereas Robert Kirkham and John Spencer, two haberdashers of London, are being persecuted by their creditors, they are to call the creditors before them and do what they can to reduce them to reason. Kirkham and Spencer offer to pay one-fifth down, and the rest in four years. This cause was recommended by Mr. Randolph, the Master of the Posts.

cxliv.
[1587. Records of the Leathersellers' Company.]

William Gardiner's name was included in an assessment for a sum of £8.

In a schedule headed "Money received of sundry persons due to them out of the hundred pounds received of the Chamberlain of London which was lent for the provision of wheat in Anno 1573" is included "Mr. Gardner, £2:10:0."

cxlv.
[1587, July 7. Patent Roll, 29 Eliz. C66/1291/1 No. 51.]

A farm for William Gardiner. Recites a grant by patent on 17 March last to John Cadye of 'Greate Wood' (48 acres), 'Kentland wood' (16 acres), 'Hatchamhillittes wood' (14 acres), 'le Springe wood' (4 acres) adjoining the field called 'Abrafeld', 'Molandspringe' (3 acres), and 'Kentlandes springe' (4 acres), all parcel of the manor of 'Hatchambarnes' in Surrey and Kent, late of the monastery of Dertford, Kent, except great trees, pretty saplings of oak, sufficient 'staddles', etc., for 21 years at a rent of 66s. 8d. during the life of Anne, late Duchess of Somerset, and after her death, of £10 19s. These letters being surrendered, the premises are hereby granted, on the advice of the Lord Treasurer and Sir Walter Mildmay, Chancellor of the Exchequer, to William Gardiner, esquire, for 21 years, at a rent of £10 19s.

cxlvi.

[1587, October. Exchequer Bills and Answers. E112/Eliz.,
Surr./27.]

William Chester of East Smithfield, Middlesex, esquire, and
Alice his wife, plaintiffs, against William Gardener, defendant.
The Chesters' Bill of Complaint. They alleged that John Stepkin, gentleman, deceased, was seized of numerous tenements
and lands (specified) in the parishes of St. Mary Matfelon, St.
Botolph, Aldgate, and Stepney, and that at the time of his
death he owed the Queen £8000; and about 17 January 19
Eliz. (1577) all those premises were seized and extended to the
Queen's use, until the debt with arrearages should be paid. By
letters patent dated 6 May 19 Eliz. the Queen demised the
premises to the plaintiffs at a yearly rent of £229:6:8, until the
£8000 should be paid. "Notwithstanding your said orators and
John Stepkin, son of the said Alice, by the persuasion of some
of their friends, and also for that there was some communication of and concerning an intermarriage to be had between the
said John Stepkin and Katherine Gardener, daughter unto one
William Gardener" by their deed dated 14 December 24 Eliz.
(1581) demised a yearly rent of £100 issuing out of the premises to the said Katherine Gardener. "By means of which deed
. . . the said William Gardener troubleth and molesteth your
said orators" and has commenced an action at the common
law against them for the said annuity, notwithstanding that
before the delivery of the said deed, John Stepkin had married
Katherine, whereby the grant is void in law. The said John
Stepkin had since died, leaving one son.

Gardiner's Answer. That after the decease of John Stepkin,
Katherine his wife was to receive the annuity of £100, but none
of it had been paid since that event; so that her present husband, in William Gardener's name, had commenced a suit
at the common law to recover it; that Katherine and John

Stepkin did not marry before the delivery of the deed in question.

The Chesters' Replication. ". . upon the faithful promises of the said Gardyner to the said John Stepkin that he would very shortly after the marriage had between the said John Stepkin and his daughter, purchase of her Majesty to and for the use of the said John Stepkin" the yearly rent of £129:6:8 reserved on the said extent, "and would also give and bestow upon the said John Stepkin many other things amounting to a very great value, [but] the said Gardyner, having by his fair promises obtained that thing which he desired, performed nothing which he promised, but endeavoured for his own private lucre and profit rather to hurt and hinder the said Stepkin than to benefit him."

cxlvii.

[1587, July. Star Chamber Proceedings, Eliz. St. Ch. 5/G25/14.]

William Gardiner, plaintiff, against Richard Rither, Henry Lane, and George Spencer, defendants.

Gardiner's Bill of Complaint. He stated that Edward Welsh owed him £100 which he did not pay; and that therefore Welsh's recognizance of £500 was forfeit in 3 Eliz. (1561). That Welsh let his lands, and after his death, two years before the lands were liable to the recognizance, they were in the possession of Richard Ryther, grocer, and James Chiball and Lawrence Browne, leathersellers. That he sued out a writ for the recovery of his money; but that Ryther, having possession of the greater part of the lands, and "seeking by all means and ways he could to devise some shift to defraud your said subject of his said just debt (being a man well experienced in forgery before that time), did intend to forge or cause to be forged" a discharge of the recognizance; and accordingly with Henry Lane, of St. Margaret's, Kent, on 1 May 28 Eliz. (1576), "not having the fear of God before their eyes but being seduced with the devil, did very wickedly and falsely forge or cause to be forged"

223

a release. Afterwards, when the suit was tried in the King's Bench, Ryther suborned Henry Lane and George Spencer to perjure themselves.

cxlviii.
[1587, Nov. 3. Star Chamber Proc. St. Ch. 5/G25/2.]

Answer of Richard Ryther. That about 3 Eliz. (1561) Edward Welsh acknowledged in Chancery a recognizance of £500 to William Gardyner, of which he was afterwards discharged. Twenty-four years after the release thus made (and about three years before the date of this answer), the said Gardyner "very craftily and covetously brought a *scire facias* upon the said recognizance," thinking that as the said Welsh was dead, either the release could not be found or that no one would be able to prove that the release was made by him. The defendant Richard Ryther, James Chiball, and Lawrence Browne were tenants of the said Edward Welsh deceased; they therefore appeared and pleaded "in bar of the said *scire facias*, the aforesaid release" made by Gardiner. The latter said it was not his deed, and put himself upon the country, and the defendants did the same. In Hilary term last the issue was tried in the King's Bench, and very sufficient matter was given in evidence on behalf of the defendants. But the complainant "without all fear [of] God very boldly stood up in open court and offered to be deposed that the same release was not his deed, and fain would have had his oath taken in that behalf if it would have been accepted". But the jury found that it was the complainant's deed, "to his great shame and discredit", whereupon verdict was given against the complainant.

Since which verdict the said complainant "hath conceived great malice against the now defendant and "against two others, honest citizens of London" who gave evidence, namely Henry Lane and George Spencer; and now, without any cause, has commenced a suit against them, charging Ryther with forging the said deed of release, and Lane and Spencer "with wilful perjury and this defendant with subornation thereof, and with other most foul practices". And further, the said Gardyner since the said verdict had brought another *scire facias* upon the recognizance against the tenants of the said Welsh; "whereupon Edmund Nashe was returned terre tenant secretly"; he appeared and pleaded a release supposed to be made to the said Welsh in bar of the said *scire facias*, and supposed to be of the same date as that pleaded by the now defendant.

All this matter was revealed to Anthony Walker, gentleman, tenant of the freehold and fee simple of the said lands; and he "greatly suspected the fraudulent dealing of the complainant" because in the last *scire facias* Edmond Welsh [*recte* Nashe] was returned terre tenant, whereas he had only a life interest in one parcel of the land. Walker took the whole matter to Sir Gilbert Gerrard, Master of the Rolls, who stayed the proceedings. Ryther described himself as "an aged man, very near four score years old, weak and sickly, and being thus in his old feeble age maliciously persecuted" by Gardiner "did set down his griefs" in a bill to the Lord Chancellor, folded like a letter, that he might be relieved from oppression, "and not to the intent to libel or injuriously to slander the said complainant". *Gardiner's Replication.* He insisted that everything alleged in his bill was true.

cxlviii *bis.*

[1587, Nov. 10. Star Chamber Proc. St. Ch. 5/G18/26.]

Gardyner against Ryther. *Deposition* of Richard Ryther, of St. Mary Magdalen, Southwark, grocer, on the behalf of the plaintiff.

16. " . . the children of Robert and Katheryn Lucye, whose names he doth not know, the plaintiff hath troubled in lands, body, or goods, by one subtle device or another" . . . "and

touching what sums of money Lucye's children should have of the said complainant . . . the said children of the said Lucye by report ought to have three thousand pound and above."
17. "that by report the plaintiff doth owe the said children of their said right three times eleven hundred pounds; but otherwise than by report this defendant doth not know the same to be true" . . nor doth of his own knowledge know "any shameful or other falsehood that the plaintiff hath used to defeat the said children of any money or other thing due to them"; but by report he hath heard that the plaintiff "by shameful falsehood defeated the said children of great sums of money".
18. "that this defendant is a poor sickly man and . . was sick about ten days past . . . when he is in health can run, leap, and skip according as any old man may do."

cxlix.

[1587/8, Jan. and Feb. Star Chamber Proc. St. Ch. 5/G30/37.]

Gardiner against Ryther. Depositions on behalf of defendant. *Deposition* of Henry Davye of Lincoln's Inn, gentleman, aged 22.

He said that he knew one John Buller because he was the tenant of his (the deponent's) father; and that William Gardyner came to Lincoln's Inn with the deponent's father's servant William Greene, and Gardyner said to them both that if they "would procure the said Bullar to break his fast with one William Hartford his cousin, he the said Hartford should accompany him . . to the same breakfast; and withal earnestly persuaded this deponent and the said Greene to give out some hard speeches of the said Gardyner, thereby to draw the said Bullar to deliver some hard speeches against him the said Mr. Gardyner, to the end that the same speeches being spoken in their hearings and presences, they might be witnesses of the same speeches, and so thereby the said Gardyner might take

226

his advantage against the said Buller. Nevertheless this deponent and the said Greene, noting a circumventious and ungodly meaning in the said Mr. Gardyner unduly to draw the said Buller into danger, did give intelligence thereof unto the said Buller, and notwithstanding the same intelligence, had a meaning as well to see the issue of this purpose as also not to lose the breakfast offered as aforesaid, went to breakfast accordingly, giving special advertisement beforehand to the said Buller to beware he did not exceed himself in speeches, and told him all the matter". At the breakfast "the said Hartford [?conversed] with the said Buller touching the said Mr. Gardyner, and proceeded to ask him whether he knew the said Mr. Gardyner; whereunto the said Buller answered he knew him too well, saying he went about to undo him and a great sort of fatherless children; whereunto the said Hartford, to draw him on to some hard speeches, as it seemed according to appointment, replied in this sort to the said Buller: 'Take heed how you deal with him, for he is the subtlest knave in all the country where he dwelleth'; and the more to draw on the said Buller to use some hard speeches against him the said Gardyner, proceeded further to say that he (the said Gardyner) little or nothing cared to forge a writing than he did to take the cup and drink; and such other like training speeches to work the said Buller to burst out into the vehemency of speech against him. But the said Buller, having advertisement and caveat given him beforehand of their traps, not only with temperance moderated his speeches, but also in express words, the more safely to be free from danger of the said complainant, said to the said Hartford that he would not so say of the said Gardyner. 'But,' said he (the said Buller), 'he hath gone about to undo a sort of fatherless children of us,' as he said before, or words of like effect".

Interrogatories to be ministered to . . Basil Johnson, gentleman, Edward Harwin, Katherine Etheropp, Sisselye Stede, Mary

Rowland, and Thomas Kinge, clerk, on the part of Richard Ryther et. al., defendants. [Selected interrogatories.]

4. Item whether do you know or have heard and by whom, that the said Stepkin in his lifetime did prefer or exhibit into the Court of Star Chamber a bill of complaint against the said Gardiner for witchcraft, sorcery, keeping of 2 toad[s], holding of irreligious opinions, or for any other matter, and for what.

7. Item what do you know or have heard and by whom that the said Gardiner held opinion or gave out speeches that he thought that there was no God, or that God hath now no government of the world, or that man need not care whether he do well or ill, for that he shall be saved or damned as he is predestined, or did hold other irreligious or unchristianlike opinions, and what were they, and whether have you at any time checked or rebuked him therefore.

Deposition of Cycelye Steed, wife of John Steed of East Smithfield, aged 44.

4. "that she heard Mr. Stypkin himself in his lifetime say that he had preferred into this honorable Court of Star Chamber a bill of complaint against the said Mr. Gardyner for very foul matter."

Deposition of Mary Rowland, daughter of John Rowland, deceased, aged 30 years.

4. "she hath heard the said Stepkin say that he had preferred such a bill into this honorable Court against the said complainant containing such bad matters as be mentioned in this Interrogatory."

5. "That Stepkin, in the time of his sickness whereof he died, would exclaim against the said Mr. Gardyner the complainant, and seemed to be of opinion and conceit that the ill usage and dealings he had received at the said complainant's hands was the very cause of his sickness; and in the extremity of his sick-

ness, when he could but even stir himself, would cry out and
say, 'O that I had him here!' (meaning the said complainant)
'He is the cause of my sickness!' "
6. That Stepkin "before he died did very christianlike forgive
the said Mr. Gardyner".
7. That Stepkin had said "that the said Mr. Gardyner was of so
devilish opinion that he thought there was no God, and that
He had no government in the world, and that no man would
care how he lived, because he was predestinated either to salvation or damnation".

Deposition of Lawrence Browne of Bermondsey Street in the
parish of St. Mary Magdalen, Surrey, leatherseller, aged 40.
3. That John Welles of his own accord bound over this deponent, Ralph and Christopher Pratt, and Robert Swan to keep
the peace; yet he had met Welles at the foot of London Bridge,
and Welles told him "that it was not Welles that was the cause
thereof, but that which Welles did in that behalf was by the
procurement of Mr. Gardyner".
5. That in Hilary or Easter term last, Gardiner had him arrested
with a *latitat* out of the King's Bench; that the deponent told
Christopher Cowper his neighbour and a friend of Gardiner's,
that he (deponent) had heard a whitster (whose name he did
not know) say "that he would acknowledge and confess his
fault to the said Raff Pratt openly in the Church, and ask ven-
geance against the said Mr. Gardyner; which when the said
Christofer Cowper had signified again unto the said Mr. Gardyner, the said Mr. Gardyner, adding no credit to this deponent's
report (or at least would not seem to give any credit thereunto),
did therefore arrest him this deponent". But that when Gardiner found that deponent meant to proceed in defending the
action, he withdrew his suit, and afterwards brought an action
of waste against him.

Deposition of Thomas Ducke of London, upholsterer, aged 40.

2. "that the said Gardyner did sue and cause this deponent to be attainted of perjury by a jury of 12 men in Southwark for testifying in a matter betwixt the said complainant and one Baker; and the point of the supposed perjury consisted in this: this deponent deposed before the Justices of Assize at Croydon in Surrey about 16 years past in the suit betwixt the said complainant and the said Baker that certain goods, as a table in a frame, stools, mattress, and such other things were lying and standing in the said complainant's house, or to such effect; and thereupon the said complainant endeavoured to prove this deponent perjured, because he supposed the said tables and such other things were not standing; and so having a jury whom he had in some awe, and some his poor neighbours, found this poor deponent guilty of perjury. And afterwards, this deponent labouring to attaint the jury (as indeed he had done if Mr. Justice Southcott had not taken up the matter), Mr. Gardyner, the complainant, unexpectedly on this deponent's part, sought an end and agreement at this deponent's hand in the matter, and thereupon the said Mr. Gardyner and this deponent did make each to other a general release or acquittance of all actions whatsoever."

Deposition of Agnes Welles, wife of John Welles of Stratford at Bow, aged 23.

2. That her husband was tenant of some lands of Ralph Pratt in Bermondsey Street; and that Gardyner "earnestly willed this deponent's husband to pay no rent for the same lands to any person or persons whatsoever, saying he would defend this deponent's husband of and from all danger or inconvenience".

3. "That the said Mr. Gardyner did persuade and set on work this deponent's husband to pretend claim and title to the said lands, and to prosecute suit for the same, persuading this deponent's husband that he had right to the said lands and would

be a mean to help him to the same lands by suit of law." But that her husband did not think he had a right to the lands till Gardyner persuaded him.

4. And that Gardyner told her husband "that if the cattle of the said Pratt came upon the said lands, that this deponent's husband should kill them, and should further use against the said Pratt all the hard means and ill usage he could"

5. That Gardyner paid the costs of the suit.

8. "That her said husband is utterly undone by those means, suits, and quarrels before specified, and thereby is enforced to fly and depart from her, leaving her and 2 children in very great want and distress." That Gardyner did not recompense her husband, and only lent him 40s.

Deposition of Ralph Pratt of St. Mary Magdalen, Bermondsey Street, citizen and leatherseller of London, aged 59.

6. "that the said Welles hath confessed to him this deponent that the said complainant had used very evil dealing towards him, and that he caused him the said Welles to abuse this deponent, for which the said Welles said he would openly in the church ask this deponent forgiveness, and say that the said Mr. Gardyner was the cause thereof and none else. And saith further that at another time at Lambeth the said Welles, before Thomas [?Moyres], Robert Swanne, and others, did ask this deponent forgiveness upon his knees for the abuse he had offered to him this deponent by means of the said Mr. Gardyner." Welles also confessed "that the said Mr. Gardyner procured him unlawfully to make a ditch or division betwixt the said two half-acres, which the said Welles did accordingly; at which time this deponent came unto him and asked the said Welles what he meant, to dig his ground and to use him so badly; whereunto he answered, 'Mr. Gardyner makes me do it. I cannot choose but do it, or I must run away. I have nothing for my pains but coarse bread,' and withal said, 'I know I

231

wrong you'; and with that threw down his spade, went his way, and said he would meddle no further in it".

Deposition of Robert Swanne of Bermondsey Street, aged 40.
4. That Gardyner told Welles, when he saw any of Pratt's cattle on the land in question, to "kill them or throw them in ditches".
6. That Welles said "that he would openly confess it in the church and ask the said Mr. Pratt forgiveness, and that he would point unto him the said Gardyner as he was in the church, and say, 'The plague of God fall upon thee! There thou art that hast made me abuse Mr. Pratt!' " That afterwards at Lambeth Welles begged Pratt's pardon on his knees, and "therewithal wept very bitterly, protesting that his conscience much moved him, that he was so miserable that unjustly he would be misled by the wicked procurement of another man".

cl.
[1588, May. Star Chamber Proc. Eliz. St. Ch. 5/G38/33.]
Gardiner against Ryther et al. Depositions on behalf of defendants.

Deposition of Edward Welshe of Darne, Kent, aged 19.
7. He stated that he had not heard "that the plaintiff did give the said Welshe [Edward Welshe the elder] a pair of hose of velvet and a felt hat lined with velvet, but he hath heard say that the plaintiff did give the said Welshe a doublet of satin; and that he was always welcome to the said Gardener, and had meat, drink, and lodging at his house, and that he was well used at the plaintiff's house for anything this deponent doth know or hath heard to the contrary".

Deposition of Joyce Clerke, widow, of St. Mary Somerset, London, aged 72.
6. That Welshe said to Harris that "he was the worse for Gardener . . and saith further that the said Welshe did say to her

that the day had been that he was a justice as well as the said Gardener".

8. "That the said Welshe, at his coming to the said Harries' house had on him an old doublet, the body whereof was canvas and the sleeves satin, rugged and torn, an old pair of velvet breeches, and an old felt hat lined with velvet. But the said Welshe did not tell her that Mr. Gardener gave him the same, neither did the said Welshe say to her that the said Mr. Gardener was not his friend, nor did say to her that the plaintiff was or had been his friend, but he said to her that he was the worse of the said Gardener; and .. further .. that when his son came to him, he would send him to Mr. Gardener for money wherewith to pay for such things as .. Harries did disburse for him in his sickness. But she heard not the said Welshe say he would send to the plaintiff to borrow money of him. And saith further that she did not hear the said Welshe make any great complaint of his estate and misery."

cli.

[1588, June. Star Chamber Proc. Eliz. St. Ch. 5/G36/1.]

Gardiner against Ryther et al. Depositions.

Deposition (on behalf of plaintiff) of Elizabeth Cobley, servant of William Gardyner, esquire, aged 30.

1. "that when the same Welshe came to her said master's house from one Mr. Saunders he was very sick and ill at ease, clothed with very poor and bare apparel and [*sic*] a very beggarly estate; whereupon her said master, taking some pity of him, did upon his own charges bestow upon him new apparel and shirts and other things necessary and convenient for him and for the recovery of his health."

2. "That her said master the complainant did bestow divers and sundry times money in physic for the health of the body of the said Welshe." And when he was better he seemed willing

to leave Gardyner's house and go to Richard Harrys of London, fruiterer; and afterwards returned to the said Gardyner's house, where he "would from time to time during his abode at her master's said house say he was indebted unto the said complainant her master, and was a man unto whom he was greatly bound and one without whom he could not live, and wished and well hoped that the said complainant her master during his the said Welshe's life would not trouble him for his debts".

Deposition (on behalf of defendants) of Alice, the wife of William Preist of Stratford at Bow, aged 70.

7. After a description of the opening of the chest containing Welshe's deeds and so forth, she said that "Mr. Gardyner hath been with her (this deponent) to know of her what she could say or depose touching the said chest of writings; and further saith that the said Gardyner the complainant did then endeavour and go about to persuade her . . . to deliver unto him the said writings (which were taken away indeed before), and further did go about to persuade her to come to one Robinson's at Stratford in the Bow to him, and there to drink with him and talk with him thereabouts, saying unto her that he would give that unto her . . . and to her said husband which should very well please and content them". But the deponent did not go to Robinson's.

Deposition (on behalf of defendants) of William Preist of Stratford at Bow, millwright, aged 78.

He said that the chest of writings was left at his house by Welshe because he boarded Welshe's children.

7. That Gardyner sent his servants divers times to come to him, promising that if he would say what was in the chest, he "would give unto him . . what recompense he would and such as should well content him," but that Gardyner did not "direct this deponent what he should say or depose in this matter or what he should keep secret".

Deposition (on behalf of defendants) of Christopher Elliott, of Stratford at Bow, schoolmaster, aged 40.

7. That Gardyner, on New Year's day last, came and asked him whether "Henry Lane had been with him, and whether that he bade him to remember whether he found any acquittance or copy of recognizance or not, and this deponent made him answer that the said Lane had not been with him to any such end. And doth utterly deny that the said Mr. Gardyner did then or at any other time indirectly deal with this deponent in any unlawful course either what to depose or what to keep secret as is supposed".

clii.

[1588, May. *Surrey Muster Rolls*, pr. Surrey Record Soc., ii, 219.]

[T]he cert[ifica]te [o]f vs William Howard esquier William More, Thomas Browne and Fraunces Carewe knightes deputie lieutenantes . . the righte honorable, the lord Charles Howard of Effingham lo: highe admyrall of England and lo: lieutenaunte of the [coun]tie of Surrey of all such horses furnished for launces and lighthorses as also Pewtronells which are founde within [. . . . .]d increased within the same since the receipte of her Majesties letters directed to his lo: and [. . . . . .M]aye 158[8].

	[launces]	lighthor[ses]	Pe[wt]ronells	Corslet[tes]
William Gardenour esquier	1.	1.	2.	

	Muskettes	Quallivers	[. . . . .]
	2.	2.	2.

cliii.

[Temp. Eliz. *Ibidem*, p. 319.]

	[lances]	lig[ht horses]
Wylliam Gardnerd esquire	j	j

cliv.

[Temp. Eliz. *Ibidem*, p. 325.]

	Launces	Lighthorses
William Gardenor esquier		j
a grey geldinge		

clv.

[1588, August. B.M. Lansdowne Manuscript 56, No. 3.]

Names of Companyes in London, mete to lend money.

Leather sellers & girdlers.

lettr	Hugh Offley	.	.	.	.	.	CCC^{11}
q	Stephen Some	.	.	.	.	.	CCC^{11}
	William Gardner	.	.	.	.	CC^{11}
q	Thomas Daunser	.	.	.	.	C^{11}
q	Thomas Herbert	.	.	.	.	C^{11}
q	Mistris Braunche widowe	.	.	.	C^{11}
	John Nelson	.	.	.	.	.	C^{11}

i^m ii^c

clvi.

[1587, December 2. Close Roll, 30 Eliz. C/54/1312.]

Walter Ralegh of Colliton Ralegh, Devon, knight, Carew
Ralegh of Cosbie, Wilts, esquire, and William Saunderson, citizen and fishmonger of London, acknowledged that they and
each of them owed William Gardyner of Barmondsey, Surrey,
esquire, £1000 to be paid on Christmas next; and if they should
not pay, the sum was to be raised on their lands and goods.
Dated 2 Dec. 1587.

"The condition of this recognizance is such that if the above
bounden Sir Walter Ralegh, knight, Carew Ralegh, and William Saunderson, or any of them, or the heirs, executors, administrators, or assigns of them or of any of them, shall truly
pay or cause to be paid unto the above named William Gardy-

ner, his executors, administrators, or assigns, the sum of £630 of lawful money of England in the fourth day of June next coming after the date above written, at the now dwelling house of the said William Gardyner in Barmondsey above written. That then this present recognizance shall be void and of none effect, or else to stand and abide in full force and strength."

clvii.

[1591, Trinity. Queen's Bench. K.B. 27/1318/388.]

England. On the Friday after the Morrow of Holy Trinity Sir Christopher Hatton, Lord Chancellor, in his proper person came into Court and produced a record of Chancery as follows: Placita in Cancellaria. Michaelmas term, 32/33 Eliz. (1590). The Queen directed her close writ to the Sheriff of Surrey, reciting the recognizance as above. A precept to warn Carew and William to be before us in our Chancery on the Octave of St. Michael, to show cause why their goods should not be levied and delivered to William Gardyner. Dated 18 September 32 Eliz. (1590). The sheriff returns that they have nothing, etc. The Queen directs a new close writ to him, dated 12 October, summoning Carew and William for the Octave of St. Martin. The sheriff returns as before.

William Gardyner asks execution against the defendants. At a hearing at Westminster, on the Quindene of Easter, 33 Eliz. (1591), counsel for the defendants says that Ralegh paid the sum of £630.

A jury of twelve £4 men of Bermondsey was to come for a trial on the Morrow of Holy Trinity, but no one came on the sheriff's writ of *venire facias*. The Court ordered distraint on them to appear three weeks after Trinity. On that day Gardyner's attorney and Carew Ralegh and William Saunderson came in person, but no jurors came. The Court ordered the trial referred to the Surrey Assizes on July 8. On that day a verdict was found for Gardyner, that he should have execution of

£1000. On Saturday after the Morrow of Ascension, 36 Eliz. (11 May 1594), Gardyner's attorney acknowledged satisfaction of the debt.

clviii.

[1589, May and June. Court of Requests Proc. Req. 2/104/34.]

Nicholas Sander of Ewell, Surrey, esquire, against William Gardener, esquire.

Sander's Bill of Complaint. "Whereas Your Majesty's said subject, having occasion to use money," in September last asked William Gardener of Southwark to lend him £100 for six months at ten per cent. William Gardener replied "that he had a very fair gelding which was both young and sound, and if he [Sander] would give him eighteen pounds for his gelding, he would let him have fourscore and two pounds more" to make up the £100. The plaintiff agreed, and two days afterwards he was given possession of the gelding, which, "never being traveled nor any way used by your said subject nor any of his servants, but led from the said Gardyner's stable in Southwark to another stable in the Spittle without Bishopsgate, died". Thereupon the plaintiff went to the defendant and told him the gelding was dead, and that he hoped he would not have to pay for him, as he was supposed to be sound. But the defendant, "neither regarding the sudden death of the said gelding, which no doubt grew by reason of some disease that he had when the said Gardyner delivered him, which thing the said Gardyner did very well know," will not only not lend the money, but is suing the plaintiff at the common law for £18 for the gelding.

Gardener's Answer. This defendant "being possessed of a very fair and serviceable gelding, and (by his servant) having the same in camp in Her Majesty's late service at Tilbury," the plaintiff was very anxious to buy it; but the defendant "utterly refused to leave or sell the same until the said service was

ended". The plaintiff wrote, and in other ways offered to buy
the gelding for fifteen or sixteen pounds, and at length decided
to buy it for £18 and to borrow £82 to make up £100. After the
delivery of the gelding, the plaintiff delayed either receiving it
or giving a recognizance for the £82, and did not pay for the
gelding; for which the defendant sued him. About five or six
days after the delivery of the gelding, the defendant sent a
servant to the plaintiff; and the servant on his return "declared unto this defendant that he was advertised that the said
complainant was rode forth of town, and that he was told by a
woman that keepeth the complainant's house that the said
gelding was dead; who demanding the cause thereof, answered
that she knew not, unless it were for want of meat, or by means
of letting of him blood".

clix.
[1589, March 31. Guildhall, Journals of the Court of
Common Council, 22/277d.]

Item by the said authority it is enacted and agreed that a
letter of attorney shall be made and the common seal of this
City thereunto put, authorising thereby William Dalby, gentleman, in the name of the Mayor and Commonalty and Citizens
of this City, to enter into certain parcels of ground lying in
St. George's Fields in Southwark and other places in the county
of Surrey, now or late in the tenure of William Gardiner,
leatherseller, or of his assigns, and in the name of the said
Mayor and the Commonalty and Citizens of this City to warn
the said William Gardiner and his assigns and all the occupiers
thereof from the possession and occupation of the same.

clx.
[1589, June 3. Dasent, *Acts of Privy Council, 1588-1589*, 237.]

A letter to Sir Owen Hopton, Sir George Barnes, knights, William Howard, Edmond Bowyer, John Parker, and William

239

Gardiner, esquires, to call before them one Nicholas Fox and Robert Morman, who by troublesome and unconscionable means molested and imprisoned one Thomas Welch. To en large Welch, examine witnesses, and settle the case according to equity.

clxi.

[1589, August 22. Dasent, *Acts of Privy Council, 1589*, 55.]

"A letter to William Howard, Thomas Vincent, Robert Lyvesey, Edward Bellingham, Edward Bowyer, and William Gard[in]er for the county of Surrey, letting them understand that whereas certen soldiours imploied in the late voyage of Portingall doe in a most disobedient sort assemble them selves together in troopes uppon the highe wayes, and do offer violence to diverse of her Majestie's subjectes, contrary to the lawes of the Realme . . ." to apprehend offenders by means of good watch, to imprison those who refuse to disperse and go home, and to furnish passports to those found to be conformable.

clxii.

[1590, Easter. Feet of Fines. C.P. 25/Surr. E. 32 Eliz.]

Between William Gardener, esquire, querent, and William Brydgewater and Agnes his wife, deforciants, and William Brydgewater, son and heir of the aforesaid William, deforciant, of the fifth part of 20 messuages, 6 gardens, and 3 acres of meadow in the parish of St. Olave, Southwark, quitclaimed for the deforciants and the heirs of Agnes to William Gardyner and his heirs for £80.

clxiii.

[1590, Easter. Queen's Bench. K.B. 27/1313/359*d*.]

Middlesex. In an action of trespass on the case, the plaintiff, John Hertford, gentleman, obtained a judgment to recover £6:0:12 against the defendants, William Gardner and Margaret his wife. Execution awarded against the goods of the defendants.

clxiv.

[1590, Easter. Exchequer of Pleas, Plea Roll 376/14.]

William Wayte, administrator of Robert Mote, late of Lambeth, Surrey, gentleman (who is said to have died intestate), comes into by his attorney on May 15 of this term and seeks by bill against Thomas Heron, gentleman, submarshal of this Exchequer, *alias* the said Thomas Heron, citizen and grocer of London, in a plea of debt of £10, alleging that Heron on 2 August, 10 Eliz. (1568) sealed and delivered two writings obligatory of £5 each, payable respectively on Easter 1569 and Easter 1570. Heron has never paid. Wayte cites his letter of administration dated 27 January 1589/90, and demands £20 damages.

clxv.

[1590, Michaelmas. Exchequer of Pleas. Plea Roll 378/25.]

October 12, 1590. In a plea similar to the foregoing, Wayte exhibits two further writings obligatory of £5 each alleged to have been made 2 August 1568 by Heron to Mote, and payable respectively on Easter 1571 and Easter 1572. Waytes cites his letter as before, and demands £20 damages for the nonpayment.

clxvi.

[1590, Michaelmas. Exchequer of Pleas, Plea Roll 378/24.]

November 28, 1590. In a plea similar to the foregoing, Wayte exhibits four more writings obligatory of £5 each alleged to have been made by Heron to Mote 2 August 1568, payable respectively on the Easters of 1573, 1574, 1575, and 1576. He again cites his letter of administration, and demands £40 damages for the nonpayment.

clxvii.

[1590, Trinity. Queen's Bench. K.B.27/1314/197.]

An action of trespass brought 20 May, 32 Eliz. (1590), by Thomas Askewe, plaintiff, against Thomas Shepperde, senior, defendant. Plaintiff alleged that one John Payne had demised a lease of a house and garden in Bermondsey to him, and that defendant wrongfully kept possession.

clxviii.
[1590, Trinity. Queen's Bench. K.B. 27/1314/197.]

William Gardner, esquire, plaintiff, brought a bill against Thomas Shepperde, senior, defendant, in a plea that on 26 March 32 Eliz. (1590) the defendant owed him £31:10:0, payable on demand. Gardner was awarded a judgment for £38 in all for the debt and damages.

clxix.
[1590, ?Michaelmas. Chancery Proc. C3/222/7.]

Askewe against Payne. *Payne's Demurrer.*

> The Demurrer of John Payne, esquire, one of the defendants, to the bill of complaint of Thomas Askewe, complainant.

The said defendant saith that the said bill of complaint exhibited against him into this honourable Court is for the most part very untrue, uncertain, and insufficient in the law to be answered unto, and the matters therein contained, framed and imagined by the said complainant of purpose (as this defendant thinketh) to vex and molest this defendant rather of malice than upon any good cause or ground of suit. The advantage of exceptions to the uncertainty and insufficiency whereof to this defendant at all times hereafter saved and reserved, for answer thereunto this defendant saith that true it is that he the said defendant was possessed for the term of two years or thereabouts of and in a certain tenement or messuage and garden with the appurtenances situate lying and being in Barmondsey in the county of Surrey; and so being thereof possessed, did permit and suffer one Thomas Shepparde to hold and enjoy the said premises as tenant at sufferance to the said defendant; by force whereof the said Thomas Shepparde was of the said premises accordingly possessed; but this defendant saith that the said now complainant, by pretence of a grant supposed to be made by the said defendant to him the said complainant of all his interest in and to the said premises, commenced suit at the common law by action of trespass against the said Thomas Shepparde in Her Majesty's Court commonly called the King's Bench; in which suit, the said parties having pleaded to issue, the same by *nisi prius* was brought down to be tried at the last Assizes holden for the county of Surrey; at which trial one William Gardiner, esquire, uncle to the said complainant, together with one Nicholas Chackley, his servant (as this defendant now remembreth his name), were produced as witnesses to prove the supposed title of the said complainant in and to the said premises; who upon their oaths publicly then and there did affirm and testify, as this defendant doth remember, that this defendant, John Payne, did assign over all his interest in his said term to the now complainant; at which time in like sort the said defendant, being produced on the part and behalf of the said Shepparde, did according to his knowledge and conscience deliver his testimony to the jury then impanelled for the trial of the said cause, that he the said defendant had not assigned all his interest and term to the said complainant, but that the said Shepparde was tenant at sufferance to the said defendant; by which testimony of the said defendant the said jurors were induced and did accordingly find that the said Shepparde was not guilty of the said trespass laid to his charge; which the said Gardiner perceiving, and seeing his testimony to be of no better credit with the said jury, hath since endeavoured and by all means possible doth seek to discredit the said defendant's testimony; for which purpose (as this defendant is induced verily to believe) the said Gardiner not only delivered very slanderous words against this defendant, charging him with perjury,

243

whereupon this defendant was moved for his purgation to bring his action of the case against the said Gardiner, but also hath (as this defendant is persuaded) procured the said complainant, being his sister's son, to prefer this frivolous and malicious bill into this honourable Court, either hoping thereby to entrap this defendant in his oath for the preserving of his own credit touching the testimony by him delivered at the trial of the said cause and thereby to procure further countenance to his said oath, or else practising to make a second oath in affirmance of the first, by being examined and deposed as a witness in this honourable Court; whereupon this defendant doth demand judgment of this honourable Court whether this defendant, after his former oath, and after a verdict in this behalf already past, shall be eftsoons compelled to make any new oath or further answer; and prayeth to be dismissed out of this honourable Court with his reasonable costs and charges in this behalf wrongfully sustained.   M: Lewis.

clxx.
[1590/1, February 5. Chancery Decrees and Orders, A1590/359.]

Thomas Askewe, plaintiff, John Payne, defendant.

The Court was informed by the Attorney-General [Sir John Popham], being of the defendant's counsel, that the plaintiff, before exhibiting his bill, had brought an action of trespass against Thomas Shepard for a tenement and garden in Bermondsey Street, which Shepard held; and that the plaintiff had taken action on a pretence that the defendant had assigned all his interest in the premises to the plaintiff, and produced William Gardyner, esquire, his uncle, to depose at the trial to that effect. The jury, upon the defendant's deposition on Shepard's behalf that he had made no such assignment, found the said Shepard not guilty. "And yet the said Gardiner, finding himself grieved that the said jury gave no more faith to his deposition, hath procured the plaintiff to exhibit a bill into this Court against the defendant for proof of a pretended assignment, contrary to the said verdict; intending thereby either to entrap the defendant upon his oath by his answer or by some examination of him in this Court, or else to procure some colour of credit to the testimony given by the said Gardyner to the jury." It was ordered that Mr. Hussey, one of the Masters, should consider whether the information be true, and the cause, upon his report, to be dismissed according to the defendant's petition.

clxxi.

[1590, November 21. State Papers Domestic, Eliz., 236, f. 54.]
Persons for loan of money [sc. to the Queen.]

Surr/	Willm Gardner of Barmondsey esqr	£20	£50 [sic]
	John Payne gent		£30
	Richard Rither		£20
	Raphe Pratt		£20
	James Chiball		£20

[Note: Only 13 other persons in the county are assessed much as £50.]

clxxii.

[1590/1, Hilary. Exchequer Bills and Answers, Eliz. and James I, Surrey. E112/Eliz. Surrey/40.]

Thomas Heron, plaintiff, against William Gardyner and William Wayte, defendants.

Heron's Bill of Complaint.

> To the right honorable Sir William Cicill knight, Lord High Treasurer of England Sir Roger Manwoode knight Lord Chief Baron of her Majesty's Court of Exchequer And to the right worshipful the rest of the Barons there

Surrey Humbly complaining sheweth unto your good Lordships, your daily orator Thomas Heron of the parish of St. Martin's in the fields near the City of London, gentleman,

Marshal of her Majesty's Court of Exchequer, That whereas about two or three and twenty years past there was a certain reckoning and account between your said orator and one Robert Mote, gentleman, deceased, for certain debt claimed by the said Mote to be due by your said orator unto the wife of the said Robert Mote, late widow of one Skyres; whereupon by mediation of Sir Nicholas Heron knight deceased, late brother to your said orator, (upon reckoning and account had) an order and end was taken between your said orator and the said Robert Mote, and all debts and duties by your said orator any way due to the said Mote or his said wife (except the sum of nine pounds) about two and twenty years past were fully paid and satisfied by the said Sir Nicholas Heron knight, for and in the behalf of your said orator unto the said Robert Mote; and afterwards the said Robert Mote, by his last will in writing, made one Johane Tayler his executrix, and, by the same his last will or otherwise, left unto her the said Johane divers lands copyhold and freehold; and about seventeen years past died, the said Johane being under age; during whose minority the administration of the goods and chattels of the said Robert Mote was committed unto one William Wilson, one of the supervisors of the will of the said Robert Mote, who, having the government of the said Johane Tayler, being under age, and of her portion of goods, and compacting with one William Gardyner of Southwark in the county of Surrey, between them both to enjoy the goods and lands of the said Johane Tayler, by compact between them the said Wilson and Gardyner, they married the said Johane to one William Wayte, a certain loose person of no reckoning or value, being wholly under the rule and commandment of the said Gardyner; after which marriage being performed, the said Gardyner (having the said Wayte at his commandment) procured the said William Wayte, and the said Johane his wife by the hard dealing of the said Wayte, for small or no consideration to convey the lands of the said

Johane unto the children of the said Gardyner; whereupon the said Johane Tayler, seeing her goods and lands to be gotten from her, consumed and wasted, not long after died; after whose death the said Gardyner procured a letter of administration of the goods and debts of the said Robert Mote unadministered, to be committed unto the said William Wayte, as an instrument by whom he hoped to make some profit; and afterwards finding some notes or bills of reckoning between the said Robert Mote and your said orator, by the procurement of the said Gardyner suit was commenced against your said orator in the name of the said William Wayte upon two bills of five pounds apiece, surmised to be made by your said orator unto the said Robert Mote; whereupon your said orator, calling the matter to remembrance, and that upon reckoning between your said orator and the said Robert Mote there remained nine pounds or thereabouts unpaid unto the said Robert Mote, upon conference and speech had with the said Gardyner, who was the whole dealer in the said cause, and used the name of the said William Wayte (being at the said Gardyner his commandment) but only as a mean to reap some profit, your said orator concluded with the said Gardyner to pay unto the said Gardyner to the use of the said Wayte nine pounds, the which your said orator did truly pay and give assurance for, being all which in law or conscience your said orator any ways ought unto the said Robert Mote, or unto the said William Wayte in the right of his said wife or otherwise. The which money being paid, and your said orator thinking all matters to be ended, and himself fully discharged from the said Wayte, and having some confidence in the good dealing of the said Gardyner, being a justice of peace, who was the only dealer in the said action, your said orator did neglect to require a general release from the said William Wayte; since which time now so it is, may it please your good Lordships, that by compact between the said Gardiner and the said William Wayte there is suit commenced

247

in her Majesty's Court of Exchequer in the name of the said William Wayte as administrator unto the said Robert Mote, against your said orator for the sum of thirty pounds contained in six several bills or writings obligatory of five pounds apiece; in the which by two several declarations it is surmised that your said orator, by six several obligations or writings obligatory, all bearing date the second day of August in the tenth year of the reign of our sovereign lady Queen Elizabeth, should become bound unto the said Robert Mote, in the said six several sums of money of five pounds apiece, amounting in the whole to the said sum of thirty pounds, which said surmised obligations are subscribed to be sealed and delivered in the presence of a notary or scrivener; whereas in deed there was never any such of the same name there subscribed, neither did your orator ever make, seal, or deliver any such obligations or bills obligatory, neither hath there been any knowledge or mention of any such bills obligatory by the space of two and twenty years and more; neither can there any due proof be produced either of the making, sealing, and delivery of them, or any of them; yet nevertheless the said William Gardyner and William Wayte, intending that the said surmised obligations bearing date so long time past (by credit and countenance of the said Gardyner, and such means as he can use) shall carry credit with a jury, without any due proof, against your said orator, the said Gardyner and Wayte have commenced and do prosecute suit thereupon at the common law against your said orator. In tender consideration of the premises, and for that your said orator can make due proof that your said orator and his said brother have fully satisfied and paid all such money, duties, and reckonings as any ways were due by your said orator unto the said Robert Mote, his executors or administrators, and for that the said Gardyner and Wayte, or any of them, are not able to make proof of any the said surmised obligations to be made, sealed, or delivered by your said orator, may it please

248

your good Lordships to grant unto your said orator the Queen's
Majesty's writ of subpena to be directed unto the said William
Gardyner and William Wayte, commanding them and either
of them thereby under a certain pain and at a certain day personally to appear before your good Lordships in Her Majesty's
Court of Exchequer Chamber, then and there to answer to the
premises, and further to stand to and abide such order and
direction therein as to your good Lordships shall seem to stand
with right, equity, and good conscience; and also to grant unto
your said orator the Queen's Majesty's writ of injunction to
be directed unto the said William Gardyner and William Wayte
and every of them, their counsellors, attorneys, and solicitors,
commanding them and every of them thereby, under a certain
pain, to surcease and stay their suits at the common law upon
the said surmised obligations, and not any further to proceed
therein until the premises shall be heard and ordered here in
this Court; and your said orator shall pray unto God for the
preservation of your good Lordships in honor long to continue
Wm Price
fiat breve de subpena secundum formam istius petitionis.

clxxiii.
[1590/1, February 5. Chancery Decrees and Orders,
A1590/359.]

John Luce, plaintiff, against William Gardyner, esquire, defendant. "The plaintiff is adjudged to pay the defendant 20s.
costs appearing in this Court upon a Subpena to rejoin, and no
replication in Court."

clxxiv.
[1590/1, Hilary. Feet of Fines. C.P. 25/Surr. H. 33 Eliz.]

Between William Gardyner, esquire, and Richard Gardyner,
gentleman, son of the said William, querents, and Edward
Newporte, gentleman, and Anne his wife, deforciants, of 24
acres of meadow in Camberwell, quitclaimed by the deforci-

ants for themselves and the heirs of Edward to William and Richard and the heirs of William for £80.

clxxv.

[1590/1, March 20. Close Roll, 33 Eliz. C54/1397.]

Between Bevill Mowlesworth, citizen and goldsmith of London, and William Gardener of Southwark, esquire, and Richard Gardener, gentleman, his son. Recites a mortgage dated 10 October 1590 by which Thomas Cure of Southwark, esquire, made over to Mowlesworth the Red Lion, a brewhouse in the High Street, in the parish of St. Saviour's, and a house adjoining it on the north, as security for the payment of £110 on 17 October 1591. For a sum unspecified, Mowlesworth makes over his rights in the property to the Gardeners. Deed enrolled 28 August 1591.

clxxvi.

[1591, Easter. Court of Wards and Liveries, Entry Book of Decrees and Orders. Wards Misc. Books 89/138, 139.]

Thomas Walker against William Gardyner.

Whereas Thomas Walker, gentleman, exhibited his bill of complaint into this most honourable Court against William Gardyner, defendant, alleging thereby amongst other things that whereas one Edward Welshe deceased was in his lifetime seized of certain lands and tenements in the counties of Surrey and Kent, part whereof being holden of the Queen's Majesty by knight's service in chief; and the said Edward Welshe, being of such estate seized, about twenty years past by good and sufficient conveyance and assurance in the law conveyed part of the said lands and tenements to one Sely Wrighte [*i.e.* Slywright], who by the like conveyance conveyed the same over to Anthonye Walker, the complainant's father, and whose heir the complainant is; and that a livery and primer seisin did grow and accrue unto the Queen's Majesty by and after the decease of the said Anthonye; and that the defendant, contrary

to all equity, did seek to sue forth execution of one recognizance of five hundred pounds, acknowledged by the said Edward on 6 June 3 Eliz. [1561] with condition for the indemnity
and saving harmless of the said defendant of one recognizance
of three hundred pounds, wherein the said defendant and the
said Edward Welshe did stand bounden to one Robertes for
payment of a lesser sum to the said Robertes, and also for the
payment of one hundred pounds to the said Gardyner at the
days and times limited in and by the condition of the said recognizance, that is to wit: £50 thereof to be paid unto the said
Gardyner the third day of August then next following, and
other fifty pounds the 20th day of September then next following; and that the said Gardyner was saved harmless by the said
Welshe against the said Robertes of the said recognizance of
three hundred pounds; and that the said Edward Welshe did
also satisfy the said sum of one hundred pounds at the days
and times limited for the payment thereof by the condition
aforesaid, and that the defendant had by his deed sufficient in
the law released and discharged the same; yet the said defendant, contrary to all equity and contrary to all good and honest
dealings, sought for to sue forth execution upon the said recognizance and to extend the land whereof Her Majesty was to
have livery and primer seisin as aforesaid, to the prejudice of
Her Majesty and to the great loss and damage of the said complainant.

Unto which bill the said defendant appeared and made his
answer and denied the said deed of release to be his deed; and
the matter proceeded until issue was joined and witnesses examined and published, and the matter proceeded to hearing,
and divers days spent in the hearing thereof; and forasmuch as
upon the full and deliberate hearing thereof it seemed unto
this most honourable Court that the said defendant was saved
harmless of the said recognizance of three hundred pounds
against the said Robertes, and that the said hundred pounds

(the nonpayment whereof the said defendant affirmed to be the cause why he would sue execution) was truly satisfied and paid unto the said defendant by the said Welshe, for the reasons and proofs hereafter particularly mentioned, viz.: for that the said recognizance of five hundred pounds being acknowledged almost thirty years past, and the said Edward Welshe lived until about these seven years last past, yet the said defendant could not prove that ever he demanded or required payment thereof, which by all likelihood he would not have forborne so long time if the same had remained unpaid; moreover for that one acquittance was showed this day in open court sealed and subscribed by the said defendant, as the plaintiff affirmed, and so it seemed unto this Court, whereby he had absolutely discharged the said recognizance of five hundred pounds; and for that likewise one other acquittance, subscribed and sealed by the defendant, as it seemed to this Court, was showed forth, testifying the payment of fifty pounds, parcel of the said sum of one hundred pounds; and also for that a copy of the said recognizance was showed in court whereon was endorsed that the same was made void, and that endorsement subscribed by the said defendant, as likewise seemed to this Court; and for that the said defendant did not nor could not show any good matter why he should take benefit of the said recognizance, but only alleged that the said acquittances were forged and were not his deeds, whereas the said release had been heretofore tried and found by a verdict of twelve men to be the said defendant's deed, and the supposition of forgery (in such as the said defendant charged therewith) heretofore examined and heard in the most honourable Court of Star Chamber, and the defendants there cleared and dismissed with their costs; upon all which matters and proofs, this Court was of opinion that the said acquittance or release showed forth in discharge of the said recognizance was the deed of the said defendant, and that there was no cause why he (the said defend-

252

ant) should sue execution upon the said recognizance. Nevertheless because it was further alleged on the part of the defendant that there was more lands liable to the said recognizance than the lands of the said complaint, and the purchasers of other of the lands of the said Edward Welshe's were not to be relieved in this Court, for which cause this Court could not take any absolute order or decree as touching the making void of the said recognizance, it is therefore *ordered* by the consent of the said defendant, that the said defendant shall permit and suffer the said complainant and his heirs to have and enjoy the profits of his land, whereof he is to sue his livery to his or their proper use, notwithstanding any execution or extent hereafter to be had or sued by colour or reason of the said recognizance; and for that the said defendant, not satisfied with the former trial by verdict at the common law, greatly desired to be referred to another trial by verdict concerning the said release, it is *ordered* and decreed by this Court with the assent of the said defendant that the said release shall receive a trial by a jury of the county of Kent (part of the lands liable to the execution lying within the said county), which jury, for the more indifferency and for avoiding of corrupt dealing in the impanelling thereof, shall be nominated and appointed by the Justices of the Assize of that county, whom this Court desireth to take so much pains. And it is further *ordered* and decreed that the trial shall be at the King's Bench bar at Westminster, and the same trial and verdict to be had and prosecuted with all effect, and to be final in the cause.

clxxvii.

[1591, July 24. Close Roll, 33 Eliz. C54/1402.]

John Stubs, citizen and fishmonger of London, acknowledged that he owed William Gardiner of Bermondsey, Surrey, esquire, £200. Dated 24 July 1591. Condition, the fulfilment of a pair of indentures made 24 July 1591 between the parties abovesaid.

clxxviii.

[1591, June 8. Patent Roll, 33 Eliz., pt. 7. C66/1362/18.]

As Samuel Thomas, the Queen's servant, had by a certain indenture dated 9 November 26 Eliz. [1584] bought from William Gardyner, esquire, all that water mill called "Sainte Johns Mylne", lying next a certain place called "Horsey Downe" in the parish of St. Olave, Surrey, and a pightel called "Harpe Leys", a close called "Crosse Leys", held of the Queen in chief, to have and to hold to the said Thomas and his heirs forever, which alienation was made without royal licence; therefore by the Queen's grace, and for 10s., the Queen pardoned the said Samuel and granted him the premises. Dated at Westminster 8 June 33 Eliz.

clxxix.

[1591, November 26. Patent Roll, 33 Eliz. pt. 8. C66/1369/26.]

As William Gardyner, esquire, by an indenture dated 29 September 24 Eliz. [1584] bought from Samuel Thomas "St. Johns Mill, Harpe Leys, and Crosse Leys" in the parish of St. Olave, Southwark, to have and to hold to the said William and his heirs forever, which alienation was made without royal licence, therefore the Queen pardoned the said William, and for 40s. granted him the same lands. Dated at Westminster 26 November.

clxxx.

[1592, June 23. Dasent, *Acts of Privy Council, 1591–1592*, 551.]

Letters to the justices of peace to prevent riots on Midsummer Eve or Night by apprentices, by placing and maintaining strong watch.

Surrey.

Mr. Gardiner Mr. Bowier Mr. Parker	for the precincts of	Newington Kentish Street Barmondsey Streete Clinck, Paris Garden and the Banckside.

clxxxi.
[1592, July 9. *Ibid.*, 1592, 19-20.]

"A letter to Mr. Harbert, Master of Requestes, Sir William More, knight, Doctor Forde, Mr. Bowyer, Mr. Parker, Mr. Gardyner, or to anie three of them." To scrutinize the examinations taken of "sondrie apprentizes and other dysordred people theire adherentes that were parties in the late greate outrage and dysorder commytted in Southwark"; to take further examinations and to send them to the Privy Council.

clxxxii.
[1592, July 15. *Ibid.*, 28-29.]

"A letter to Mr. Rookebie, Master of Requestes, Mr. Sollycitour Generall, Sir George Barnes, Sir Richard Martin, knightes, George Moore, Mr. Bowyer, Mr. Gardyner, esquires, Justices of Peace in the county of Surrey, Mr. Daniell, Mr. Dale, Mr. Fuller and Mr. Buckley, councellours at lawe, or to anie six, four, or three of them." To consider of the examinations taken "of the apprentices and others that were at the great disorder and outrage that latelie was commytted in Southwark" and to make a speedy report, that order may be taken for the punishment of offenders.

clxxxiii.
[1592, June 17. Close Roll, 34 Eliz. C54/1430.]

Nicholas Saunder of Ewell, Surrey, esquire, for £2,000, sells to William Gardiner of Bermondsey, Surrey, esquire, and William Gardiner his son, the "mannor, farme, or tenemente of Lagham otherwise called Langham Parke," with all its appurtenances, which came to Nicholas Saunder after the death of his father, the late Nicholas Saunder, esquire, and "all that parke called Lagham alias Langham Parke", containing 600 acres in "Godston alias Wolkensted, Tanriche alias Tanrigge, and Crohurste", which were sold 27 March 27 Eliz. (1585) to the elder Saunder by Richard Brookman, of London, gentleman. The Gardiners are to be discharged and saved harmless from all extents on a recognizance made 5 May 12 Eliz. (1570) by which Robert Cooke, gentleman, acknowledged that he owed 300 marks to Julian Fisher, widow, of Godstone. To the Gardiners is assured the yearly rent of 40 marks due on a lease made by Nicholas Saunder the son, 28 December 1590, to one James Dodd, of a parcel of the premises for seven years. Saunder warrants the Gardiners for two years from all other claims. Deed enrolled 9 November 1592.

clxxxiv.
[1592. Close Roll, 34 Eliz. C54/1435.]

William Gardyner of Bermondsey, Surrey, esquire, acknowledged that he owed £600 to Nicholas Saunder of Ewell, Surrey, esquire. To be defeasanced if £500 is paid on 8 November next in "the nowe mansion of Margaret Saunder widdow scituate within Sainct Maryspittle without Baishopsgate London".

clxxxv.
[1592, May and Sept. Star Chamber Proc. St. Ch. 5/L4/40.]

Henry Lane and Richard Rither, plaintiffs, against William Gardner, esquire, defendant. *Depositions.*

Deposition, 8 May 34 Eliz. (1592), of William Gardyner of Bermondsey Street, Surrey, esquire.

1. That the release shown to him "was not this deponent's release or acquittance, as he very well knew and was assured in his conscience".

7. That Alice Priest was examined as a witness before Mr. Jones, one of the examiners in Chancery. "This defendant doth well remember that he did send unto the said Alyce to come to be examined and to declare the truth of her knowledge on this defendant's behalf and no more," and that she "had not

any thing for her pains or travel taken in that behalf, except it were her charges in coming to and from her dwelling house".
8. ". . but this defendant is very sure that he did not confer with the said Alyce Pryeste touching her examination, neither did this defendant give or promise to give unto the said Alyce Pryeste any gift or reward to depose or come to be examined . . other than her charges aforesaid, neither did the defendant use any persuasions or threatening words or speeches unto the said Alyce thereby to draw . . her upon her said examination in the Chancery to deny, contrary, or to thwart her said former deposition orderly and duly taken."
9. That before the said Alice was last examined, the defendant "did request Mr. Younge, a Justice of peace, to call the said Alyce Pryeste before him and to examine her" as to whether the defendant asked her to deliver him a chest or writing of Welsh's. That upon the verdict being given against him, he sued out a new *scire facias*, and the reason why the matter was brought to trial in Surrey "was because this defendant was informed by his learned counsel that it was best it should be there tried because the lands in question did lie within the county"
11. "Albeit he taketh himself not compellable to answer thereunto, saith that neither this defendant nor any other to his knowledge did deal or practise with the said John Hasellrigg, then undersheriff of the said county of Surrey, to return any panel or jury for trial of the said issue at the denominations of this defendant, as is supposed; howbeit the defendant did request the said undersheriff to return some honest men to be of the said jury, whose names this defendant might perchance declare unto the said undersheriff; which this defendant hopeth he might lawfully do. But this defendant doth deny that he . . or any other by his means or to his knowledge did give or promise to give any rewards, gifts, or promises to the said undersheriff for to do the same otherwise than as he lawfully might."
14. He "doth utterly deny that any . . . speeches used by this

defendant to the said Draper tended to persuade the said Draper to deny the said supposed release to be his deed".

Deposition, 13 September 34 Eliz. (1592), of John Miller of St. Mary Magdalen, Bermondsey, leatherseller, aged 51.

1. He said he had known William Gardyner for 40 years, and that "the said William Gardyner is reputed and accounted amongst his neighbours to be of good and honest conversation, and to be a just and true man in his words, promises, and challenges".

2. That he heard Gardyner say to Rither in the parish church of Bermondsey, before seven or eight of the parishioners, "that he, the said Rither, was by a judgment of the same Court [Star Chamber] committed to the Fleet for libelling against the said Mr. Gardyner," and that Rither replied "that the said Mr. Gardyner did so overweighed him [*sic*] the said Ryther in the said honourable Court of Star Chamber with friends and money that he could have no right".

Deposition of John Jefferson of Bermondsey, leatherseller, aged 44.

2. He gave the words that passed between Gardiner and Rither as follows: "Rither, you know what you should have, if you had right: you should be committed to the Fleet." Rither replied, "You overweighed me with money and friendship."

clxxxvi.
[1592, May. Star Chamber Proc. St. Ch. 5/L43/31.]

Henry Lane and Richard Rither, plaintiffs, against William Gardiner, defendant. Depositions on behalf of the defendant.

Deposition, 25 May 34 Eliz. (1592), of Thomas Mayowe of Darent, Kent, husbandman, aged 27.

7. He said "that about 7 weeks last past and more, one Swillson . . . did tell this deponent that Mr. Gardyner and Mr. Young, a justice of peace, had caused and procured a woman to be ex-

amined and to forswear herself [?] directly against that which she had sworn before".

clxxxvii.

[1592, August. Star Chamber Proc. St. Ch. 5/L35/10.]

Henry Lane and Richard Rither, plaintiffs, against William Gardyner, esquire, defendant.

Depositions concerning a suit between Walker and Gardyner in the Court of Wards, in which a book of acquittances with Gardyner's signature was produced to compare with his signature on the deed of release of the bond of £500 to Welsh (which release Gardyner said was forged). Deponents say that no proof could be found that the signatures were the same.

Deposition of Nicholas Chaukley, servant of William Gardyner, aged 23.

He said that Ryther told him he was weary of the suit, and would like to come to a settlement with Gardyner; the deponent therefore arranged a meeting between them: "this deponent's said master and the said Rither met together upon certain grounds of this deponent's said master called the Graunge, beyond Southwark, where they walked and talked together a good while. But what words passed between them this deponent cannot tell, by reason he stood a good space distant from them, saving that at the time of the departure of the said Rither from the said Mr. Gardyner, the said Ryther used these words or the like in effect, viz.: 'Will you? then get it as you can, and I will defend it as I may.' "

clxxxviii.

[1592, November 25. Star Chamber Proc. St. Ch. 5/R15/10.]

Richard Ryther and Henry Lane, plaintiffs, against William Gardener and Henry Draper, defendants.

259

The *Rejoinder* of William Gardener and Henry Draper, defendants, to the replication of Richard Ryther and Henry Lane, plaintiffs.

They say that everything in their answer was true "and in no sort craftily or cautelously contrived in words or terms to shadow the truth": that the bill of complaint and the replication "and every the matters, causes, circumstances and things therein contained, be very false and frivolous, untrue, uncertain," etc. (The defendants were accused of perjury and subornation of perjury, etc.)

clxxxix.

[1593/4, 25 January. Hawarde, *Les Reportes del Cases in Camera Stellata*, 1, 2.]

In Camera Stellata die Veneris 25 Januarij 1593, Elizab. 36, adonque presente, Sur Keeper, Archeuesque del Canterberye, Ch. Just. de Banco, Ch. Baron d'exchequer, L. Stafford, L. Bukherst, Sr Thomas Hennage vice-chamberlein, Sr John Fortescue, chaunceller d'exchequer.

It was moved between Lane, plaintiff, and Gardiner and others, defendants. The case was for perjury, for this that Gardiner, in the Court of Wards upon proof there that he had sealed, subscribed and delivered a 'generall relleasse' to one Ryder, now dead, had deposed that it was not his deed; and so in this Court, being heard at St Albon's, it was ordered for the default of the plaintiff that he could not come to his books which were in a house in London in which seven persons had died of the plague between October last and January, and this was now moved to stay the hearing, but it could not prevail; and so, on the default of the plaintiff for want of the books, they proceeded to hear the cause. Serjeant Yelverton and Serjeant Healle with the plaintiff. It was ordered by the whole Court that Gardiner, the defendant, be dismissed by the great favour of the court.

cxc.

[1593, March 14. Close Roll, 35 Eliz. C54/1462.]

John Pope of Stanwell, Middlesex, gentleman (son and heir of
Paul Pope, late citizen and scrivener of London), for £450,
sells to William Gardyner of Barmondsey, Surrey, esquire, and
William Gardyner his son, the messuage and appurtenances in
the parish of St. Mary Magdalene, Barmondsey, occupied by
the late Raulfe Walker, and seven tenements and yards there
in the respective occupations of Edward Wilkinson, 'letherseller', Nicholas Wise, 'straunger', Richard Crofte, 'Cord-
wainer', Hughe Lane, 'pointmaker', William Daye, 'Smyth',
Agnes Horsham, 'widowe', and Richard Smyth, 'weaver'; also
an orchard used for a whiting place, now or late in the tenure
of Thomas Burton, ' Pointmaker'; one garden plot in the tenure
of Richard Wall, Arnold Wood, and William Domer; and one
pightel of land now an orchard, with a yard adjoining, in the
tenure of the said William Domer, John Marrowe, 'Gardyner',
and Thomas Forden, 'letherseller', adjacent to 'the howse of
William Walker in Barmondseystreete on the south part and
vpon the land leading to certaine tenementes belonging to the
said William Gardyner on the north part and the hige waie on
the west part and the landes of Rauffe Pratt on the east part'.
Pope covenants that neither he nor his father received of
William Walker or Elizabeth his wife the sum of £310 mentioned to be paid in a proviso contained in a pair of indentures
dated 6 October 30 Eliz. (1588) between the said Walkers and
Paul Pope. Deed acknowledged by John Pope in Chancery, 3
November 1593, and enrolled 15 March 1593/4.

cxci.

[1593, April 17. Dasent, *Acts of Privy Council, 1592–1593*, 192.]

A letter to Mr. Gardiner, Mr. Yonge, and Mr. Keale, appointed
by the Privy Council to distribute to "divers souldiers and
marryners hurt and maymed in her Majesty's services" two

shillings each every Saturday for twenty weeks, "giving straight chardge unto them to forbeare to demaunde almes in the streetes or els where duringe the contynewaunce of this allow-aunce, uppon paine, being so taken begginge, to loose the bene-fitt therof and to be whipped as rogues and vagaboundes ... And therefore you maie do well to devyde your selves so as one maie paie seche as are of London, an other those that are of Mydlesex and the third make payment to the rest that are of Southwark, which wee referr to your dyscrecions".

cxcii.
[1593, November 2. Close Roll, 35 Eliz. C54/1460.]

John Pope of Stanwell, Middlesex, gentleman, acknowledged that he owed £900 to William Gardyner of Bermondsey, Sur-rey, esquire, to be paid on the Feast of St. Andrew next (30 November 1593); dated 3 November 1593. To be defeasanced if the conditions mentioned in a pair of indentures of bargain and sale dated 2 November 1593, between the said John Pope and the said William Gardyner and William Gardyner his son, are fulfilled.

cxciii.
[1593/4, March 10. Close Roll, 35 Eliz. C54/1462.]

Henry Saunder of the Inner Temple, gentleman, and Nicholas Saunder of Ewell, Surrey, esquire (sons of the late Nicholas Saunder of Surrey, esquire), for £660, sell to William Gardiner the younger, of Bermondsey, Surrey, gentleman, and William Waite of the same, yeoman, the Rectory and Parsonage of Ewell, and that water mill called 'the nether mill' with two closes adjoining, in reversion after the death of Margaret Saun-der, widow of Nicholas Saunder, deceased. Provided that if the said Margaret die before 13 March 1594/5, Gardiner and Waite on request shall regrant the premises to Nicholas Saunder for £660 to hold until the said 13 March 1594/5 at the yearly rent of a peppercorn. Provided always that if the Saunders on 13 March 1594/5 shall pay to Gardiner and Waite £660 at the elder Gardiner's house in Bermondsey, this indenture shall be void and of none effect.

cxciv.
[1593/4, March 10. Close Roll, 36 Eliz. C54/1483.]

Nicholas Saunder of Ewell, Surrey, esquire, and Henry Saunder of the Inner Temple, London, gentleman, two of the sons of Nicholas Saunder of Ewell, esquire, deceased, acknowledged that they owed William Gardyner the elder of Bermondsey, Surrey, esquire, £600, to be paid on the Feast of the Nativity of St. John the Baptist next (24 June 1594). To be defeasanced on the fulfilment of the articles contained in a pair of indentures of bargain and sale of the same date, between the said Nicholas and Henry Saunder and William Gardyner the younger of Bermondsey, gentleman, and William Waite of Bermondsey, yeoman.

cxcv.
[1593/4, March 10. Close Roll, 36 Eliz. C54/1485.]

Another entry of the recognizance last mentioned.

cxcvi.
[1594, March 30. Close Roll, 36 Eliz. C54/1485.]

Nicholas Saunder of Ewell, Surrey, esquire, acknowledged that he owed Henry Saunder of the Inner Temple, gentleman, £500. To be defeasanced if the said Nicholas fulfils the conditions of a certain deed indented bearing the same date.

cxcvii.
[1593/4, March 17. State Papers, Domestic, Eliz. 248/33.]

William Waad, Clerk of the Privy Council, writes to Sir Robert Cecil: ". . . your Honour may perceive by this certificate from

Mr. Gardener that the search was not well performed by him, notwithstanding the instructions he had besides the letter. And in that part of Southwark which doth appertain to London, there was no search made at all."

cxcviii.

[1594, June 22. Close Rcll, 36 Eliz. C54/1485.]

Richard Cowper of Capell, Surrey, gentleman, and John Younge of Chichester, Sussex, gentleman, acknowledged that they owed £200 to William Gardyner of Bermondsey, Surrey, esquire. To be defeasanced on the payment of £105 to the said William Gardyner at his house in the parish of St. Mary Magdalen, Bermondsey, on December 27 next.

cxcix.

[1593/4, January 25 and February 11. Chancery Proc.,
Ser. II. 240/27.]

William Gardiner, plaintiff, against William Withens, Thomas Newman, and John Thompson, defendants.

Gardiner's Bill, sworn 25 January 1593/4.

To the right honourable Sir John Puckering, knight, Lord Keeper of the Great Seal of England.

In most humble manner complaining showeth unto your honourable good Lordship your orator Willyam Gardiner of Barmondsey in the county of Surrey, esquire, that whereas Thomas Neweman and John Thomson, by the trust which your orator reposed in them and of the good assurance he conceived of their faithful dealing towards him, had received full and absolute authority from your orator to buy divers and sundry houses in Barmonse streete in the said county of Surrey to your orator's use then being to be sold by one John Hobson; and accordingly they did, about five years last past, buy to the use of your orator the said houses in Barmonse aforesaid for the sum of £520 or thereabouts of lawful money of England,

264

the most part being in hand paid to the said Hobson, of your orator's money which they had in their hands, and the rest your orator was bound to pay at a short day after; and the said Neweman and Thomson, having received into their or either of their hands and custodies the assurance or assurances of the said houses, lands, or tenements, and your orator having divers and sundry times demanded the same, they the said Neweman and Thomson most fraudulently, contrary to the trust in them reposed and contrary to their faithful promise on that behalf made, did detain, keep, and wrongfully withhold not only the assurance or assurances of the said houses and the rents, issues, and profits of the said lands by the space of a year or two, but also demised and let several leases of the same to divers persons for fines to the value of a great sum of money, contrary to all right, equity, and good conscience; and after, your orator demanding account of the rents and profits thereof by them received, the said Newman and Thomson made answer that they would neither pay any money nor make any account for the same except your orator would give them a general acquittance and so to trust them of their credit to answer and satisfy your orator; which your orator (nothing doubting any such deceit) made to them or one of them a general acquittance as he required; after which acquittance so made, the said Neweman and Thomson, neither respecting their credit nor caring to keep their promise, not only sold the said land committed of trust unto them to one Robert Wythens and Willyam Wythens his son, with whom they were chiefly compacted to deceive your orator, but also untruthfully denied either to render an account of their indirect proceedings or to pay that which was due to your orator; the said Neweman adding withal further, that he would not care to deceive his own father to do Wythens good. These their deceitful dealings and falsified promises notwithstanding, so it is, if it may please your good Lordship, the said Neweman, under the greatest show of friendship studying to use his uttermost deceit, when-as your orator bought of one John Stubbes, about four or five years last past, one messuage or tenement with certain land belonging to the same, situate in Eltam, for the sum of £600 of lawful money of England, sending the said Newman to the said Stubbes to take notice of the covenants and to make a draught of the assurance between the said Stubbes and your orator, the said Newman going accordingly and taking notice thereof as aforesaid, for his own private lucre and commodity, without respect of credit or care of good conscience, and contrary to all right, in the end did convey the land to the said Robert and William Wythens or one of them for the said sum of £600, the said Robert Wythens giving the said Newman ten pounds to deceive your orator; and the said Newman and Thomson or one of them would say they had greatly augmented the said Wythens, and not refrain to tell it openly, that when they first dealt with him he had not above two or three thousand pounds; but now by their endeavours in putting the same money to usury, they had made him worth near twenty thousand pounds. And whereas your orator willed the said Newman and Thomson (having although a very good opinion in them) to buy of one Mr. Neweport divers lands in Camberwell, and carefully to look into the title of the said lands and tenements, and to the assurance thereof promising them what bargain they made he would accomplish the same; and they seeing your orator so addicted to them as to believe their words and protestations, whereas they bought it for £140, they did most unconscionably and unjustly put in the writing £160; and also to the further loss of your orator, whereas they assuredly knew the assurance of the said lands and tenements to him to be made was worth little or nothing, by reason the land was entailed long before the same assurance then to him made, yet they to deceive your orator did disburse his money therein, contrary to equal and honest dealing, and to your orator's

great loss and damage thereby. In tender consideration whereof, and for that your orator hath no remedy by the ordinary
course of the common laws of this realm for to recover any recompense against the said Thomas Newman and John Thomson for the said deceits and fraudulent dealings by them used
against him, that therefore it may please your good Lordship
of your accustomed goodness to grant unto your said orator her
Majesty's most gracious writ of subpena to the said Willyam
Wythens, Thomas Newman, and John Thomson and every of
them to be directed, commanding them and every of them
thereby at a certain day and under a certain pain therein to be
limited, personally to be and appear before your good Lordship in her Majesty's honourable court of Chancery, then and
there directly to answer unto the premises and further to stand
to and abide such order and direction therein as to your good
Lordship shall seem consonant to equity and good conscience;
and your orator shall daily pray for the prosperous preservation of your Lordship's honourable estate long to continue.

Jo. Spurling

The *Answers* of Newman, Thompson, and Withens, sworn 11
February 1593/4.

> The joint and several answers of Thomas Newman,
> John Thompson, and William Withens defendants,
> to the surmised bill of William Gardener complainant.

The said defendants by protestation say that the said bill of
complaint is contrived, imagined, and devised by the said complainant of his own malicious, troublesome, and envious nature
to the intent rather wrongfully and unjustly to vex, molest,
and trouble the said defendants than upon any just cause or
good ground of suit that the said complainant hath against
the said defendants, as the common use and custom of the
said complainant is to deal with all or the most part of men
with whom he ever had any dealings—still complaining of
those whom himself oppresseth and offereth wrong unto; and

further by like protestation say that the matters in the said
bill of complaint are very frivolous, slanderous, and untrue,
such as are not meet to trouble this honourable Court withal,
and such as if they were true are properly determinable at and
by the common law and not in this honourable Court; for all
which causes, these defendants do demand judgment of this
honourable Court whether they shall be compelled, adjudged,
or ordered to make any further answer thereunto; yet if the
said defendants shall be constrained to make further answer to
the said bill, then, the advantage of exceptions to the insufficiency of the said bill always to the said defendants reserved,
the said defendants severally say as ensueth: *And first*, the said
Thomas Newman saith that one John Hobson, citizen and
haberdasher of London, now well-nigh eight years past did
convey and assure, for the sum of £500 or thereabouts, unto
him the said Thomas Newman and the said John Thompson
(one other of the said defendants) by the appointment of the
said complainant, (and, as this defendant Thomas Newman
ver[il]y believeth and thinketh, rather upon a fraudulent device, intent, and purpose of the said complainant to defeat the
wife of the said complainant of her dower at the common law
therein, than upon any trust or confidence he reposed in him
this defendant or the other defendant John Thompson), divers
and sundry houses and tenements in Barmondsey street in the
county of Surrey; but chiefly, because the said houses and tenements were inhabited with honest poor people and near neighbours to the said complainant, to make instruments of the said
defendants Thomas Newman and John Thompson to enhance
the rents of the said tenements in most unconscionable sort to
satisfy his greedy desire, to the impoverishing of some of the
poor tenants, and great defamation of this defendant Thomas
Newman, who because he dealt in that case with the tenants
more than the other defendant, John Thompson, did many
times endure many bitter exclamations and curses at some of

the tenants' hands; and by that means the said complainant
reaped the gain, and the said defendant the shame; and for
that this defendant Thomas Newman perceived that he should
rather reap discredit and shame by dealing with the letting of
the said houses, and enhancing the rents, than any honesty,
good report, or gain, because the said complainant would cause
him this defendant Thomas Newman many times to agree with
a tenant for the lease of some one of the said houses for a fine
and rent certain, and, the agreement being made, would not
suffer him to proceed, but deny the agreement again, to the
shame and great grief of mind of him this defendant Thomas
Newman, he the said Thomas Newman thereupon grew weary
with dealing any more with the said tenants and tenements, as
he had just cause to do; whereupon the said complainant (about
a year or more after the said houses and tenements were so to
him this defendant and the said other defendant John Thompson conveyed) bargained and agreed with the said Robert
Withens, named in the said bill of complaint, that he this
defendant Thomas Newman and the other defendant John
Thompson should for the sum of £520, which was paid by the
said Robert Withens or by his appointment to the said complainant, convey and assure the said houses and tenements to
the said Robert Withens and his heirs or such other person or
persons as the said Robert Withens should appoint; and thereupon he this said defendant Thomas Newman and the said
other defendant John Thompson, upon the request and by the
appointment and consent of the said complainant, did convey
the said houses and tenements to the said Robert Withens and
William Withens his son, one other of the defendants; and the
said complainant having long before the sale made to the said
Robert Withens and William Withens received from this defendant Thomas Newman all such sum and sums of money,
rents, and fines as he this defendant Thomas Newman had by
any means received out of or concerning the said houses or

tenements, without concealing to this defendant's knowledge any one penny thereof, did about the month of December Anno 1587 make, enseal, and deliver as the deed of him the said complainant, one general acquittance or release to him this defendant Thomas Newman, as meet and right was for him so to do; and further this defendant Thomas Newman saith that the other defendant John Thompson did, for the said complainant, bargain with Mr. Newporte named in the said bill of complaint for certain lands and tenements in Camberwell or thereabouts for a certain sum of money (which now this defendant Thomas Newman doth not well remember, but he thinketh for the sum of £160) and that by the appointment of the said complainant; and the said Newporte, having received the said £160 for the said lands, gave to the said defendant John Thompson £20 for driving the said bargain and making the conveyances thereof between the said complainant and the said Mr. Newporte, for this defendant Thomas Newman received the moiety thereof from the said Thompson, being a copartner in all gains, earnings, and profits; without that, that the said Thomas Newman and the other defendant John Thompson, having received into their or either of their hands and custodies the assurance or assurances of the said houses, lands, and tenements as above to them conveyed by the said John Hobson, did wrongfully detain, keep, and withhold the same and the rents, issues, and profits of the said lands from the said complainant, he having divers times demanded the same, as the said complainant hath most shamelessly and slanderously alleged in the said bill of complaint; for that he this defendant Thomas Newman hath for his part answered and paid to the said complainant or to some other to his use all such rents, fines, and issues and profits of the same houses and tenements as ever came to this defendant Thomas Newman his hands until the time that the same lands and tenements were conveyed as above to the said Robert Withens and William Withens, and long before the release

made by the said complainant to him this defendant Thomas
Newman; and without that, that the said defendants Thomas
Newman and John Thompson did ever make any leases of any
part of the said lands, houses, or tenements to any person or
persons before the said conveyance made to the said Robert
and William Withens but such as the complainant did first
agree unto, and received or might receive the fines and profits
thereof to his own use without any denial or gainsaying of the
said defendants Thomas Newman and John Thompson or
either of them; and without that, that the said defendants
Thomas Newman and John Thompson, upon the demand of
any account of the rents and profits of the same lands received
by them, the said defendants Thomas Newman and John
Thompson, made answer that they would neither pay any
money nor make any account for the same except the said
complainant would make them a general acquittance, for that
this defendant Thomas Newman, who received the most part
of the rents and profits of the said lands and tenements, if not
all, had paid and satisfied the same unto the said complainant
long time before the said acquittance made to him this said
defendant Thomas Newman; and without that, that the said
defendants Thomas Newman and John Thompson were compacted with the said Robert Withens and William Withens to
deceive the said complainant, and so, not regarding their credit
or promise, sold the said lands and tenements to them the said
Robert Withens and William Withens his son, as the said complainant most audaciously, to the great slander of the said defendants Thomas Newman and John Thompson, hath surmised: for that the said complainant himself hath bidden God
give them (the said Robert and William Withens) joy of their
bargain since the same houses and tenements were to them
conveyed by the said Thomas Newman and John Thompson;
and without that, that to this said defendant Thomas Newman
his knowledge, the said complainant did buy of the said John

Stubs, named in the said bill, one messuage or tenement with certain lands belonging to the same situate in Eltham for the sum of £600, and sent this defendant the said Thomas Newman to take notice of the covenants and to make a draught of the assurance between the said Stubs and the said complainant, or that this said defendant Thomas Newman, going accordingly and taking notice thereof, did convey the said lands to the said Robert and William Withens or one of them for the said sum of £600, the said Robert Withens giving to this defendant £10 to deceive the said complainant, as the said complainant most untruly hath alleged; but true it is that the said complainant would have had this defendant Thomas Newman buy the said house and lands at Eltham of the said Stubs for £600, which the said Stubs refused to sell the same at the said price; and at length the said house and land of the said Stubs and the goods therein being extended upon by the sheriff of Kent upon a statute merchant or of the staple, and the body of the said Stubs taken and carried to prison to the Compter in Southworke, the said complainant (as many times it hath been his cunning and shifting devices to work upon advantages, and when a poor man is falling, utterly to press him down) sent to this said defendant Thomas Newman, praying him to go to the said Stubs to the Compter (assuring himself that now the said Stubs being in this extremity would yield to his price); yet was he prevented of his lewd expectation by the providence of God, as this defendant verily thinketh and believeth; for before this said defendant could come to the said Stubs to bargain with him for the said house and land for the use of the said complainant, the foresaid Robert Withens and Margarett his wife had gotten to the said Stubs and bought the said house and land and goods and chattels and cattles then extended about the same for the sum of £700 or thereabouts, without the privity or knowledge of this defendant Thomas Newman; and yet the said Robert Withens had been offered the same house and

272

land by this said defendant Thomas Newman long before, who then refused to buy the same at the then motion of this said defendant Thomas Newman; and without that, that the said complainant, to the remembrance of this defendant Thomas Newman, willed this defendant Thomas Newman to buy of the said Mr. Newporte the said lands in Camberwell; neither would this defendant Thomas have dealt therein if he had been thereunto required, knowing the said complainant to be a man of such an evil mind and conversation, that with one and the self-same breath he would speak a word and deny it again; for so hath he often served this defendant Thomas Newman, to his great grief and shame; and without that, that he this defendant Thomas Newman [did] know the said lands or tenements to be little or nothing worth by reason the same were entailed; for he this defendant Thomas Newman never looked into the title thereof; and without that, that he this defendant Thomas Newman did disburse the money of the said complainant for the same without the privity of the said complainant to the great loss and damage of him the said complainant, as the said complainant most wrongfully hath also surmised; and without that, that any other matter, cause, or thing in the said bill of complaint contained which concerneth this defendant, and material to be answered unto, and not sufficiently answered, traversed, confessed, or denied, is true.

And the said John Thompson for answer to the said bill, for so much as him concerneth, saith that the said John Hobson by the appointment of the said William Gardiner, almost now eight years past, did convey and assure unto the foresaid defendant Thomas Newman and him this defendant John Thompson certain houses and tenements in Barmondsey streete aforesaid, and that rather (as he this defendant verily thinketh) to the intent to defeat his wife of her dower therein, and to raise and enhance the rents thereof to satisfy his greedy desire, and to avoid the exclamations of the poor tenants that dwelt therein, being his near neighbours, than upon any great confidence or trust he had in them the said defendants Thomas Newman and John Thompson; and yet this said defendant John Thompson saith that he and the other defendant Thomas Newman have more honestly performed the trust in them reposed than he thinketh the said complainant would have done if the like had been committed unto him, for that he this defendant John Thompson saith to his remembrance he hath justly and truly paid and satisfied to the said complainant all such sum and sums of money, rents, fines, and profits whatsoever which by any means ever came to his this defendant's John Thompson's hands out of or concerning the said houses or tenements; and the said complainant, having about six years past sold to the said Robert Withens and William Withens the said houses and tenements for £520 or thereabouts, which was truly paid to the said complainant by the said Robert Withens or by his appointment, he this defendant John Thompson and the other defendant Thomas Newman conveyed the same houses and tenements upon the request of the said complainant and by his appointment and with his consent to him the said Robert Withens and William Withens his son; and further the said defendant John Thompson saith that true it is that he the same John Thompson by the appointment, at the request, and with the consent of the said complainant, did bargain and agree with the said Mr. Newporte for the said lands, being in or about Camberwell as he thinketh, and albeit the said complainant had given full commission to him this defendant John Thompson to buy the said lands for him the said complainant although they should cost £200, yet this said defendant John Thompson, doing as faithfully therein for the said complainant as if the same had concerned himself, bought the said lands for £160 of the said Mr. Newporte, which lands were accordingly assured to the said complainant or by his appointment in such good sort and with such good liking of the title and assurance as the complainant then held himself well contented and satisfied withal; and the said Mr. Newporte of his own good and well disposed mind, thinking he had sold the same lands for so much as they were worth, bestowed on this defendant John Thompson for his pains taking in driving the said bargain and in respect of much travel and making the conveyances, the sum of £20; whereat it seemeth the said complainant to grudge, for that his nature is, for aught this defendant John Thompson could ever perceive, to grieve that any man should live or gain by anything that he hath to deal in; and yet this defendant verily thinketh he better deserved £40 at the said complainant's hands than £10 at Mr. Newporte's hand, for that he this defendant, since the said lands were sold by the said Mr. Newporte, hath offered the said complainant £320 or thereabouts for the same; without that, that he this defendant JohnThompson was compacted with the said Robert Withens and William Withens to deceive the said complainant, as the said complainant most untruly hath surmised; and without that, that he this defendant John Thompson denied to render account or to pay that which was due to the said complainant concerning the same houses and tenements, as the said complainant most untruly allegeth; and without that, that he this said defendant John Thompson did buy for the said complainant of the said Mr. Newporte the said lands in Camberwell for £140, or knew the title of the said lands to be worse by any entail thereof made, other than such as the said John Thompson had made the said complainant privy of to the uttermost of the knowledge and skill this said defendant John Thompson had in the same title; and without that, that this said defendant John Thompson did, to deceive the said complainant, disburse the money of the said complainant for the said lands, but had the full assent, consent, and good will of the said complainant to do the same; and without that, that any other matter, cause, or thing, in the said surmised bill of complaint contained, that concerneth this said defendant John Thompson, and material to be answered unto and not sufficiently answered, traversed, confessed, or denied, is true.

And the said William Withens, one other of the said defendants, concerning so much of the said bill as toucheth him, for answer saith that the said Robert Withens his father, about six years past, bought of the said complainant divers and sundry houses, lands, and tenements in Barmondsey streete aforesaid for the sum of £520, which was justly and truly paid and satisfied him the said complainant before any assurance had or made to the said Robert Withens and him this defendant William Withens, for that the assurance was to be made by the other two defendants Thomas Newman and John Thompson, of whose honest, just, and true dealings the said Robert Withens and he this defendant William Withens have had so good, long, and perfect trial, that they made no haste to demand the said assurance, but at their best leisures to convey the same; who have accordingly performed the faithful trust to them therein reposed; and the said complainant, at the time of the assuring of the same lands and tenements, and at other times since, bad God give this defendant William Withens and his said father Robert Withens joy of their bargain, and never until now of late by the said bill of complaint found any fault with the said defendants Thomas Newman and John Thompson concerning the same lands and tenements in Barmondsey streete, albeit he this defendant hath been oftentimes in all their companies together; without that, that the said Thomas Newman and John Thompson were compacted with him this defendant William Withens and the said Robert Withens his father or either of them to deceive the said complainant as he most falsely and unjustly hath surmised; and without that, that the said Thomas Newman did convey any lands to the said Robert Withens and him this defendant William Withens lying at Eltham, other than by drawing and engrossing certain conveyances of certain lands and goods in Eltham aforesaid, which one John Stubbs, citizen and fishmonger of London, bargained and sold unto the said Robert Withens for the sum of £700 or thereabouts, which was paid to the said John Stubs or to such as he appointed accordingly; and without that, that the said Robert Withens ever gave the said Thomas Newman £10 to deceive the said complainant of the said bargain as the said complainant most wrongfully hath alleged, for the said Robert Withens bargained and agreed himself with the said Stubs for the said land, and afterwards sent for the said Newman to draw and make up the conveyances between them; and without that, that any other matter or thing in the said bill contained concerning this defendant William Withens, material to be answered unto, and not sufficiently answered, traversed, confessed, or denied, is true; most humbly beseeching your honourable Lordship, the premises duly considered, the rather for that the said complainant hath as aforesaid imagined and devised the said bill of very malice to put your said suppliants to great charges, and not upon any just cause so to do, that it would please your Honour to dismiss the said defendants out of this honourable court with their costs and charges which by the unjust vexations of the said complainant they have been forced to disburse and lay out.

Lewkenor

Gardyner's *Replication.*

> The Replication of William Gardyner Esquire complainant to the joint and several answers of Thomas Newman, John Thompson, [*sic*] defendants.

The said complainant for replication saith in all and every matter, thing, and things, as he before in his said bill of complaint hath said, and doth and will aver, verify, maintain, and prove the same to be just, certain, and true, in such sort, manner, and form, as therein the same bin very certainly and

277

truly set forth and declared; and that the same bill is framed upon good ground of suit which this complainant hath against the said defendants, and not contrived, imagined, and devised to the intent wrongfully and unjustly to vex, molest, and trouble the said defendants, as in their said answer is very untruly and slanderously expressed and alleged; without that, that the said John Hobson named in the said answer did assure unto the said Thompson and Newman by this complainant's appointment divers houses and tenements in Barmondsey streate in the said answer mentioned upon a fraudulent intent and purpose of this complainant's to defeat his wife of her dower at the common law therein, or to enhance the rents of the said tenements in such sort, manner, and form, as in the said answer is most falsely and slanderously suggested and surmised; and without that, that this complainant hath many times caused the said Newman to agree with a tenant for a lease of some one of the said houses for a fine and rent certain, and, the agreement being made, would not suffer him to proceed, but denied that agreement again, in any other sort than as this complainant might so do lawfully; and without that, that the said Newman and Thompson upon the request and by the appointment and consent of this complainant, did convey the said houses and tenements to the said Robert Withens and William Withens his son, specified in the said answer, or that this complainant, long before the sale made to the said Robert Withens and William Withens, received from the said Newman all such sum and sums of money, rents, and fines, as the said Newman had by any means received concerning the said houses or tenements, or that the said complainant did receive of the said Robert Withens £520 upon the sale of the said tenements, as in the said answer is untruly alleged; or that this complainant hath bidden God give the said Robert Withens and William Withens joy of their bargain, in such sort, manner, and form, as in the said answer is untruly suggested and alleged; and without that, that the said Newporte gave to the said Thompson £20 for driving of the said bargain and making the conveyance of certain lands and tenements in Camerwell in the county of Surrey between this complainant and the said Newporte, in such sort, manner, and form as in the said answer is untruly alleged, or that it hath been many times this complainant's cunning and shifting devices to work upon advantages, that when a poor man is falling, utterly to press him down, or that this complainant is of such an evil mind and conversation as in the said answer is most falsely, lewdly, and slanderously suggested and alleged; and without that, that this complainant willed the said Thompson to buy the said lands of the said Mr. Newporte (named in the said answer) although the same should cost £200, or that the said Thompson dealt as faithfully therein for this complainant as if the same had concerned himself, or that the said lands were accordingly assured to this complainant, or by his appointment, in such sort, as in the said answer is untruly suggested and alleged; and without that, that any other matter, thing, or things contained in the said answers, material or effectual in the law to be replied unto, and herein not sufficiently replied unto, denied, traversed, or confessed and avoided, is true; all which said matters and things this complainant is and will be always ready to aver and prove, as this honourable Court shall award; and prayeth, as he before in his said bill of complaint hath prayed.

ffuller

cc.

[1594, October and November.
Chanc. Town Depositions. C24/243.]

William Gardyner, plaintiff, against Thomas Newman and John Thompson, defendants. Depositions on behalf of the defendants.

279

Deposition of Margaret Withens of London, aged 60.

2. That the defendants conveyed to Robert Wythens, her husband, deceased, and William his son and heir, certain messuages in the parish of St. Mary Magdalen, Bermondsey, which were on Gardyner's lands; and that the defendants' names were used by him only in trust. After the possession of the tenements was given, "this deponent, her said husband and son, and the now defendants going homewards by the said Gardner's house in Barmondsey Street, they were all of them invited to dinner by Gardener; and at this deponent's coming into Gardner's house, the said Gardner, welcoming this deponent with a kiss, therewith used these or the like words in effect, viz.: 'God give you joy of your good bargain! I am sure you are now in possession of it.' 'And so are you of our money,' quoth this deponent, 'but,' said this deponent to Gardner, 'if my husband would have been ruled by me, he should not have dealt with you; for,' quoth this deponent, 'Mr. Gardener, you have taken all the fines aforehand, and the tenements are a sort of ragged houses little worth,' or speeches of like effect."

3. That Robert Withens kept possession of this property till his death, a period of seven or eight years, "in all which time this deponent, being often in Gardner's company, never heard him make claim unto the said lands or any part thereof, or say that he was not paid or fully satisfied", or that the conveyance had been made without his consent; on the contrary, that "she many times heard the said Gardner say (as well unto her said husband as to herself) that they had a good bargain at his hands of the said houses; unto which speech this deponent would and did still answer him as before, or to like effect".

About eight years before the date of this deposition, a certain John Stubbs sold land in Eltham, Kent, to the deponent's husband; she would however not allow Newman to deal for her, but went herself to Stubbs, who was then in prison in Southwark; and afterwards at the Bull, a tavern in Southwark, the deponent's husband and Stubbs concluded the bargain; "for this deponent did then speak and tell her said husband that if Newman were acquainted with it, he would drive the bargain for him and let others have it when he had done; and that if he were ruled by Newman, he should never buy land, for that it was against Newman's profit that the money which he had the disposing of should be laid out upon land; in regard whereof, this deponent (not trusting Newman) dealt in the said bargain herself with Stubbs". At the conclusion of the bargain, Newman was sent for to do the writing; and "she well remembreth that the said Gardner, about the time of the said purchase making, seemed very desirous to have had that bargain after this deponent's said husband had gone through with it; whereupon this deponent's said husband offered him to forgo it for £10, but Mr. Gardner would not give it".

Deposition of John Bennet of London, vintner, aged 50.
2. That William Gardner and Robert Withens often met at the deponent's house in Grace Church Street, and that he "hath heard them many times speak of the purchase of the tenements mentioned in the Interrogatory; at which times the said Gardener would and did say that the said Withens had a great bargain at his hands of those lands, and that they were better worth than his money; but Mr. Wythens still said they were a sort of rotten decayed houses, and that he made little account of the bargain", but that Gardener, even in the absence of Withens, maintained "what a great bargain he sold to Mr. Withens".
3. That Gardner often admitted that it was he who sold the said tenements, though "the assurance thereof was made by the said Newman and Thompson;. . . and the said Mr. Gardener ever seemed to like well and to ratify what was done concerning the sale of the said lands to Wythens, bidding him many

times in this deponent's hearing, God give him joy of the bargain, notwithstanding that in merriment, jesting-wise, would
say that he had a great bargain at his hands": and that "they
often met and were very merry together at this deponent's
house, as familiar friends might be".

Deposition of Thomas Stephens of Bermondsey Street, mari-
ner, aged 50.

4. To the interrogatory, "whether do you know or have heard
that the said William Gardyner at any time did say he re-
pented he had sold the said messuages, lands, and tenements
to the said Robert Wythens, or any other like words in effect",
he deposed: "That it may be that the said complainant hath
used speeches to this deponent to the effect mentioned in the
interrogatory"; but that about a year past, when speaking
about a small parcel of ground which Gardyner leased to the
deponent, he (the deponent) told him "that the same ground
was rated very dear, and that he (this deponent) paid no more
rent for his dwelling house (meaning his said house for which
this deponent payeth rent to the said William Wythens) than
he demanded for that parcel of ground (in quantity above
one acre): 'why,' quoth Gardner, 'if I had not been, you had
never had it (meaning this deponent's said house) at so easy a
rent'."

cci.

[1593–1594. Court of Requests Proc. Req. 2/214/4.]

William Gardyner, plaintiff, against Richard Gurney, and
others, defendants. Depositions on behalf of the plaintiff.

Deposition of John Stubbes of St. Olave, Southwark, brewer,
aged 52. That he was tenant of the brewhouse called 'the sign

of the James' in Southwark, sometime the inheritance of William Beeston, and late of Robert Smith. The brewhouse was offered for sale two or three years before to Richard Gurney and Robert Withens, at a price of £700 or £800, and that the plaintiff Gardiner wanted to buy it. About five years before the date of this deposition (10 November 1594), this deponent offered some houses and lands in Eltham, Kent, to the plaintiff, who sent Newman and Withens to conclude the bargain. The property was sold to Withens for £700, about £400 of which they had kept back.

Deposition of Lawrence Wytheralle of St. Stephen's, Walbrook, merchant, aged 40. That he had heard that Richard Gurney bought the messuage in question from Smythe; and that a letter was written to Gurney in the name of Ralph Raven to warn him before he made the bargain, "and that he should beware of the said Smythe for fear of ill dealing", and that he "was a deceitful crafty man".

Deposition of Nicholas Chalkley, servant of William Gardener of Bermondsey, aged 24. That either Thompson or Newman told the plaintiff that Mr. Gurney, an alderman of London, was bargaining with Thompson for the messuage, and that Gardyner said "he would never have to do with the said Mr. Gurney for the said purchase by any means", but if the purchase were made by Newman or Thompson, he would have it from them.

Depositions on behalf of the defendants.

Deposition of William Wolley of St. Nicholas Acon, Lombard Street, scrivener, aged 26. That "William Gardener went divers times from his word upon the foresaid bargain [with Gurney for the brewhouse]".

Deposition of Robert Smythe of Bromley, Middlesex, gentleman, aged 50. That he said to Gurney, " 'I fear that if these lands or tenements shall come by any ways to the said Tompson and Newman, that then the said Tompson and Newman would convey the same to Gardyner, to whom by no means I would be willing that the said lands should come'. Whereupon, and upon the faithful promise of the said Gurney that the said lands and tenements should come unto the use of one of his daughters in marriage (as he then said) and not otherwise, he (this said deponent) did seal the said second conveyance and not the first"; and that Gurney paid him £200, and became bound in £600 more to the deponent, with Tompson and Newman as sureties. That John Stubbes came from Gardyner to know how much he would sell the property for, and that he asked £900 or £1000. "That he (this said deponent) did tell the said Thompson and Newman that he feared that he (the said Tompsonne) wrought to have the said messuages or tenements and premises for the said Gardyner, for that the said conveyance was ingrossed in their names; affirming that if he wist it were so, then he would never seal the books, for that he would not by any means have to deal with the said Gardyner."

ccii.

[1594, Easter. Court of Requests Proc. Req. 2/152/12.]

Richard, son of William Stone, late citizen and haberdasher of London, plaintiff, against William Gardyner of Bermondsey, esquire, defendant.

Stone's *Bill of Complaint.* That about a year and a half before, the plaintiff's father had exhibited a bill by which he showed that about a year earlier he had become bound by obligation to Gardiner (for the debt of Richard Grey) for the payment of £100 with interest at ten per cent. About February before the

284

bill was exhibited, Gardyner told William Stone that the money had not been paid. The said William then paid the money, and Gardyner promised to give up the bond, but did not do so, and it still remained in the hands of one Robert Lee; and that the £100 was not due to Gardyner when he demanded it. Newman and Thompson the scriveners had induced Stone to give the bond.

Gardyner's *Answer*, sworn 3 May 1594. He said that the bill "was devised and imagined by the procurement or privity of John Thomson . . . for some causeless displeasure and malice which he beareth to this defendant, as he hath just cause to suspect, and the rather for that the said Thomson, as it seemeth, hath either by his folly or deceit abused the said Stone to the defrauding of him of one hundred pounds".

In his earlier answer to William Stone's bill of complaint (dated 16 November 1592), Thompson and Newman, being scriveners, had in their hands £100 of the defendant's to employ for his benefit. And about a year before, Tompson had told the defendant that he had lent this money to William Stone, who was unknown to the defendant. Tompson said that Stone "was a man that had been called upon to be Sheriff of London, and that he would warrant the money", which was lent for but a quarter of a year. And the defendant told Tompson that he had concluded an agreement with Nicholas Sanders, esquire, for a certain purchase, and asked him and Newman to give him some of his own money for this purchase. And they declared that the money lent to Mr. Stone had already come in.

The defendant told them to give this £100 to Mr. Sanders in part payment of the purchase. The defendant has been informed that the debt alleged to be due to Lee is owing upon a deed made a year and a half ago, but the plaintiff says that he became bound to Grey only a year ago; therefore the £100 paid to Sanders could not be due to Lee.

The defendant had neither seen the complainant nor had the bond, but Newman and Tompson often kept his deeds for him. And he had never received the £102 10s.

Depositions taken in January and May, 1593, subsequent to the bill of complaint of William Stone against Gardiner. Depositions on behalf of the plaintiff.

Deposition of William Wolley, servant of John Tompson, aged 23. That William Gardyner, in February last past, came to his master's shop and asked to have the money due to him called in so that he could pay Nicholas Sanders, and told the deponent to go to Stone for the money, "and promised him . . . recompense for his pains". But on being asked for the bond, Gardyner said he could not find it as yet. And, believing Gardyner, the deponent's master had borrowed £100 from Anne Owen, gentlewoman, to pay Gardyner. Afterwards Gardyner was asked for the bond at least twelve times, and sometimes he answered that he could not find it, and sometimes that he had given it to the deponent or to his master.

Deposition of Robert Lee of St. James, Garlick Hythe, merchant, aged 50. That about 17 May 1591 he lent £100 on Stone's bond, and that the money had never been paid. Afterwards he went with Tompson to Gardyner's house at Bermondsey, where Tompson told Gardyner "that he had wrongfully received" the money, and asked him to make restitution to Lee. But Gardyner refused to do anything.

Deposition of John Thompson of St. Michael Cornhill, scrivener, aged 38. That in February Gardyner came to his shop and told him to lend Mr. Sanders £600 upon lands called Lagham, and therefore to call in all money due to him. Gardyner "never left urging and calling upon this deponent to procure payment". And when paid, Gardyner never gave back the bond, but always made excuses: sometimes saying he had forgotten it, or had given it to Wolley, or that he did not know to whom he had delivered it, or that he had mislaid it, or that he never had it, or had lost it.

cciii.

[1593/4, January 28.

Court of Requests Proc. Req. 2/153/36.]

Stone against Gardyner. Deposition on behalf of defendant.

Deposition of John Thompson. That after Stone had paid £102 10s, Gardyner and Sanders came to him for the money; and he asked Gardyner "if he had brought Stone's bond with him. Whereunto he then answered that he had forgotten it, but he would bring it the next day." And afterwards, when the deponent urged him to give up the bond, he "would sometimes say that he had forgotten to bring it, and sometimes that he had delivered it to one Wolley", who declared that "he had it not at any time"; then Gardyner said "he had delivered it he could not tell to whom, and that he did tell this deponent that he never had the said bond, but he would look for the same better, and if he could find it he would deliver it".

cciv.

[1594, Michaelmas. Feet of Fines. C.P. 25/Surr. M. 36/7 Eliz.]

Between William Gardyner, esquire, and William Gardyner, gentleman, querents, and John Pope, gentleman, and Dorothy his wife, deforciants, of 10 messuages and gardens, 4 orchards, and 4 acres of land in Bermondsey, quitclaimed by the deforciants for themselves and the heirs of John to the querents and the heirs of William Gardyner, esquire, for £120.

ccv.

[1594, Michaelmas. Common Pleas. C.P. 40/1538/1512d.]

London. William Gardyner, esquire, and Margaret his wife, executrix of the will of Frement Abraham, late citizen and merchant taylor of London, plaintiffs, against Edward Bowes of London, esquire, defendant, for the recovery of a debt of £17:12:2, and damages of 97s. Execution order by default of defendant.

ccvi.

[1594, Michaelmas. Queen's Bench. K.B. 27/1331/548.]

William Gardyner, plaintiff, against Henry Lane, defendant.

By the plaintiff's bill it was alleged that Edward Welshe of Lymesfield, Surrey, esquire, on 6 June 3 Eliz. (1561) acknowledged that he owed William Gardyner, citizen and leatherseller of London, £500, which he was to pay on the feast of the Nativity of St. John the Baptist next, but he had not paid the said sum.

William Gardyner came on the Morrow of the Purification, 36 Eliz., but Edward Welshe did not. Various writs were issued to discover the heirs of Welshe, and to discover why the money should not be raised on the lands which had been his.

On the Octave of St. Michael, 36 Eliz., Henry Lane, gentleman, tenant of half the manor of St. Margaret's, and of other lands in Kent which had been the property of the said Edward Welshe, appeared and said that on 8 June 6 Eliz. (1564) William Gardyner, by a certain release, remised to the said Edward, his heirs, etc., the aforesaid £500.

William Gardyner said that the release in bar of the aforesaid plea was not made. A day was given. The jurors did not come.

ccvii.

[Temp. Elizabeth. Loseley Park. Loseley MS. 1044.]

(Copy of the oath to be administered to the Sheriff of Surrey and Sussex on his appointment.)

Ye shall swear that well and truly ye shall serve the Queen in the office of the Sheriff in the counties of Surrey and Sussex and do the Queen's profit in all things that belongeth to you to do, by way of your office, as far forth as you can or may; ye shall truly keep the Queen's rights and all that belongeth to the Crown; ye shall not assent to decrease, to lessing, ne to concealment of the Queen's rights or of her franchises. And whensoever you shall have knowledge that the Queen's rights or the rights of her Crown bin concealed or withdrawn, be it in lands, rents, franchises, or suits, or any other things, ye shall do your true endeavour to make them to be restored to the Queen again; and if you may not do it, ye shall certify the Queen or some of the Council thereof (such as you hold for certain will say it unto the Queen); ye shall not respect the Queen's debts for any gifts or favour, where ye may raise them without great grievance of the debtors; ye shall truly and righteously treat the people of your Sheriffwick, and do right as well to poor as to rich in all that belongeth to your office; ye shall do no wrong to any man for any gift or other behest, or promise of goods for favour, nor bate he shall disturb no man's right; ye shall truly acquit at the Exchequer all those of whom ye shall any thing receive of the Queen's debts; ye shall nothing take whereby the Queen may lose, or whereby that right may be letted or disturbed, or the Queen's debts delayed; ye shall truly return and truly serve all the Queen's writs as far forth as shall be to your cunning; ye shall not have to be your undersheriff any of the Sheriff's clerks of the last year past; ye shall take no Bailiff into your service but such as you will answer for; ye shall make each of your Bailiffs to make such oath as you make yourself in that that belongeth to their occupation; ye shall receive no writ by you nor any of yours unsealed, nor any sealed under the seal of any Justice save of Justice in Eyre or Justice assigned in the same shire where ye be Sheriff in, or other Justices having power and authority to make any writs unto you by the law of the land or of Justice of Newgate; ye shall make your Bailiffs of true and sufficient men in the county; also you shall do all your power and diligence to destroy and make to cease all manner heresies and errors commonly called 'lollaries' [Lollardries] within your Bailiwick from time to time to all your power, and assist and to be helping to all the ordinaries and commissaries of Holy Church, and favour and maintain them as oftentimes as ye shall be required by the said ordinaries and commissaries; ye shall be dwelling in your own proper person within your Bailiwick for the time ye shall be in the same office, except ye be otherwise licensed by the Queen; ye shall not let your Sheriff-wick nor any Bailiwick thereof to any man; ye shall truly set and return reasonable and due issues of them that be within your Bailiwick, after their estate and haviour, and make your panels yourself of such persons as be most next most sufficient and not suspected nor procured, as is ordained by the Statutes, and over this in eschewing and restraint of the manslaughters, robberies, and other manifold grievous offences that be done daily, namely by such as name themselves soldiers and by other vagrants, the which increase in number and multiply so that the Queen's true subjects may not sure ride nor go to do such things as they have to do, to their intolerable hurt and hindrance; ye shall truly and effectually, with all diligence possible to your power, execute the Statutes, as the Statutes of Winchester and of vagabonds. All these things ye shall truly observe and keep as God help you and by the contents of this book.

ccviii.

[1594, November 3. Chancery. Sheriffs' Rolls. C227/11A.]

Surrey and Sussex	Walterus Covert Miles Nicholaus Parker Miles Willelmus Gardener Armiger	Ricardus Blunt Armiger *Willelmus Gardener Armiger Ricardus Leeche Armiger

Nomina Vicecomitum de tribus annis vltimo preteritis	Nomina eorum qui per dominos de Consilio erant pro Vicecomitibus nominati ad Scaccarium in CrastinoAnimarum anno regni Elizabeth nunc Regine tricesimo sexto.

[In the roll for the year following—C227/13—Richard Leeche's name is pricked.]

ccix.

[1595-1596. Exchequer Pipe Rolls. E372/441, 442.]

Gardiner's charges as Sheriff of Surrey and Sussex appear in various places on the Pipe Rolls for 37 and 38 Elizabeth.

ccx.

[1595, April 20. Close Roll, 37 Eliz. C54/1501.]

Richard Cowper of Capell, Surrey, gentleman, for £1600, sells to William Gardyner the elder of Barmondsey, esquire, Nicholas Smithe of Westminster, gentleman, and William Gardyner the younger, gentleman, the mansion house called Sandplace in Darkinge, Surrey, and all 'buildinges, barnes, stables, yardes, orchards, gardins, landes, tenementes, meadowes, pastures, feedinges, woodes, vnderwoodes, trees, coppices, commons, waters, fishinges, sheep courses, sheepwalkes, rentes, seruices, free warrens, easementes, profittes, commodities and hereditamentes whatsoeuer' heretofore granted to John Cowper, 'serieant at the lawe', by John Carell, esquire; and all the lands, etc., in Darkinge heretofore demised by the said Richard Cowper to Lawrence Courtoppe of Darkinge, gentleman. Deed acknowledged by Richard Cowper, gentleman, in Chancery, 19 May 1595, and enrolled 25 May 1595.

ccxi.

[1595, Hilary. Feet of Fines. C.P. 25/Surrey H. 37 Eliz.]

Between William Gardyner, esquire, querent, and Richard Treene and Joan his wife, deforciants, of 9 messuages, 2 cottages, and 2 gardens in the parish of St. Saviour, Southwark, quitclaimed by the deforciants for themselves and the heirs of Richard to William and his heirs for £100.

ccxii.

[1595, Trinity. Common Pleas. C.P. 40/1554/2266d.]

Thomas Luke, *alias* Awdley, of Southwark, butcher, attached to answer William Gardener, esquire, in a plea of trespass. Gardiner charges him with breaking his close at Bermondsey, and taking 40 cartloads of hay, valued at £30.

On the same membrane is the record of a similar suit of Gardiner's against Stephen Poore, of Southwark, butcher.

In another plea (on the same membrane) Richard Mills of London, butcher, is attached to answer William Gardener, esquire. Gardiner charges that Mills depastured cattle in his close at Bermondsey, where they consumed grass to the value of £20. There is a later entry of this suit in Michaelmas term, 37/8 Eliz.: C.P. 40/1561/2878.

ccxiii.

[1595, Michaelmas. Common Pleas. C.P. 40/1561/2878.]

William Gardener, esquire, of St. Mary Magdalen, Bermondsey, plaintiff, against Edmund Readinge, of Deptford, Kent, yeoman. Concerning an indenture dated 30 April 34 Eliz. (1592), by which the plaintiff sold to the defendant all the underwoods and trees growing in Great Hatcham Wood, containing 50 acres, lying in the parish of Deptford, forever, except one parcel of woodland (4 acres) adjacent to the high road and abutting on Brick Hill. The defendant undertook to repair the fences etc., but the plaintiff says that he did not repair them. A day given.

ccxiv.

[1595/6, Hilary. Queen's Bench. K.B. 27/1336/689.]

In Michaelmas term last, Alice Lanckton, widow, brought a bill against William Gardner, esquire, Sheriff of Surrey. She said that a certain John Hankyn, by a writing obligatory dated 30 July 35 Eliz. (1593), was bound to her in a debt of £20, payable on demand. When he did not pay the money on being asked, Alice brought suit against him, 28 January 37 Eliz. (1594/5), and got a writ to attach him, directed to Gardner as Sheriff of Surrey. But Gardner failed to produce Hankyn, and on the issue of subsequent writs, has repeatedly failed to do so. Alice accuses him of scheming to defraud her, and asks £30 damages. A jury inquired into the case at Westminster, and found that Alice had been damnified by Gardner's negligence. It was considered that she should recover damages and costs totalling £5:6:8 against Gardner.

ccxv.

[1595, December 23. Close Roll, 37 Eliz. C54/1516.]

Richard Cooper of Capell, Surrey, gentleman, John Younge of Chichester, Sussex, gentleman, and Arthur Langworth of Ringmere, Sussex, esquire, acknowledged that they owed £400 to William Gardyner of Bermondsey, Surrey, esquire, to be paid on the Feast of the Purification next ensuing. Dated 23 December, 38 Eliz. Condition, £205 to be paid to William Gardy-

293

ner at his house in the parish of St. Mary Magdalen, Bermondsey, 25 March next.

ccxvi.
[1595/6, Hilary. Common Pleas. C.P. 40/1563/1041.]

Surrey. William Gardener, esquire, Sheriff of the county aforesaid, plaintiff, against Laurence West of Farneham, Surrey, brewer, defendant. Gardener said that West, on 6 October 37 Eliz. (1595), at Woking, by his deed held himself bound to the plaintiff in a debt of £20, which he refused to pay. It was considered that Gardner should recover his debt, and damages of 13s. 4d.

ccxvii.
[1596, November. Wards Miscellaneous Books, 233.]

Wards, return of sheriffs' process.
"Anno xxxvii Eliz. R. Sussex. 50^{ll} Willm Gardiner esquier late shereif of the said Countie for his insufficiente retorne of her Ma^{tes} proces in Anno pd . . . L^{ll}

Surr. 50^{ll} The saide Wm Gardiner esquier [as before] . . . . . . L^{ll}
29no Novembr 1596 This vppon thexaiacon of the vndershreefe is myttigated vnto C^s. Sol. Rec. 30 Nov 1596 [etc.]."

ccxviii.
[1595, August 23. Star Chamber Proc. St. Ch. 5/G19/28.]

William Gardyner, esquire, complainant, against John Thompson, Thomas Newman, and others, defendants. Deposition on behalf of complainant. Interrogatories and deposition of William Wayte.

Interrogatories to be ministered to William Wayte on the part and behalf of William Gardyner [etc.]
1. Inprimis whether do you know that one Mr. Ferrers who hath married the wife of one John Smythe deceased, late ser-

vant to the Lord Chief Justice of England, or any other by his appointment, did pay to you one hundred pounds due to the plaintiff in May 1593 by a bond made to one William Smythe. 2. Item whether do you know or remember that the said plaintiff did in the aforesaid May 1593 or thereabouts send you to the said Thompson for one hundred and five pounds or thereabouts which the said Thompson did then owe to the plaintiff; And whether do you know or remember that the said plaintiff did deliver unto you one bill or bond of Thompson's hand for the payment thereof, and who paid you the same money, to your now remembrance; And whether did you seek the said Thompson divers and sundry times to have the said money about the said month of May 1593, as you know or remember.

Wayte's Deposition. Willyam Waight of Barmondsey Street within the County of Surrey, yeoman, of the age of forty years or thereabouts, [etc.].
To the first interrogatory this deponent saith that neither the said Mr. Ferrers in this interrogatory mentioned nor any other by his appointment, to his knowledge, did pay to him this deponent one hundred pounds due to the complainant.
To the second interrogatory this deponent saith that the said complainant did in May 1593 or thereabouts, as this deponent now remembreth, send him this deponent to John Thomson, one of the defendants in this cause, for one hundred and five pounds or thereabouts which the said Thomson did then owe to the said complainant, as the said complainant then told this deponent; and this deponent saith that the said plaintiff did then deliver unto him this deponent a bill or a b[ond] (which or both this deponent doth not [?clearly] remember) under the said Thomson's hand, for the payment of the said money; And further this deponent saith that one Harry, whose surname he doth not now remember, being then the servant of Thomas Newman (one other of the defendants), did (as this deponent

now remembreth) pay unto him this deponent the said sum of one hundred and five pounds before mentioned; And further this deponent saith that he this deponent did at divers and sundry times about the month of May 1593, as this deponent now remembreth, seek for the said Thomson, to have received of him the said Thomson the said sum of one hundred and five pounds before mentioned.

Other depositions in the suit are contained in the following: St. Ch. 5/G35/13; G8/21; G8/18.

ccxix.

[1595, Michaelmas. Common Pleas. C.P. 40/1561/2876.]

Gardiner against Thompson. John Thompson of London, scrivener, was attached to answer William Gardiner in a plea that whereas Thompson had £100 of Gardiner's to lend at ten per cent., and accordingly lent it to William Stone of London, haberdasher (now deceased), for a certain term, and afterwards Stone had paid the £100 to one Nicholas Saunders, esquire, for a debt of Gardiner's, Thompson (conspiring with Stone to defraud Gardiner), in the name of Stone but at the costs of Thompson, exhibited a bill of complaint against Gardiner at Hertford, before the Master of Requests, with the intention of defrauding Gardiner of the £100; falsely suggesting in the bill that Stone, about a year earlier, at the request of one Richard Gray, gentleman, had become solely bound for the security of payment of £100 with interest at 10 per cent., to such person and at such time as Gray, Thompson, and a certain Thomas Newman should appoint, Stone carelessly trusting Gray; and further suggesting in the bill that Gardiner, in the February preceding, had affirmed that he held the said obligation of Stone's, and had demanded the £100, which Stone accordingly paid to Gardiner, with 50s. as interest for three months, on Gardiner's promise to give him the bond; a promise which was never kept, and could not be kept, since Stone now had perfect intelligence that his obligation was in the hands of one Robert Lee, merchant; and that although Gardiner knew all this, and that the £102 10s. was none of his debt, he refused to repay the sum to Stone, which was in all equity due to Stone. This bill was brought by Stone in the Court of Requests at the costs of Thompson. Later, on 3 May 1593, in the same suit, Thompson falsely deposed that about 11 November 1590 he had received £100 from Gardiner to be lent to Richard Gray on the obligation of Gray and Stone, to be repaid in six months (13 May following); which £100 and interest were not paid on the very day (as he Thompson thought) but within a few days afterward, and were then lent, by the appointment of Gardiner, to John Smith, late servant to the late Chief Justice of England; whereas in truth neither the said £100 nor any part thereof was paid to the said John Smith by the appointment of the said Gardiner.

After this examination of Thompson, Stone had died; and Thompson, knowing that the administration of Stone's goods was granted to [Richard Stone], he brought a bill of revivor in this person's name in the Court of Requests against Gardiner. Whereupon, on 14 June 1594, by the said Court it was ordered that Gardiner, on his peril, should bring and deliver the £100 then in question on or before the Monday next following: the sum to remain in the hands of the Court until further order; by which Gardiner not only underwent divers great labours, and was obliged to spend huge sums of money in defence of the premises, but also was frequently arrested and detained in prison by order of the Court of Requests for the non-payment of the said £100, and was in danger by this pretext of losing £102 10s. of his own money. Gardiner wishes to prove that Stone in his lifetime did not pay him (Gardiner) the £102 10s. mentioned, nor any money; he charges that Thompson has tried to defraud him; and claims damages of £200.

297

The defendant John Thompson denies the accusation. A day given.

ccxx.

[1595/6, January 23. Star Chamber Proc. St. Ch. 5/G14/23.]

William Gardyner, plaintiff, against Andrew Graye, defendant. *Deposition* of Andrew Gray of the Middle Temple, esquire, aged 64. He said that he had been bound with Stone for the debt of Richard Gray, gentleman; that "at the last Hartforde term" William Stone went to his lodgings there and consulted him about a suit commenced by him against Gardyner for the "wrongful receiving of the sum of one hundred pounds", and said that he would send the defendant Thompson with further instructions. The deponent did not tell Richard Stone to put in a bill of revivor.

ccxxi

[1596, Easter. Queen's Bench. K.B. 27/1337/708.]

Middlesex. In Michaelmas term last past, John Thompson, citizen and scrivener of London, brought a bill in a plea of trespass against William Gardiner, esquire, as follows: Whereas William Stone, late of Westminster, by an obligation had stood bound (to some person unknown to Stone) in £150 conditioned on the payment of £102 10s. to this person unknown on 19 August 1591, at the shop of John Thompson in St. Michael Cornhill; and whereas afterwards (20 February 1591/2) Stone had delivered the £102 10s. to Thompson to pay to the person mentioned, and the obligation thereupon to be cancelled; nevertheless William Gardiner, moved by his perverse and most wicked malice to deceive and defraud Thompson, on the last day of February, 1591/2, pretending that he was the unknown person mentioned, craftily demanded the said sum of £102 10s.; and Thompson, believing him in his simplicity and good will, gave him the money. On 10 July 1592 this fraud of Gardiner's came to the notice of Thompson, for he then learned that a certain Henry Lee was the true person to whom the obligation had been made. Thompson thereupon paid Lee £102 10s. of his own proper money; and he now asks £200 damages of Gardiner. The defendant Gardiner denied the charge of fraud.

A trial by jury held on Wednesday and Saturday three weeks after Easter, in Westminster Hall before Sir John Popham, C.J., and John Povey. The jurors find Gardiner guilty, and assess damages in all at £116 10s. Writ of error received 25 May 1596.

ccxxii.

[1596, Easter. Queen's Bench. K.B. 27/1337/369.]

Middlesex. In Michaelmas term last past Thomas Newman and John Thompson, citizens and scriveners of London, brought a bill against William Gardiner, esquire, in a plea of trespass as follows: That Gardiner, 15 March 1585/6, in consideration of their drawing an indenture of sale between John Hobson and themselves (in secret trust for Gardiner) had agreed to pay them a reasonable sum for their work; they estimate this at £5. Also charges for drawing other deeds, as follows: 17 March 1585/6, for a deed of feoffment, Hobson to Newman and Thompson in trust for Gardiner, 13s. 4d. 10 July 1586, for a deed of conveyance of the above to Robert Withens, £5. 7 October 1589, for an indenture between Gardiner and his wife Margaret of the one part and Newman and Thompson and a certain William Wayte of the other, by which Gardiner agreed and granted with Newman, Thompson, and Wayte to acknowledge a fine of all and singular his lands, tenements, and hereditaments in the county of Surrey, which fine should be for divers uses and with divers provisions in the indenture specified, £3:6:8. 31 October 1589, for an indenture between Gardiner and a person to Newman and Thompson unknown, concerning divers agreements between Gardiner and Margaret his wife for the payment of £1,500 as in the indenture is specified, 10s. 2 January 1589/90, for an indenture between Gardiner and Richard Gardiner, his son, by which Gardiner granted to Rich-

299

ard and his heirs the remainder of all his lands and tenements after his death, with divers other remainders, and with a certain proviso of revocation of that indenture therein specified, £5. 10 April 1590, for a deed poll by which Gardiner witnessed his mind concerning the revocation of the indenture last mentioned, 30s. 17 June 1591, for an indenture between Nicholas Saunder of the one part and William Gardiner and William Gardiner his son of the other, by which Saunder sold to the Gardiners the manor of Lagham *alias* Langham Park in Surrey, £6:13:4. 8 January 1590/1, for an indenture between Edward Newport and Richard Baker of the one part, and William Gardiner and Richard Gardiner, his son and heir, of the other, by which the parties of the first part sell to the parties of the second part divers parcels of meadow land and pasture in Camberwell, Surrey, late in the occupation of one Edward Fowle, £6:13:4. 10 February 1590/1, for an indenture between Robert Smith and Frances his wife, of the one part, and Newman and Thompson, of the other, by which the parties of the first part sell to the latter on a secret trust for Gardiner, the 'James' or 'St. James' brewhouse in Bermondsey Street, St. Olave's, Southwark, in the tenure of John Stubbes, and an ale brewhouse next adjoining the 'James', late in the occupation of John Bowles, and three messuages in the several occupations of Robert Humble, Thomas Massy, Thomas Huntington, and John Wyndsore, in Bermondsey Street, £6:13:4. 20 February 1590/1, for an indenture whereby Newman and Thompson lease the property mentioned in the last indenture to Gardiner for 100 years, 20s. 20 May 1591, for two writings: one by which Robert Smyth sold divers implements in the brewhouses mentioned to Newman and Thompson on a secret trust for Gardiner; and the other by which Newman and Thompson sold them to Gardiner, 13s. 4d. 1 March 1590/1, for an indenture between Newman and Thompson of the first part, and Richard Gardiner, son of William Gardiner, of the other, by which it is witnessed that Newman and Thompson have sold the tenements last mentioned to Richard Gardiner, 33s. 4d. These separate sums come in all to £44:6:8 [I make it £41:16:8],which Gardiner has not paid, although they demanded payment on 1 March 1594/5. They ask £80 damages.

Gardiner denies the charge. A day given.

ccxxiii.

[1595/6, February 12. Chancery Proc., Eliz. C2 Eliz./G1/48.]

William Gardyner of Bermondsey, Surrey, esquire, plaintiff, against Thomas Newman and John Thompson, defendants.

Gardiner's Bill of Complaint. That the plaintiff, "by bargaining and dealing in the world after a good and lawful sort, hath heretofore had occasion to deal with scriveners for the making of certain deeds and writings, and (amongst others) being acquainted with Thomas Newman and John Thompson, scriveners of London, whom he thought to be honest and credible persons and such as he might safely trust", he had employed them about nine years before as scriveners, and also to do other work for him, by which they "did gain and receive divers great sums of money". He had always paid them for their writings when each deed was sealed. But now the said defendants, knowing how long it was since they had been employed by the plaintiff, caused him to be arrested by process out of the Queen's Bench, for the nonpayment of money he had promised them; and in particular [as in the document preceding], amounting in all to £44:6:8; the said Newman and Thompson "hoping (of their unconscionable, false, wicked, and covetous dispositions) by extremity of law to recover" the said sum, "which they most unreasonably, unjustly, impudently, and falsely do demand". There were in all 13 deeds, some of which should not have cost more than twelve pence or two shillings, and some the plaintiff did not tell them to write. They had been paid for everything.

The *Answer* of Thomas Newman and John Thompson. Newman said that he had been kept so busy writing the said deeds that he "could scarce . . . take rest or eat his meat for the importunacy of the complainant". In the defendants' names, the plaintiff had obtained the property of John Hobson on a secret trust for his (the plaintiff's) use, "so done of purpose, as this defendant remembreth, by the complainant to deprive or defraud his wife of dower if she survived him". In the matter of the sale of property to Robert Withens, the complainant had sued the defendants "of a malicious, false, and insatiable conscience". "The complainant had fraudulently and unjustly received one hundred and odd pounds of right due to Robert Lee of London, alderman."

ccxxiv.

[1595/6, Hilary. Queen's Bench. K.B. 27/1336/225.]

Surrey. In Michaelmas term last past William Gardiner of Barmondsey, Surrey, esquire, brought a bill against Thomas Newman and John Thompson, citizens and scriveners of London, for breach of agreement; showing a writing dated 21 July 1588 at St. George's, Southwark, made by the defendants, by which, for £420 already paid, they had that day sold to Gardiner the following jewels:

'one honye combe of golde', 'one booke and one coller of golde', the collar containing 20 'buttons' of which six are set with 'a Dyamonde a peece', nine with two 'pearles a peece', four with 'one rubye a peece', 'the other lacking hys stone', and the book set with 14 'Rubyes', 14 'Turkeys', and 2 'Saphers', weighing together 14 ounces. Also three pieces of gold chain set with 'pearle', weighing together 19 ounces. Also 3 dozen and ten 'buttons of golde', and two 'olde iewelles of golde', weighing together 18 ounces; also 42 'buttons of golde' set with 'one dyamonde a peece', 'one rynge sett with a dyamonde', 'one feire Aggett sett in golde', 'one rynge sett with fower diamondes';

302

also 'a locke sett with 49 diamondes'; also 'one crosbowe of golde sett wth 27 dyamondes and one rubye'; also 'one paire of tonges of golde' set with 'syxe Dyamondes, xxvi rubyes, & one pearle pendant'; also 'one brydle of golde' set with 24 'diamondes', 4 'rubyes', and 'twoe pearles pendant': also 'one rounde iewell of golde' set with 21 'diamondes' and 8 'rubyes'; provided that if on or before 21 January next after the date of the writing they paid Gardiner £420, at the shop of the said John Thompson in Cornhill, that then the sale should be void. Gardiner alleges that the money was not paid as agreed, and demands £600 damages. Newman and Thompson maintain that the money was duly paid. At a jury trial held 11 February 1596/7, Gardiner failed to appear and prosecute his suit. The Court awarded Newman and Thompson £4 damages, and an execution against Gardiner.

ccxxv.
[No date. Chancery Proc., Eliz. C2 Eliz./T7/27.]

John Thompson and Thomas Newman, plaintiffs, against William Gardiner, defendant. The plaintiffs recite the hypothecation of the jewels as in the preceding suit, and maintain that they paid Gardiner the £420 for their redemption on or before 21 January next after the date of the writing, and that Gardiner "well knoweth he lent the same money to other persons" afterwards. They ask an injunction against Gardiner to restrain him from proceeding in his suit against them at the common law.

ccxxvi.
[1595, 1596. Chancery Proc., Eliz. C2 Eliz./L7/60.]

Richard Leech, plaintiff, against William Gardener, defendant.

Leech's Bill of Complaint. Sworn 17 November 1595.

To the right honourable Sir John Puckering, knight, Lord Keeper of the great Seal of England.

Humbly complaining showeth unto your good Lordship your

303

daily orator Richard Leech of Sheiffeilde in the county of Sussex, esquire, that whereas Nicholas Sawnders of Ewell in the county of Surrey, esquire, was lawfully seized in his demesne as of fee of and in the manor, farm, or tenement of Lagham *alias* Langham Parke, containing by estimation 600 acres, in the said county of Surrey, and of and in the lands, tenements, and hereditaments thereunto belonging, now of the yearly value of £100 at the least, and also of and in the rectory or parsonage of Ewell in the said county, and of and in two watermills in Ewell aforesaid with all and singular their appurtenances, of the like yearly value of £100 at the least, and of and in divers other lands and tenements to your said orator unknown; and the said Nicholas so being thereof seized, together with Nicholas Saunders, son and heir apparent of the said Nicholas, 24 July 29 Eliz. [1587] became bound by recognizance in the nature of a statute staple in the sum of £400 unto Sir Nicholas Woodruffe, knight, citizen and alderman of London, and thereupon indentures of defeasance were made, as your said orator hath credibly heard, between the said Nicholas the father and Nicholas the son of the one party, and the said Sir Nicholas Woodruffe of the other party, whereby it was between them concluded and agreed that upon the payment of £200 or thereabouts at a certain time and place in the said indentures set down, that the said recognizance should be void; which said lesser sum was accordingly paid; and afterwards the said Nicholas Saunders the father, of all and singular the said premises died as aforesaid seized, and the same by lawful course of inheritance, or else by some conveyance unto your said orator unknown, came unto the said Nicholas the son, being son and heir of the said Nicholas the father; who, after the decease of the said Nicholas his father, entered into all and singular the said premises with appurtenances, and was lawfully thereof seized in his demesne as of fee; and so being seized, the said Nicholas for and in consideration of the sum of £500 of good and lawful money of England unto him well and truly paid by your said orator, by his deed bearing date 24 September 31 Eliz. [1589], granted for himself and his heirs unto your Lordship's said orator and his heirs, one annuity or yearly rent of £50 to be issuing and going out of the said manor, farm, or tenement of Lagham *alias* Langham Parke, with clause of distress for non-payment thereof, as in and by the said deed more fully and at large it doth and may appear; and for the better security and sure enjoying of the said annuity, he the said Nicholas the son, 1 November 31 Eliz. [1589], became bound unto your Lordship's said orator in the sum of £1000 by recognizance in the nature of a statute staple, acknowledged before Sir Christofer Wray, knight, then Lord Chief Justice of England; by virtue of which said grant your Lordship's said orator was of the said rent lawfully seized in his demesne as of fee; and the same was afterwards duly paid unto your said orator according to the purport of the said deed, until about June 34 Eliz. [1592]; and then one William Gardener of Sowthwarke esquire, and now high Sheriff of her Majesty's counties of Sussex and Surrey, well perceiving that the said Nicholas Saunders began to grow very prodigal and unthrifty, greatly laboured with the said Nicholas Saunders to purchase of him the said manor, farm, or tenement of Lagham *alias* Langham Parke, which he easily obtained; and because he well knew of the said yearly annuity or rent charge of £50 granted out of the same unto your said orator and his heirs, and of the said recognizance of £1000 acknowledged for the payment thereof, and understood that the said recognizance of £400 was uncancelled though in truth satisfied, it was concluded between the said Willyam Gardner and the said Nicholas Saunders that the said Willyam should retain £500 or thereabouts, or some other good sum of money in his own hands of the money which he should have paid for the said purchase, towards the discharge and payment of the said £50 per annum, or towards a composition to be made for the same; and also should retain in his hands out of the said money payable for the purchase of the said lands £400, or some other sum of money, for his indemnity and saving harmless touching the said uncancelled recognizance of £400, if any danger should happen by reason thereof to accrue; and by reason hereof the said Gardner, growing acquainted with the said Nicholas Sawnders, not long after purchased likewise of him the said rectory of Ewell and the said mills, being in effect the whole living of the said Sawnders.

Now so it is, if it may please your good Lordship, that the said William Gardner, having purchased and got unto himself in manner the whole lands and living of the said Nicholas Saunders the son, and devising and imagining with himself how and by what means he might defeat your Lordship's said orator not only of his just annuity or yearly rent of £50 aforesaid, but also how to avoid the said recognizance of £1000, notwithstanding that the said Gardner well knew and was made acquainted by the said Saunders of the said annuity as aforesaid, and also of the said recognizance of £1000, and for the payment thereof accordingly there was left in his hands as aforesaid the sum of £500 at the least, fraudulently combined and confederated himself with the said Nicholas Saunders and with one Nicholas Smyth of Westminster, gentleman, and upon conference between them had how and by what means they might best defraud your Lordship's said orator of the said annuity and of the execution of the said recognizance of £1000, notwithstanding that they, the said Gardener, Saunders, and Smyth, well knew that the said former recognizance of £400 acknowledged as aforesaid to the said Sir Nicholas was in verity and right paid and satisfied, but yet left uncancelled and undeformed; and not regarding the laws and statutes of this realm made and provided against maintenance, champarty, and the buying and selling of debts, made great suit unto the said Sir Nicholas Woodruff to assign over the said recognizance of £400

unto the said Nicholas Smyth, being a man nearly allied unto
the said Gardner, and upon great entreaty and persuasions
used unto the said Sir Nicholas, that it was a thing that might
be greatly beneficial unto the said Nicholas Sawnders and no
way hurtful to any man, about February 35 Eliz. [1592/3] procured the said Sir Nicholas, not knowing of the said annuity
of £50 per annum nor of the said recognizance of £1000, neither
being in any sort made privy unto this practise, privily for little
or no consideration (and such as was, was paid by the said
Gardener), to assign over the said recognizance of £400 unto
the said Nicholas Smyth; which was done by the said Sir Nicholas at the only costs and charges of the said Gardener and
Saunders or one of them, and hath ever since lain hid and been
concealed, until that now of late your Lordship's said orator
was compelled to sue forth a writ of extent upon the said recognizance of £1000 (in regard that the said annuity of £50
hath been long unpaid unto him) directed unto the said William
Gardner, for the extending of the lands of the said Saunders;
which the said William Gardener to execute did delay and pro-
tract until within very few days of the return of the said writ
of extent; and in the mean season at his own costs and charges
sued out another writ of extent upon the said recognizance of
£400 to himself (being Sheriff of the said counties of Sussex and
Surrey) directed, and hath with all post haste caused an inquiry thereupon to be made by inhabitants within the Borough
of Sowthwarke, neighbors unto the said William Gardener, and
such as have no knowledge of the value of the said lands late
the said Nicholas Saunders', and hath by indirect means procured the inquirers thereof to extend the said manor, farm, or
tenement of Lagham *alias* Langham Parke, being worth £100
per annum, at the yearly value but of £10; and the said rectory
of Ewell and the said mills there, being worth likewise £100
per annum, at the yearly value of £6:13:4 at the most, of purpose to hold the said lands long in extent, and by this fraud

307

and collusion to debar and defeat your Lordship's said orator
from his said just annuity of £50 per annum, and to suspend
the execution of the said recognizance of £1000; and now
laboureth exceedingly to get out a *liberate* upon the said extent
thus as aforesaid by himself procured, executed and returned
contrary to all equity, right, or good conscience.

In tender consideration whereof, and forasmuch as your Lordship's said orator hath no remedy by the common laws of this
realm to relieve himself against the said defendant touching
the said extent by the said Gardener fraudulently procured as
aforesaid, nor can avoid the same but by the order of your
good Lordship in this honourable Court, may it therefore please
your good Lordship to grant unto your Lordship's said orator
her Majesty's most gracious writ of subpena to the said Willyam Gardener to be directed, thereby straitly charging and
commanding him at a certain day and under a certain pain
therein to be limited, personally to appear before your good
Lordship in her Majesty's high Court of Chancery, then and
there particularly to answer unto the premises and to set down
expressly upon his oath what money was at any time left in
the hands of, or abated unto the said Gardener for and towards
the payment and discharge of the said annuity and of the said
several recognizances or any of them, and whether the said
debt of £400 be fully satisfied, yea or no, and how much thereof
in right and conscience is now due; and upon what consideration and whose instance the said recognizance was assigned
over unto the said Smyth by the said Sir Nicholas Woodruffe,
and to whose use, and who did bear and pay the charges of the
said assignment; and also of the said fraudulent extent, and
who is the follower and suer forth thereof; and farther to stand
unto such order therein as to your good Lordship shall seem
agreeable to equity and right; and that it may likewise please
your good Lordship in the mean season to make stay of the
liberate to be pursued forth upon the said fraudulent and un-

conscionable extent. And your Lordship's said orator will always pray unto God for the happy preservation of your good Lordship with increase of all honour.

E. Pelham

Gardiner's Answer. Sworn 27 November 1595.

[Abstract]   Gardiner says that after he had paid Saunders £1400 of the purchase price of £1900, he learned that the estate was variously charged and encumbered; whereupon, in Michaelmas term 35 Eliz. (1592), he complained in Chancery against Saunders that he or his father had "contrived divers leases, grants, estates, and conveyances of the premises or some part thereof to one John Hunte, Humfrey Squyre, John Greymes, William Browker, John Lambe, William Heath, and Robert Baxter or to some of them"; and had "charged and encumbered the premises with divers statutes and recognizances; as namely to Henry Prannell of the Middle Temple, gent., in £400 or thereabouts, and to one Luke Gardon *alias* Ward in the sum of 1000 marks, and to one Richard Wilkinson, gent., in £440 or thereabouts, and to one John [?] Ramsey in £100 or thereabouts, and to one Valentine Saunders in £1200 or thereabouts, and to one John Ballett in £250 or thereabouts, and to one Edward alias Edmund Gresham in 1000 marks or thereabouts, and to Sir John Harte, knight, by the name of John Harte, citizen and alderman of London, in £2000 or thereabouts, and to one Sir Nicholas Woodroff, knight, in £400 or thereabouts, and to the said Sir Nicholas Woodroff, knight, in £300". That afterwards Saunders confessed to Gardiner that the premises were charged with the recognizance of £400 to Sir Nicholas Woodruff, and with an annuity of £50 granted to Leech, and with a recognizance to Leech of £1000. "Upon which intelligence . . this defendant thought it expedient for him to get the said statute or recognizance so made to the said Sir Nicholas Woodroff as aforesaid discharged or assigned over to him this defendant, and to that end this defendant did require and call upon the said Nicholas Saunder to be a mean to accomplish the same"; Saunders thereupon made an indenture dated 20 February 35 Eliz. (1593) with Gardiner and Nicholas Smith, agreeing to get Woodruff to make over the recognizance of £400 (which was dated 24 July 29 Eliz. [1587]) to Gardiner or his nominee before 31 March next following. He says that Woodruff did so on payment of £200. He admits that he sued out the writ of extent, and caused a jury to inquire into the value of Lagham Park and the rectory of Ewell, and that this jury valued them at £10 and £6:8:4 by the year respectively.

Gardiner's further Answer. Sworn 29 April 1596.

> The answer of William Gardener esquire, defendant, to so much of the bill of complaint of Richard Leech esquire as by an order in this most honourable court the said William Gardener is enjoined to make further answer unto.

The said defendant saith that where it is ordered in this most honourable court that this defendant shall directly and certainly answer for what consideration the statute or recognizance of £400 was assigned by Sir Nicholas Woodrooffe to Nicholas Smithe, and whether any money and how much was left in this defendant's hands, or to be by him retained, for his indemnity and saving harmless touching the said statute or recognizance of £400, this defendant thereto saith that, so far as he now can call it to his remembrance (being long since the said recognizance was assigned over to the said Nicholas Smithe), the same was so assigned to the said Nicholas Smithe for and in consideration of the sum of £240 at the least, which this defendant did pay to the said Sir Nicholas Woodrooffe, to his best remembrance; and this defendant having understanding that the lands, tenements, and hereditaments sold unto this defendant and William Gardener his son by the said Nicholas Saunders were (contrary to the faithful promise, bargain, and covenants

of the said Nicholas Saunders) subject as well to divers and
sundry other statutes, recognizances, charges, and encumbrances as to this statute, and knowing withal that he had and
was to pay for the said premises the sum of £1900 of lawful
English money, whereof he then had paid to the said Nicholas
Saunders £1400 beforehand, and was to pay unto him £500
more, residue of the said £1900, at a certain day between this
defendant and the said Nicholas Saunders agreed upon, and
should (that notwithstanding) reap no benefit of the said premises, because they were subject and liable to such and so
many statutes, recognizances, former encumbrances, and other
charges, as the same were likely to remain a very long time in
extent, and this defendant to reap no commodity by the said
land, this defendant thereupon, to the intent to be the more
certainly assured of every particular charge or encumbrance
wherewith the said premises might be charged, and to the end
to be relieved by the aid of this most honourable court in such
sort as he should not be enforced to pay unto the said Nicholas
Saunders any part of the said sum of £500 in regard that the
said premises were subject to such and so many encumbrances,
this defendant therefore did exhibit his bill of complaint into
this most honourable court against the said Nicholas Saunders,
to the intent that he the said Nicholas Saunders should upon
his oath discover how he had encumbered the said premises,
and that by order in this most honourable court this defendant
might be so far relieved as that he might still retain in his hands
the said sum of £500, to the intent therewith in some part to
discharge the said statutes, recognizances, and other charges
which might be imposed and charged upon the said premises;
and this defendant did beside not only make or cause to be
made an attachment of the said sum of £500 according to the
custom of the City of London, but also meant to have arrested
or to have caused to be arrested the said Nicholas Saunders as
well upon certain statutes of £3000 or thereabouts, as for the

breach of such covenants as the said Nicholas Saunders had
entered into to this defendant; howbeit this defendant, upon
composition made with the said Sir Nicholas Woodroofe concerning the said statute of £400 and the payment of the said
£240, which was assented unto by the said Nicholas Saunders,
did not only satisfy and pay to and for the debt of the said
Nicholas Saunders (and that by the assent and consent of the
said Nicholas Saunders) the said sum of £500 residue of the
said sum of £1900, which sum of £500 this defendant might
very well have retained in his hands (as he thinketh) upon the
said attachment thereof made as is aforesaid, and hoped likewise to have been relieved therein in this honourable court by
reason of his said bill exhibited for that purpose, and have had
besides by the law the benefit of the statutes or recognizances
for the breach of the covenants; and which sum of £500 this
defendant would not have paid to or for the debt of the said
Nicholas Saunders if the said statute or recognizance of £400
had not been set over to the said Nicholas Smithe by the said
Sir Nicholas Woodroofe, so as in consideration of the setting
over of the said statute to the said Nicholas Smithe in such sort
as is aforesaid, this defendant did then forbear and lose such
benefit and advantage as he might lawfully and justly have
taken against the said Nicholas Saunders by reason of the said
attachment made as is aforesaid by way of retaining of the
said sum of £500, and of his proceeding upon the said bill in
this honourable court; and also such benefit as he might have
further reaped upon the said statutes of £3000 and for the
breach of the said covenants, by reason that the said Nicholas
Saunders had broken such covenants with this defendant as
before that the said Nicholas Saunders had entered into unto
this defendant; and therefore, forasmuch as this defendant did
forbear to take such benefit as is aforesaid against the said
Nicholas Saunders for that the said statute or recognizance of
£400 was so set over to the said Nicholas Smith as is aforesaid,

there is no reason to the contrary (as this defendant hopeth) but that the said Nicholas Smith may lawfully take the advantage of the said statute or recognizance; for by all law and conscience it is lawful (as this defendant verily thinketh) for him that hath purchased and paid for land so dearly, to get in any statutes or recognizances that the land is charged with to protect him against after statutes, and especially as the case of this defendant standeth, who might then have satisfied himself in some reasonable sort for the charges that lay upon the land; all which he hath now in effect lost, for the £500 he hath paid and satisfied, and now can not sue the said Nicholas Saunders for he is gone to the sea, and hath been a great while; and if he were returned, yet he is a man of little or no ability to satisfy anything (as this defendant thinketh); all which matters the said defendant is ready to aver and prove as this most honourable court shall award, and prayeth as before in his former answer he hath prayed.

Yelverton

Leech's Replication.

> The Replication of Richard Leeche, Esquire, complainant, to the several Answers of Willyam Gardener, Esquire, defendant.

The said complainant, saving unto himself now and at all times hereafter all advantages and exceptions to the uncertainty and insufficiency of the said answers, by way of replication doth and will aver all and every thing in his said bill of complaint to be certain, just, and true, in such manner and form as in and by the same is set forth and declared; and that the said Nicholas Saunders the father was seized of the manor, lands, and tenements in the bill named in his demesne as of fee, and that he and the said Nicholas Saunders the son so became bound by recognizance in the nature of a statute staple in the sum of £400 unto the said Sir Nicholas Woodruffe knight, and defeasance thereof made upon the payment of £200 or such like sum, as in and by the said bill is truly set forth and alleged; and that the said manor of Lagham *alias* Langham Parke came after the decease of the said Nicholas Sawnders the father unto the said Nicholas the son, and that he was thereof seized in his demesne as of fee; and so being seized, granted for the consideration in the said bill truly set forth, the said annuity or rent charge of £50 per annum unto the said complainant and his heirs, with clause of distress for non-payment thereof in the said lands, and entered into the said recognizance of £1000 of the nature of a statute staple unto the said complainant for the true payment thereof in such manner and form as in and by the said bill is likewise truly set forth and alleged; and that the said complainant was by force of the said grant lawfully seized of the said rent charge, and the same was justly paid unto the said complainant until the said defendant practised and went about to purchase the said manor of Lagham; and also the said complainant saith that the said defendant well knew of the said rent charge and recognizance of £1000; and understanding that the said recognizance of £400 was uncancelled (and yet the money thereupon due was satisfied), it was agreed between the said Sawnders the son and the said defendant at the time of the sale of the said manor of Lagham unto the said defendant, that he should retain such money in his hands out of the said purchase for and towards the payment and discharge of the said recognizance of £400, and for his indemnity touching the same, as in the said bill is likewise truly set forth and alleged; and that the said defendant, insinuating himself with the said Nicholas Saunders the son, hath purchased of him the said rectory of Ewell, and in effect the whole lands and living of the said Sawnders; and that the said defendant, after that he had purchased the said lands and living, devising how to defraud the said complainant of his said rent of £50 per annum, and of the said recognizance of £1000 (notwithstanding he well knew both of the said annuity

314

or rent charge and also of the said recognizance of £1000 before
he purchased the said manor of Lagham of the said Sawnders,
and that money was left in his hands by the said Sawnders for
the payment thereof), did fraudulently confederate himself
with the said Saunders and with the said Nicholas Smyth the
other defendant, and all of them (knowing that the said recognizance of £400 was satisfied but yet left uncancelled), did
(contrary to the laws and statutes of this realm touching maintenance, champarty, and buying and selling of debts) labour
unto the said Sir Nicholas Woodruffe to assign the said recognizance of £400 unto the said Nicholas Smythe, being a
man very nearly allied unto the said Gardener; and that the
said Sir Nicholas, upon the reasons and considerations in the
said bill set forth (and not knowing of the said practice intended against the said complainant), did assign over the said
recognizance of £400 unto the said Smythe in such manner and
form as in the said bill of complaint is truly set forth and
alleged; and that the said assignment lay hid and unknown by
the space of three years, and nothing done upon the said recognizance of £400, until the said complainant was enforced at
his great costs and charges to sue forth an extent upon his said
recognizance of £1000, in regard the said rent charge was long
behind and unpaid, and thereby to extend the said manor of
Lagham and other the lands late of the said Nicholas Sawnders
sold unto the said defendant. And that the writ of *extendi
facias* was directed unto the said William Gardener, being then
High Sheriff of the county of Sussex, and that he protracted
and delayed the execution thereof until within short time of
the return thereof, and in the meantime sued forth, at his own
proper costs and charges, a writ of extent upon the said recognizance of £400, directed unto himself; and that thereupon
he made an inquiry in such manner and form as in the said bill
of complaint is truly set forth and declared, and caused the
jurors (being his neighbours in Southwarke) to extend the said

315

manor and park of Lagham at £10 per annum (being worth £100 per annum), and the said rectory of Ewell and the mills there, mentioned in the said bill, at £6:14:4 (being worth likewise £100 per annum), and made speedy return of the said writ, and sued forth with all expedition a writ of *liberate* upon the same, purposely to defraud the said complainant of his said rent of £50 per annum, and utterly to defeat him of the benefit of the said recognizance of £1000, as in and by the said bill of complaint is most truly and plainly set forth and alleged; and this complainant further replieth and saith that although the said jury, upon the inquiry taken for him, had valued the said manor and park of Lagham at £10 per annum, yet that ought to be no precedent unto the said defendant, for that if the same were given in extent unto the said complainant, it should be rated to him at less by £50 per annum than the very value thereof, in regard of his said rent charge going and issuing out of the same; and if the extenders for the said complainant found the said manor and park at £10 per annum, it was upon the reason of the charge issuing out thereof unto the said complainant; but the extenders and jury sworn to extend for the said defendant upon the said statute of £400 had no reason or ground to extend the said manor and park at £10 per annum, whenas the said defendant hath confessed and set forth upon his oath that he did pay £1900 for the same, and therefore must needs in common presumption be of the yearly value in the said bill set forth and declared; and therefore, and for that the said defendant hath in his answer upon his corporal oath confessed that shortly after he purchased the said manor and park of Lagham of the said Sawnders, that he was informed of divers former and secret estates and of divers charges and encumbrances wherewith the said manor and lands were charged as in the said answer is particularly set forth (all which, or the most of them, the said complainant verily thinketh were before that time paid and discharged), and for

316

GARDINER DOCUMENTS

that it likewise appeareth by the defendant's own showing that
the said defendant for the searching out of the truth thereof
exhibited his bill of complaint in this most honourable court
against the said Nicholas Saunders, and that the said William
Gardener took out process upon the said bill against the said
Sawnders, and that thereupon the said Gardener and Sawnders
came unto a conference about the same, and upon the said
conference the said Sawnders confessed unto the said defendant
the said recognizance of £400 acknowledged unto the said Sir
Nicholas Woodruff, and also confessed and acknowledged that
he had upon the consideration of £500 paid unto him by the
said now complainant, granted unto him a rent charge in fee
of £50 per annum out of the said manor and park of Lagham,
and had bound himself in the said recognizance of £1000 for
the performance thereof; and also forasmuch as the said defendant hath further in his said answer confessed that thereupon he procured the said Sawnders to be a means unto the
said Sir Nicholas Woodruffe to assign over the said recognizance of £400 unto the said Smythe, and urged the said Saunders
to enter into very strait covenants for the effecting thereof,
and that thereupon the said Gardener, by and with the consent
of the said Sawnders, made composition that the said recognizance should be assigned by the said Sir Nicholas Woodruffe
unto the said Smythe, and that the same was assigned accordingly; and for that the said Gardener hath likewise confessed
by the said answer that he, knowing that he had paid £1400
unto the said Sawnders for the said manor and park of Lagham
with the appurtenances, and that he was to pay £500 more,
did cause the said £500 to be attached in his own hands, and
hath thereby likewise confessed that by that means he might
have satisfied and paid the said rent charge unto your said
orator, and could further have relieved himself upon the breach
of divers covenants broken by the said Sawnders; and also by
the forfeiture of one recognizance in the nature of a statute

317

staple of £3000, acknowledged by the said Sawnders unto the said defendant for the performance of the said covenants broken as aforesaid, which courses the said defendant had greatest reason in conscience to have pursued, as he hath confessed he did not, but by reason of the confederacy aforesaid, and plot laid and devised against the said complainant, how and by what means to wrest him unconscionably from his just rent of £50 per annum, and from all benefit to be had by any extent upon the said recognizance of £1000, by and with the consent of the said Sawnders, compounded as aforesaid with the said Sir Nicholas Woodruffe for the setting over of the said recognizance of £400 unto the said Smythe to the use of the said Gardener, as by the said answer appeareth; and forasmuch as the said defendant hath confessed that upon this plot and practice executed he eased the said Sawnders from the lawful and ordinary courses of law, which upon breach of the covenants or forfeiture of the said great recognizance of £3000 he the said defendant purposed and might have taken against the said Sawnders, and apparently confesseth that therefore he hopeth to enjoy the benefit of the said extent upon the said recognizance of £400 extended at the low rate of £10 per annum, and undervalued as aforesaid, which tendeth apparently to the utter loss of the said complainant's just rent of £50 per annum and to the frustrating and utter avoiding of the said recognizance of £1000, so as the said complainant shall never come to be relieved thereby, and the rather for that the said defendant hath in his answer confessed that the said Sawnders is gone to the sea, and is become of small value, and so the said complainant every way remediless, and by the pack and confederacy aforesaid, utterly defeated of his said rent and of all benefit to be had by virtue of the said recognizance of £1000, except he may be relieved by your good Lordship in this most honourable court; and therefore the said complainant hopeth and most humbly prayeth that in regard of the premises and in

regard it appeareth upon the said defendant's own showing
that he well knew of the said rent and recognizance granted
and acknowledged to the said complainant before he departed
with the said £500 out of his hands, whereby (as also by the
breach of the covenants made unto the said defendant and of
the forfeiture of the said recognizance of £3000) the said defendant likewise hath confessed that he might have relieved
himself, and hath in effect confessed that he waived those re-
medies, and joined himself with the said Sawnders and Smythe
to avoid and debar the said complainant both of his said rent
and also of the advantage of his said recognizance of £1000,
that this honourable court will set down such order whereby the
said complainant may have and enjoy the said rent of £50 per
annum, and have the same duly paid unto him according to
equity and good conscience; without that, that it is true that
any former estate or estates was made or granted of the said
manor and premises, or that the said manor and park was in
truth encumbered and charged with the said statutes and recognizances in the said answer recited and mentioned, or with
any other, except only the said statute of £400 unto the said
Sir Nicholas Woodruffe, which this complainant verily thinketh
was long since satisfied or discharged, and except the said recognizance of £1000 acknowledged unto the said complainant,
or that the said Nicholas Sawnders the son did, before or upon
the said bargain and sale of the said manor and park of Lagham
unto the said defendant, protest and solemnly vow and assure
the said defendant that neither the said Nicholas Saunders,
nor the said Nicholas his father or either of them, had any way
charged or encumbered the premises or any part thereof otherwise than the said Nicholas did make known unto the said
defendant, which was the said rent of £50 per annum and the
said recognizance of £1000, or that the said Mrs. Sawnders,
late wife of the said Nicholas Sawnders the father, hath any
estate in the said rectory of Ewell or the mills there, as in the

said answer is untruly surmised, or that the said writ of extent sued forth by the said complainant was executed before the said writ of extent sued out by the said defendant, or that the said Nicholas Sawnders the son, before the time of the said grant of the rent charge of £50 per annum as aforesaid, had granted his interest in the said rectory and mills unto the said Henry Sawnders his brother in such manner and form as in the said answer is untruly set forth, or that the said defendant hath paid the said £400 unto the said Sir Nicholas Woodruffe upon the assignment of the recognizance of £400 aforesaid or any part thereof of his own money, or that there was cause why he should so do, for such money as was paid (if any were paid at all) was money that the said defendant owed unto the said Sawnders, or that the said defendant did satisfy and pay to and for the debt of the said Nicholas Sawnders (and that by the assent and consent of the said Nicholas Saunders) the said sum of £500 in such manner and form as in the said answer is untruly alleged; and without that, that any other matter or thing in the said answer contained material or effectual for the said complainant to reply unto, and not in this replication confessed and avoided or else traversed and denied, is true; all which matters the said complainant is ready to aver and prove, and humbly prayeth as in his said bill he hath formerly prayed.

Amherst

ccxxvii.

[1596, November. Chancery Town Depositions. C24/254/29.]

Leech against Gardiner. Interrogatories and depositions on behalf of Gardiner. The two deponents are Henry Allison, of St. Olave's, Southwark, scrivener, aged 56, and Nicholas Chalkley of Bermondsey, servant unto the defendant, aged 27. Allison was Gardiner's scrivener, and Chalkley, one of his servants.

ccxxviii.

[1596/7, February 14. Chancery Proc., Eliz. C2 Eliz./L1/38.]

Charitye Leeche, widow, plaintiff, against William Gardiner, esquire, defendant. As Richard Leech's widow, Charitye brings a bill of revivor of his suit against Gardiner, and in it repeats her late husbands charges, as given above.

ccxxix.

[1595/6, Hilary. Feet of Fines. C.P. 25/Surr. H. 38 Eliz.]

Between William Gardener, esquire, querent, and Richard Cowper, gentleman, and Elizabeth his wife, deforciants, of two messuages, gardens, and orchards, and 330 acres of land in Dorking, warranted by the deforciants for themselves and the heirs of Richard against the heirs of John Cowper, late serjeant at law, to William and his heirs forever, for £120.

ccxxx.

[1596, 1597. Court of Requests, Order Books. Req. 1/47.]

Roger Manners, esquire, and Edward Catesbie and Margaret his wife, plaintiffs, against William Gardyner, esquire, and Margaret his wife, defendants.

1596, 14 June. The defendants to make answer on their oaths to the points of such exceptions as had been put into Court, before the 21st of this month at their peril.

1596, 15 November. The messenger of the Court with all convenient speed to bring in the body of William Gardyner to answer for his contempts; on his appearance, the Court would proceed to take order for his punishment.

1596, 19 November. Ordered, in the presence of William Gardyner, that there should be a hearing on the coming Friday. William Gardyner promised in open Court to bring with him 20 marks, according to a former order, to be disposed of as the Court should think fit.

1597, 4 May. Gardyner had not paid the 20 marks.

1597, 9 May. William Gardyner submitted to perform such order and decree as the Court should make, and he gave to the plaintiff 20s., "towards the relief of his present necessities". Hearing ordered for the twelfth day of Trinity term.

1597, 9 June. Unless the defendants showed good matter to the contrary on Tuesday next, a decree would be made that they should pay the plaintiffs £73:6:8, as part of the money demanded, which (it was alleged) had come into the hands of Frement Abraham.

1597, 26 November. The decree against the defendants to be drawn up and signed, but execution thereof suspended until counsel had considered the writings brought in by Roger Manners.

ccxxxi.

[1596, Michaelmas. Queen's Bench. K.B. 27/1340/425.]

Surrey. In Easter term last William Gardyner, esquire, brought a bill in a plea of trespass against Francis Langley, setting forth the loyalty, good name, etc., of the said William and his children, and showing that he was a justice of peace appointed to hear and determine divers felonies, etc., in the county of Surrey for divers years, and that he carried on a business of buying and selling with the Queen's subjects; and that Francis Langley, knowing all this, maliciously slandered him: on 22 May 38 Eliz. (1596) at Croydon, Langley had falsely and maliciously said, "he is a false knave and a false perjured knave, and I will prove him so": which, being publicly said, damaged the said William in £1000.

Now on the Saturday after the Octave of St. Michael, Francis Langley . . . said that in Trinity term, 22 Eliz. (1580), a certain Thomas Walker, son and heir of Anthony Walker, then deceased, exhibited his bill in the Court of Wards and Liveries against the said William Gardyner, alleging amongst other things that the said Anthony had bought from —— Slywright, gentleman, divers messuages, etc., in Barmesey Strete in South-warke, which had formerly belonged to Edward Welsh. After the death of the said Anthony the third part of this property descended to the said Thomas Walker, and was held of the Queen in chief by knight service, and the said Thomas was of age. And that Edward Welsh (long before Anthony bought the property) had become bound to the said William Gardyner in a recognizance for £500, dated 6 June 3 Eliz. (1561) [conditions recited], and that afterwards Gardyner had released this recognizance to Welsh. Nevertheless in Michaelmas term, 27 Eliz. Gardyner had tried to procure an execution of the recognizance. Walker, complaining against the wrong thus offered by Gardyner, asked for an injunction to restrain him from proceeding at the common law. In his sworn answer to this bill, Gardyner said that he was assured in his conscience that he had never made a release to Welsh. Being examined on his oath on 5 February 33 Eliz. (1590/1) Gardyner was shown a release, made to Edward Welsh in acquittance of the bond dated 6 June 1561; he denied that it was his deed. Therefore the said Gardyner had wilfully perjured himself in the Court of Wards, and the said Francis afterwards said the above words concerning the said William Gardiner. A day given.

ccxxxii.
[1596, Michaelmas. Queen's Bench. K.B. 27/1340/433.]

A similar suit, likewise entered in Easter term, except that the date of Langley's uttering the slanderous words is given as 21 May 1596. Gardiner asks £1000 damages on this new charge. Langley's defence is the same as before. A day given.

ccxxxiii.
[1596, Michaelmas. Common Pleas. C.P. 40/1578/2638.]

Francis Langley of Southwark, gentleman, attached to answer William Gardener, esquire, on a charge that at Croydon,

1 June 1596, he slanderously said of Gardener, "he is a false knave, a false forsworn knave and a perjured knave". Gardener asks £200 damages. Langley's defence is the same as in the two suits preceding. A day given.

ccxxxiv.
[1596, Trinity. Queen's Bench. K.B. 27/1338/473d.]

Middlesex. William Gardiner, esquire, late sheriff of Sussex, plaintiff, against Thomas Eason, of Baybushe, Sussex, yeoman, defendant, in a plea of debt for £20.

ccxxxv.
[1596, Trinity. Feet of Fines. C.P. 25/Surr. T. 38 Eliz.]

Between William Gardyner, querent, and Thomas Tryne and Anne his wife, and Richard Tryne, deforciants, of two acres of meadow in Camberwell and Deptford, warranted against the heirs of Richard and Thomas to William for £40.

ccxxxvi.
[1596, September 24. Patent Roll, 38 Eliz., pt. 13. C66/1455.]

A farm for William Gardiner. Recites patent of 7 July 1587; on surrender of which and on payment of £3 fine, there is hereby a new grant of confirmation to Gardiner of the farm, parcel of Hatcham Barns Wood.

ccxxxvii.
[1596, November 5. Chancery Decrees and Orders.
Vol. 1596A, 397.]

Elizabeth Fowle, widow, and others, plaintiffs, against William Gardyner, defendant. This day sennight given to the defendant to answer or else to be attached.

ccxxxviii.

[1596, November 13. Chancery Proc., Eliz. C2 Eliz./F1/63.]

Elizabeth Fowle, widow, and Edward Fowle, formerly of Peckham, plaintiffs, against William Gardiner, esquire, defendant. *Gardiner's Answer*. The suit concerns an inn, and mentions the scriveners Newman and Thompson.

ccxxxix.

[1596/7, March 6. Court of Requests Proc. Req. 2/119/4.]

William Gardyner of Bermondsey, esquire, plaintiff, against James White and Jane Ferrys or Ferrers, defendants.

Gardyner's Bill. Alleges that John Thompson had £100 of Gardyner's, which he lent on 13 February 1590/1 to John Smith, gentleman, late servant to Sir Christopher Wray, late Lord Chief Justice of England, for three months, payable 15 May following at Thompson's shop in Cornhill, with 50 shillings interest; and for this payment John Smith and James White became bound to William Smyth of London, gentleman (in trust for Gardyner). The sum was not paid; but on 16 May Thompson took another bond of them of £150 for payment of the £100 in six months (17 November following). So they kept on the debt from half-year to half-year until John Smith died, and afterwards in the name of his executrix Jane Smith, now Ferrers. Gardyner says that they have somehow got possession of the bond and cancelled it, but that he has not received the money.

Demurrer of defendants. Demur on the ground that they have been examined on these points in a Star Chamber suit.

ccxl.

[1597, April 18. Court of Requests, Order Book. Req. 1/48.]

The defendants, on their previous examination in the Court of Star Chamber, had confessed that the money was paid. Ordered to amend their answers on that point.

ccxli.

[1597, April 27. Court of Requests Proc. Req. 2/57/16.]

Gardyner against White and Ferrers. Further answer of defendants. They insist that the debt on which Gardyner sues was paid.

ccxlii.

[1597, June 2. Court of Requests Proc. Req. 2/149/2, 149/27.]

Roger Manners, esquire, and others, plaintiffs, against William Gardiner and Margaret his wife, defendants. Depositions touching divers sums paid by plaintiff to Frement Abraham, and the payment of certain annuities by defendants.

ccxliii.

[1597, Trinity. Exchequer, Barons' Depositions. E133/1323.]

William Gardiner, plaintiff, against Edward Adams and his wife Mary, late wife of Thomas Palfreyman. Depositions concerning wood felled in the royal manor of Hatcham Barns.

ccxliv.

[1597, Michaelmas. Common Pleas. C.P. 40/1601/3293.]

On 18 June 27 Eliz. (1585), at Westminster, Thomas Gardiner the younger of London, gentleman, wished to borrow £100 from a certain Ralph Ratcliffe of London, mercer, and to evade the act of 13 Eliz. against usury, Ratcliffe delivered to the said Thomas divers pieces of velvet, satin, and taffeta, worth £60, for which the latter was to pay £100 on 20 November following. Ratcliffe would thus receive £40 for the use of his money, contrary to the statute, which allowed no more than ten per cent. interest. The said Thomas gave Ratcliffe his bond for £200 for the payment of £100. Afterwards the said Ratcliffe sued the said Thomas for the £200, which he recovered, with 20s. damages. Thereupon Thomas petitioned the Queen for

remedy, who ordered the case to be heard by the Justices of
the Bench on 1 July 1597.

Therefore on 1 July, to the house of Edmund Anderson, Chief
Justice of the Common Bench, in Charterhouse churchyard,
came the said Thomas Gardener, by William Cragg his attorney, and William Gardener of Bermondsey, Surrey, esquire,
John Jefferson, citizen and leatherseller of London, Richard
Swifte, citizen and leatherseller of London, and Stephen Mayn-
ford of Southwark, gentleman, and mainperned the said
Thomas in £400. A writ of venire facias issued to the Sheriff
of Sussex.

ccxlv.

[Temp. Elizabeth. Exchequer Bills and Answers.
E112/Eliz./Surrey 60.]

William Gardner, esquire, plaintiff, against John Rider and
William Stere, defandants. Concerning lands late belonging to
the Monastery of St. Saviour's, Bermondsey. These documents
are reported missing at the Record Office.

ccxlvi.

[1597. Exchequer Bills and Answers. E112/Eliz./Surrey 59.]

William Gardyner of Bermondsey, Surrey, esquire, plaintiff,
against Edmunde Bowyer of Camberwell, esquire, defendant.
Gardyner's Bill. That Robert, sometime Abbot of the Monastery of Bermondsey, was seized of the Grange of Bermondsey,
and by indenture, dated 1 May 26 Hen. VIII, demised the same
to Ralph Wryne, gentleman, and Helen his wife, for 60 years
next following, at a yearly rent of £48. By letters patent of
19 March 18 Eliz. (1575/6), the said Grange was demised to
William Gardyner at the same rent after the end, forfeiture,
or avoidance of the term of 60 years, for a term of 21 years.
The Wrynes' lease expired at Michaelmas 36 Eliz. (1594), and

the complainant entered into possession. Since which time the plaintiff let one close of land in the parish of St. Mary Magdalen, Bermondsey, near the 'Floude ditche', called 'the Ponde Close' or 'the Conye Yard', containing two acres, lying on the west side of the great barn belonging to the said Grange, for a term of years to one Edward Quarrell. But a certain Edmund Bowyer of Camberwell, esquire, pretends that the Pond Close belongs to his parsonage of Camberwell, and not to the Grange, and has brought an action for trespass against the said Quarrell in the King's Bench.

Bowyer's Answer. That the Abbot of Bermondsey by indenture dated 2 April 29 Hen. VIII, granted to William Gardner of Bermondsey, husbandman, the plaintiff's father, all the tithes belonging to the parsonage of Camberwell, with the exception of the glebe land called 'the parsonage landes' and also the said barn and a piece of ground on its west side, for a term of 50 years, at a yearly rent of £10. And the said William Gardner, being so possessed, by indenture dated 27 April 34 Henry VIII, demised all his title and interest in the said premises to Robert Draper of Camberwell, gentleman, the defendant's grandfather. And the said Robert Draper, by his deed dated 28 April 34 Hen. VIII, demised the said barn and parcel of land to the said William Gardyner, the plaintiff's father, for a term of 46 years, reserving to himself "one half-year, parcel of the said fifty years" at the end of the term, at a yearly rent of a red rose. The Queen, by her letters patent of 7 August 15 Eliz., granted the tithes and the same lands to William Greerley for 21 years at the expiration of the lease to William Gardner. Also the Queen, by letters patent of 12 January 32 Eliz., for the sum of £440, granted to Edmund Bowyer, the defendant, and Katherine his wife, the rectory of Camberwell, with the said barn and the parcel of ground on the west side.

ccxlvii.

[1597, Trinity. Exchequer Bills and Answers.
E112/Eliz./Surr. 63.]

Edmund Bowyer of Camberwell, esquire, and Katherine his
wife, plaintiffs, against William Gardiner, esquire, and Edward
Quarrell, defendants.

The Bowyers' Bill. Recites the grants as in the preceding suit,
and claims that Pond Close was granted to him with the parsonage of Camberwell. Alleges that Gardiner, "of his covetous
and insatiable mind, hath not only defaced the bounds of the
said parcel of ground by extirping the trees standing and growing" there, but also levelled the ditches, "to the procurement
of perjury in setting forth the true Bounds".
Gardiner's Answer. Denies everything in the bill and declares
that Bowyer defaced the bounds, etc.

ccxlviii.

[1597, July 28. Dasent, *Acts of Privy Council, 1597*,
pp. 313, 314.]

Order to Middlesex justices, transmitting the Queen's will that
plays be forbidden during the summer, and that the stages
and galleries of the Curtain and the Theatre be plucked down;
no plays to be allowed within three miles of the City until All-
hallowtide next.
"The like to Mr. Bowier, Willian Gardyner, and Bartholomew Scott, esquires, and the rest of the Justices of Surrey, requiring them to take the like order for the playhouses in the
Banckside, in Southwarke or elsewhere in the said county
within iii miles of London."

ccxlix.

[1597. Close Roll, 39 Elizabeth. C54/1570.]

John Pope of Stanwell, Middlesex, gentleman, acknowledged
that he owed William Gardyner the elder of Bermondsey,

Surrey, esquire, £40 to be paid at Whitsun. Condition, £20 to be paid on 20 September.

ccl.

[1597, September 1. Prerogative Court of Canterbury. Somerset House. 113 Cobbham.]

[Copy of the will of William Gardiner. In the margin of the first page of the will in the entry book is the note, "xv^{to} February 1598 lata est Sm̄a pro valore Codicilli dc̄i def."]

In the name of God Amen. The first day of September in the nine and thirtieth year of the reign of our Sovereign Lady Elizabeth by the grace of God Queen of England, France, and Ireland, Defender of the Faith, &c., I, William Gardiner of Bermondsey in the county of Surrey, esquire, being whole in mind and of perfect remembrance, thanks be unto God for the same, do make and ordain this my last will and testament in manner and form following, viz.: First I give and bequeath my soul to Almighty God, my maker, and to Jesus Christ, my only Saviour and Redeemer, and my body to the earth from whence it came, to be buried in the parish church of St. Mary Magdalen's in Bermondsey aforesaid, whereof I am a parishioner; And for the disposition of my goods, chattels, lands, tenements, possessions, and hereditaments wherewith it hath pleased God to bless me in this present life, I devise, give, and bequeath them in manner and form following, viz.: First I give unto my executors my mansion house wherein I now dwell, together with the use of all the furniture and household stuff used with and in the same, to have and to hold for the space of two months next after my decease; Item, I give unto my executors the Manor of Wardalls with the appurtenances in the county of Kent, and all those lands, tenements, and hereditaments heretofore by me conveyed unto the use of Christopher Gardiner my son, deceased, and my now mansion house wherein I now dwell, with

the gardens, backsides, and close with the same occupied after
the decease of my wife; And also all my Manor of Sandplace in
Dorking in the said county of Surrey, after the term of three
years next after my decease; And also all other my free lands,
tenements, and hereditaments hereafter in this my last will
willed and bequeathed unto Christofer Gardiner, the son of
Xρofer Gardiner my son, deceased (the interest of my wife for
term of her life by virtue of this my last will excepted and reserved); And also all my interest and leases of the Manor of
Bermondsey and Bermondsey Grange, in the county of Surrey,
and of Hatcham Barne Woods in the county of Kent; And also
the reversion of the Parsonage of Ewell with the appurtenances
in the county of Surrey after the death of Mistress Saunders,
widow; And also my interest and leases of certain tenements
called 'the White Horse and Wallnuttre' situate within the
parish of Saint Olave's in the borough of Southwark or elsewhere within the county of Surrey; And my interest and leases
of certain houses and gardens called 'the Ile of Duckes' in the
parish of Saint Olave's aforesaid, bought of one Fee, and my
interest and lease of a certain meadow or marsh ground lying
in Popler Marsh which I have from my Lord Wentworthe,
deceased, and my interest and lease of the brewhouse called
'Pickle heringe' in the parish of St. Olave's aforesaid, to have
and to hold the said manors, lands, tenements, and hereditaments, and all the leases and premises aforesaid with the appurtenances unto my said executors for and during the term
of twelve years next after my decease, for and towards the
payment of my debts and legacies, and performance of this my
present last will and testament; And my mind and will is that
if my said executors at any time before the end of the said
twelve years shall have levied, received, and gathered so much
money of the issues and clear yearly rents of the said manors,
lands, tenements, hereditaments, and leases as will amount
unto the full payment of all my debts and legacies in and by

this my present last will and testament given and bequeathed, and my said executors fully satisfied of all such sums of money as they have expended or laid out touching the execution of this my will, or in any sort been at, or charged withal, then I will, and my mind is, that the said manors, lands, tenements, hereditaments, and leases, and every of them, immediately after the said term of twelve years, or after so much money received and gathered as is aforesaid, shall severally remain as they be hereafter in this my present last will given, bequeathed, limited, or appointed. Item, I will and bequeath unto Margaret, now my wife, fourteen hundred pounds of lawful English money, to be paid unto her by my executors within two years next after my decease for and in consideration hereafter by this my last will expressed and declared. Item, I do bequeath unto the said Margaret my wife absolutely to her own use all such household stuff and plate now being at or within my now mansion house in Bermondsey aforesaid as were hers at the time of marriage between me and my said wife; And also I give and bequeath unto her the use and occupation only of all my other household stuff and plate whatsoever remaining in my said mansion house so long as she shall be a widow and keep herself unmarried. Item, I will and bequeath unto the said Margaret my wife, after the said two months as aforesaid, my mansion house aforesaid, with the gardens and backsides to the same belonging, and one close lying on the backside, now used by me with the said house, and all the tenements or houses over against the said mansion house whereof she now receiveth ⌐ e rents, and also all those my tenements or houses situate between the said mansion house and the tenement called 'the Maidenhed', to have and to hold the premises aforesaid with the appurtenances to her, the said Margaret, and her assigns, for and during the term of her natural life; provided always and upon condition that if she, the said Margaret my wife, shall at any time hereafter make any claim or title to any other

332

my lands, tenements, possessions, [or] hereditaments, or make claim to any other goods and chattels whatsoever by reason of her right of dower, jointure, joint purchase, thirds, or any other right or custom whatsoever other than to those gifts and bequeaths [bequests] to her before by this my present last will given, willed, or bequeathed, then I will that all the gifts, legacies, and bequeaths to her before given, willed, or bequeathed shall be utterly void and of none effect, and that she shall receive no benefit by the same; provided also that if the said Margaret my wife, upon reasonable request to be made unto her by my executors or any other unto whom by this my present last will and testament I shall will, devise, or bequeath any of my lands, tenements, possessions, hereditaments, leases, goods, and chattels whatsoever, shall refuse or do not in convenient time release, surrender, and give up to them and every of them (upon reasonable request to be made as aforesaid), at their costs and charges, all her right, title, and interest of dower, jointure, joint purchase, and thirds, and other her right whatsoever of, in, and to my said lands, tenements, possessions, hereditaments, leases, goods, and chattels (other than in and to those gifts, legacies, and bequests to her before by this my present last will and testament given, willed, or bequeathed), then I will that all the gifts, legacies, and bequests to her as aforesaid given, willed, or bequeathed, shall be utterly void and of none effect. Item, I will and bequeath unto Christofer Gardiner, the son of Christofer Gardiner my son, deceased, all such lands, tenements, and hereditaments as were conveyed by me unto Nicholas Fuller and others in trust to the use of the said Christofer Gardiner my son, and also my manor of Sandplace in Dorking in the county of Surrey with the appurtenances, to have and to hold the said manor, lands, tenements, and hereditaments with the appurtenances to him, the said Christopher Gardiner, and to the heirs males of his body lawfully begotten; and for default of such issue, to Thomas

Gardiner my son, and to the heirs males of his body lawfully begotten; and for default of such issue, to the use of William Gardiner my son, and to the heirs males of his body lawfully begotten; and for default of such issue, then to remain to the right heirs of me, the said William Gardiner, for ever. But my will and meaning is that during the minority of the said Christofer Gardiner, that my executors have the setting and letting, government and disposition of all such the legacies, bequests, and his inheritances, until he come unto the age of one and twenty years, and then to yield him a true account of all such profits, rents, and revenues only received by them to his use, taking their reasonable allowances for such charges as they shall be at about the same. Item, I will and bequeath unto Francis Gardiner, the daughter of the said Christofer Gardiner my son, deceased, five hundred pounds, to be paid unto her by my executors when she shall attain to the age of one and twenty years, or at the day of her marriage, which of them shall first happen, if she so long live. Item, I will and bequeath unto Judith Gardiner, late wife of Christofer Gardiner my son, deceased, until the said Christofer her son and Francis her daughter shall come unto the age of one and twenty years, thirty pounds yearly for five years next ensuing after my decease, and after those five years, forty pounds yearly until their age aforesaid, for and towards the education and bringing up of the said Christofer and Frauncis during their minority as aforesaid; and my will and mind is that if either of them should decease or that the said Frauncis should happen to marry before the said age, that the said sum and sums should remain for the education of such as were living and unmarried. Item, I will and bequeath unto William Gardiner, the son of Thomas Gardiner my son, all my lands, tenements, hereditaments, and woods with the appurtenances in Peckham and Camberwell in the said county of Surrey, and also all that my Manor of Wardalls with the appurtenances in Deptford in the county of Kent, and also all those woods called 'Caltons Woodes' with the appurtenances in the counties of Kent and Surrey, to have and to hold the said manors, lands, tenements, hereditaments, and woods with the appurtenances to the said William Gardiner and to the heirs males of his body lawfully begotten; and for default of such issue, to the use of such other issue male as the said Thomas Gardiner my son shall hereafter have of his body lawfully begotten, and to the heirs males of the body of such issue male (of my said son Thomas) lawfully begotten; and for default of such issue, to the use of Christofer Gardiner and to the heirs males of his body lawfully begotten; and for default of such issue, to the use of William Gardiner my son and the heirs males of his body lawfully begotten; and for default of such issue, to remain to the right heirs of me, the said William Gardiner, for ever. And further my will and mind is that if the said William Gardiner, son of the said Thomas Gardiner, die without issue male of his body, and he, the said Thomas Gardiner, surviving and having no other issue male then living, then I will and bequeath that all the premises bequeathed to William his son shall be unto the said Thomas Gardiner and to the heirs males of his body lawfully begotten; and for default of such issue, to the said Christofer Gardiner, and to the heirs males of his body lawfully begotten; and for default of such issue, to William Gardiner my son and to the heirs males of his body lawfully begotten; and for default of such issue, to the right heirs of me, the said William Gardiner, for ever. Item, I give and bequeath unto the said William Gardiner, son of Thomas Gardiner my son, after the end and expiration of such interest as aforesaid bequeathed unto my said executors for the performance of this, my last will and testament, the use and occupation of all my leases of the Manor of Bermondsey and Bermondsey Grange with the appurtenances, and of Hatcham Barne Woods in the county of Kent, and all the term of years in the same leases yet to come and unexpired (if the said William shall so long live); and if it fortune him, the said William Gardiner, to die before the term of years of the same leases unexpired, then I will and bequeath that all the use and occupation of the residue of the term of years in the said leases or any of them, shall remain and be to the use of the heirs males of the body of the said William Gardiner lawfully begotten for and during the residue of the years in the said leases that shall be unexpired at the time of the death of the said William Gardiner; and if he, the said William Gardiner, die without issue (the said term unexpired), then I will and bequeath the occupation and use thereof unto the said Thomas Gardiner, for and during his natural life; provided always, and my will and meaning is, that if Thomas Gardiner my son at any time become out of debt, or shall not owe or be indebted in any sum or sums in all amounting above one hundred pounds, then I will and bequeath that he, the said Thomas Gardiner my said son, shall first have, hold, and enjoy all and singular my said lands, tenements, hereditaments, and woods in Camberwell and Peckham, and also the said Manor of Wardalls with the appurtenances, and all those woods called 'Caltons Woodes' and all the leases and terms of years in the same, of the Manor of Bermondsey and Bermondsey Grange, and of Hatcham Barne Woods with the appurtenances, before willed and bequeathed to the said William Gardiner, to him the said Thomas, likewise after the term of twelve years before given to my executors; and after his decease, to remain to the heirs males of his body lawfully begotten, with remainders over as is before limited and appointed; provided always, and my mind is, that Stephen Maineford shall have a lease of a tenement and certain lands, parcel of my said lands and tenements in Peckham and Camberwell, late in the tenure of one William Plogge, deceased, for and during the term of one and twenty years from and after the feast of St. Michael next after my decease, yielding and paying therefore yearly twenty

336

pounds, at the four most usual feasts in the year by even portions, unto them who by force of this my last will and testament otherwise shall have estate of the same tenement and lands. Item, I will and bequeath unto Margarett Gardiner, Frauncis, and Catherin Gardiner, three of the daughters of the said Thomas Gardiner my son, to each of them five hundred marks, to be paid by my executors unto the said Thomas Gardiner their father, to be by him kept and employed to the best use of his said daughters until they shall attain unto the age of one and twenty years, or until the day of their marriage, which shall happen first, and then to be paid unto them as they shall severally attain to the age aforesaid or as they shall be married as aforesaid; and if any of the daughters of my son Thomas shall die before she or they shall have their portions due and payable, then I will that their portions be equally divided amongst the sister or sisters of them surviving. Item, I will and bequeath unto William Gardiner my son, over and besides all such lands, tenements, and leases before by me assured unto him in marriage with Mr. Serjeant Yelverton's daughter, being part in possession and part in reversion after my decease, these parcels following, viz.: the reversion of the Parsonage of Ewell with the appurtenances in the county of Surrey, and a water-mill there when it happeneth, to have and to hold the said Parsonage of Ewell with the appurtenances and the mill unto the said William Gardiner and to his heirs for ever; and also I give and bequeath to my said son William Gardiner one hundred pounds towards the renewing of a lease of certain tenements and grounds in Rederith in the county of Surrey, which I have already assured unto him. Item, I will and bequeath unto the said William Gardiner my son, after such interest expired as aforesaid made unto my executors, my interest and leases of certain tenements called 'the White Horse' and 'the Wallnuttree', situate within the parish of St. Olave's in the borough of Southwark in the county of Surrey, and also my interest and lease of certain woods in Kent which I lately bought of one John Johnson, and also my interest and lease of the 'Ile of Duckes', bought of one Fee, and all the terms of years in the foresaid several leases contained yet to come and unexpired; provided also, and my will is, that if Edward Fowle, his executors or assigns, do pay to my said executors within [blank] next after my decease the sum of [blank] That then also the bequest before made to my executors and my said son William of my lease and interest of 'the Wallnuttree' in Southwark shall be likewise utterly void, and that then I will that my said executors shall assign to the said Edward Fowle, his executors and assigns, the lease of the same 'Wallnuttree', and my meaning is, that the money that is to be paid by the same Edward Fowle, my executors to have it towards the payment of my debts and performance of the legacies in this my will. Item, I will and bequeath unto Anne Perrot, my daughter, my manor or capital messuage called Sandplace in Dorking with the appurtenances in the county of Surrey, to her during the term of three years next following after my decease. Item, I will and bequeath unto the said Anne Perot, my daughter, four hundred pounds. Item, I will and bequeath unto Dorothie Perot, daughter of the said Anne, three hundred pounds, to be paid at her day of marriage or at some other convenient time. Item, I will and bequeath unto every of the other children of the said Anne Perot my daughter, one hundred pounds apiece, viz.: to William Perott one hundred pounds, to Frauncis Perot one hundred pounds, to Ursula Perot one hundred pounds, and to Symon Perot one hundred pounds, to be paid unto the said Anne Perot my daughter, to be employed to the best use of her said children until they shall severally attain to their ages of one and twenty years, or until the day of the marriage of the said daughters, which of them shall first happen; and if any of my daughter's children aforesaid do chance to die before their portions shall be due as aforesaid, then I will and my mind is

338

that his and their portions so deceasing shall be equally divided amongst the rest of the children of the said Anne then surviving at the time when his or their portions so deceasing should have been due and payable. Item, I will and bequeath unto my executors all recognizances, statutes, bonds, and writings entered into, acknowledged, and made unto me or any other to my use by Symon Perot, gentleman, deceased. And my will and mind is that they, my said executors, shall receive and take the benefit thereof to the only use of the said Anne Perot my daughter, and that they shall pay unto the said Anne Perot all such money or other profit as shall be recovered, levied, or received by virtue of the said recognizances, statutes, bonds, and writings, or any of them. Item, I will and bequeath unto Katherin Smith my daughter, now wife of Nicholas Smith, esquire, to the use of her during her life and of the children of the said Nicholas and Catherin after her decease (if any of the years of these leases following shall be unexpired), all that lease and term of years in the same of all those tenements, houses, and lands with the appurtenances in Bermondsey Street or elsewhere which I have made unto me from the President and Fellows of Magdalen College in Oxford, and also one lease and term of years in the same unexpired of all the marsh lands or meadows lying in Popler Marsh, which I have from my Lord Wentworthe. Item, I will and bequeath unto John Stipkin, Christofer Smithe, William Smithe, John Smithe, and Francis Smithe, the sons and daughter of the said Catherin my daughter, six hundred pounds, viz.: to each of her said sons one hundred pounds apiece, and two hundred pounds to her daughter Fraunces, to be paid unto the said Catherin my daughter to the use of her said sons and daughter to employ every of their portions for them until her said sons shall severally attain unto their age of one and twenty years, and her said daughter unto the age of one and twenty years or the day of her marriage, which shall first happen; and if any of the said children of my daughter Catherin shall die before their portions be due, then I will that his and their portions shall be equally divided amongst such of the children of my daughter Catherin which she now hath by the said Nicholas Smithe as shall be then surviving at the time when his or their portions so deceasing should have been due and payable. Item, I will and bequeath unto William Waite, John Waite, Richard Waite, and Margaret Wayte, sons and daughters of William Waite the elder, one hundred and threescore pounds between them, viz.: to every of them forty pounds apiece, to be paid unto the said sons as they shall attain unto the age of one and twenty years, and to the said daughter at her age of one and twenty years or at the day of her marriage, which shall first happen; and if any of the said children of the said William Wayte shall die before his or their portion shall be due, then I will that his or their portions so deceasing shall be equally divided amongst the rest of the children of the said William Waite the elder surviving. Item, I will and bequeath unto Margarett Atkinson, the daughter of [blank] Atkinson my niece, thirty pounds, to be paid unto her when she shall attain unto the age of one and twenty years, or the day of her marriage, which shall first happen. Item, I will and bequeath unto Frissell Banckes, the daughter of Elizabeth Banckes, my niece, thirty pounds, to be paid unto her at the age of one and twenty years or at the day of her marriage, which shall first happen. Item, I will and bequeath unto the right honourable Sir John Fortescue, knight, Chancellor of the Queen's Majesty's Exchequer, and one of Her Highness' most honourable Privy Council, twenty pounds and my stoned horse. Item, I will and bequeath unto Sir Edmond Anderson, knight, Lord Chief Justice of Her Majesty's Court of Common Pleas, twenty pounds and my bay trotting gelding. Item, I will and bequeath unto John Jefferson twenty marks. Item, I will and my mind is that the said John Jefferson shall have a lease in reversion for one and twenty years of the house wherein he now dwelleth, and also a lease in reversion of 'Dove-house Meade' for one and thirty years at such rent as they be now letten, after the expiration of such interest and term as yet are unexpired. Item, I will and bequeath unto Titus Morris of the city of Norwich, my very good friend, thirteen pounds, six shillings, eight pence. Item, I will and bequeath unto Gods-call, merchant of London, three pounds. Item, I will and bequeath unto the poor people of the parish of Saint Thomas in Southwark, three pounds, six shillings, eight pence. Item, I will and bequeath unto the poor of the parish of Saint Saviour's in Southwark, five pounds. Item, I will and bequeath unto the prisoners in the Compter in Southwark, forty shillings. Item, to the poor in the Hospitals of Christ Church in London and Saint Thomas in Southwark, twenty pounds, viz. to either of them, ten pounds. Item, to the prisoners in the White Lion, the Marshalsey, and King's Bench in Southwark, fifteen pounds, viz. to each of them prisons [sic], five pounds. Item, I will and bequeath unto Mr. Steere, minister of the parish of Saint Mary Magdalen's in Bermondsey, forty shillings or a ring of that value. Item, I will and bequeath unto the churchwardens of the parish church of Saint Mary Magdalen's aforesaid, to buy therewith a Communion cup to be used in the said church, six pounds, thirteen shillings, four pence. Item, I will and bequeath unto the poor of the said parish of Saint Mary Magdalen's, ten pounds, to be distributed amongst them by my executors presently after my decease. Item, I will and bequeath unto the poor people of the said parish of Saint Mary Magdalen's for ever, ten pounds yearly to be issuing, levied, perceived, and taken, and yearly to be paid out of all my houses situate in Bermondsey Street, built upon the causey there. Item, I will and bequeath unto Abraham Loadinge, five pounds. Item, I will and bequeath unto Edward Wilson, forty shillings. Item, I will and bequeath unto Edward Gateward, forty shillings. Item, I will and bequeath unto Richard Rider, clerk, five pounds. Item, I will and bequeath unto Nicholas Chalkeley, six pounds, thirteen shillings, four pence, and George Rooper, my servant, forty shillings. Item, unto Marie, my maidservant, six pounds, thirteen shillings, four pence. Item, to Isabell, my other maidservant, forty shillings. Item, I will and bequeath unto William Hall, sometime my servant, six pounds, thirteen shillings, four pence. Item, I will and bequeath unto Edward Brasier, servant unto Thomas Gardiner my son, forty shillings. Item, I will and bequeath unto John Luce, my brother-in-law, six pounds, thirteen shillings, four pence. Item, I will and bequeath unto Christofer Gardiner, the son of Xρofer Gardiner my son, deceased, all the residue of my fee simple lands, tenements, and hereditaments whatsoever in this my present last will and testament before not willed and bequeathed, to have and to hold the same to him the said Christofer Gardiner and to the heirs males of his body lawfully begotten; and for default of such issue, to the use of Thomas Gardiner my son and the heirs males of his body lawfully begotten; and for default of such issue, to the use of William Gardiner my son, and of the heirs males of his body lawfully begotten; and for default of such issue, to remain to the right heirs of me, the said William Gardiner, for ever; provided always, and my intent and meaning is, that if the said Christofer Gardiner or his heirs or Judith Gardiner his mother, or any other for them, or any of them to their use by their privity, assent, or appointment, shall at any time hereafter go about to impeach, recover, or get the possession of any the lands, tenements, and hereditaments, or any part thereof, that were heretofore conveyed by me unto the use of Christofer Gardiner, my son deceased, as aforesaid, by force of any assurance or conveyance heretofore made to the said Christofer contrary to the intent and meaning of this my last will and testament, then I will that my bequest of my fee simple lands, tenements, and hereditaments aforesaid, and also the bequest of my manor of Sandplace in Dorking with the appurtenances before in this my last will and testament willed and bequeathed unto the said Xρofer Gardiner, son of Christofer Gardiner my son, deceased, and all other bequests or legacies before in this my last will willed and bequeathed unto the said Xρofer, Judith, and to Francis Gardiner her daughter, shall be utterly void and of none effect. And then I will that the said lands, tenements, and hereditaments, and my said manor of Sandplace in Dorking with the appurtenances, to him the said Christofer before given and bequeathed, shall remain and be to my executors and their heirs, to be sold by them to the best proof towards the payment of my debts and legacies and performance of this my last will and testament. And my mind and will is, and I do by these presents bequeath unto my said executors after the performance of this my last will and testament, that my said executors shall have all such lands, tenements, and hereditaments bequeathed unto the said Xρofer during his minority, yielding an account for the same at the full age of the said Xρofer, deducting unto them all such reasonable charges and expenses whatsoever that they shall or have expended about the same; provided always, and my mind, will, and meaning is, that Kellem Hedley and [blank] Gardiner, my tenants, and their two wives shall not be put forth of the tenements wherein they now dwell during their natural lives, paying the rent they now pay for the same. All the residue of my goods movable and immovable, chattels, household stuff, plate, implements, and jewels whatsoever, excepting two gold chains given unto my two sons Thomas and William, of what nature and kind soever they be of, in this my present testament and last will not willed or bequeathed, I wholly give and bequeath them unto my executors; and I do ordain, make, and appoint William Gardiner my son and Nicholas Smithe, esquire, my son-in-law, executors of this my last will and testament, charging them as they will answer before God to see this my last will and testament performed and executed according to the true intent and meaning thereof, as I hope they will according to the trust and confidence I repose in them; and that they see my funerals performed, and my body decently to be brought unto the ground as fitteth one of my degree and calling; provided always, that if any of mine executors, without the assent of the rest of the executors, or else without the assent of one of them, together with the assent of the said right honourable Sir John Fortescue, shall do or cause to be done any act or acts, thing, or things, touching any of my goods, money, chattels, or debts, by force of his executorship, amounting to the value of five pounds or more, that then he so doing shall be, and shall be adjudged to be, from the beginning, none of my executor, nor shall receive any benefit or advantage of any legacy given to him with the rest of the executors as executors or in the name of executors, any thing before to the contrary in any wise notwithstanding; and that all controversies arising between my executors or any other concerning this my said will, shall be ordered by the said Sir John Fortescue and Sir Edmond Anderson. In witness whereof, to this my present testament and last will, I, the said William Gardiner, have set my hand and seal the six and twentieth day of September in the nine and thirtieth year of the reign of our most gracious Sovereign Lady, Queen Elizabeth, Annoque Domini 1597. This will was sealed and published by the above named William Gardiner the testator the day and year last above mentioned in the presence of us Nicholas Fuller, Nicholas Chalkeley, George Bacon, George Rooper.

[Codicil.]

Whereas by my last will and testament in writing, dated the first day of this instant month of September, amongst other things in the legacies therein willed or bequeathed to my wife, I have added two provisos or conditions to the same legacies which are thought very strait and dangerous, therefore I will that the same provisos and conditions be both void and of no

344

force; and that my said wife shall have the legacies therein to her bequeathed in such manner as the same are therein to her bequeathed, upon these conditions following and not upon any other condition, that is to say, that if she shall arrest, sue, implead, or cause to be arrested, sued, or impleaded, mine executors or any of them, or any claiming under them, or mine heir, or any claiming by, from, or under mine estate, for any money, goods, chattels, lands, or tenements, upon any title, right, or interest derived from me or by her intermarriage with me, other than for the money, goods, chattels, lands, and tenements, or any of them, devised or bequeathed to her by my said last will and testament, or if she shall refuse to make such release or releases, surrender or surrenders, to my heirs, executors, or assigns, of all and every my goods, chattels, lands, and tenements, or of any part thereof (other than of such as are devised unto her by my said will), as the Lord Chief Justice of the Common Pleas at Westminster for the time being shall think meet to be made unto them and every or any of them, and shall subscribe his name thereunto in testimony of his assent or liking thereof, or if that she do not within six days next after notice to her given thereof and the said release or surrender to her tendered, duly and lawfully seal and deliver the same as her deed or deeds, then and from thenceforth the legacies to her given, bequeathed, limited, or appointed by my said will shall be void and of no force, any thing therein to the contrary in any wise notwithstanding. And where I have by my said will devised to Christofer Gardiner my son's son, and to the heirs males of his body lawfully begotten, with divers remainders over, the manor of Sandplace in Dorking in the county of Surrey, which manor with the appurtenances before in my said will I have bequeathed to my said executors amongst other things for twelve years for the payment of my debts and performance of my will, so as some contrariety appeareth which may breed controversy hereafter, therefore I do by this

345

Codicil annexed to my will as part thereof declare, will, and devise, touching the said manor of Sandplace with the appurtenances, that Anne Perrot my daughter shall have the same for and during the term of three years next after my decease, and that after the said three years expired, mine executors shall have the same manor of Sandplace with the appurtenances for and during nine years, residue of the said twelve years, for the payment of my debts and legacies, if in the mean time the same be not fully paid or satisfied, as in my will I have expressed; and that after those estates, interests, or terms ended, then to remain to the said Christofer Gardiner, my son's son, and to the heirs males of his body lawfully begotten, with the remainders over in such sort as in my said will is declared. And I do likewise declare, will, and devise that the legacies by me made of the manor of Wardalls, the lands in Poplar Marsh and of any other thing or things which I have in the former part of my will devised to mine executors for twelve years as above, and after I have devised to any other person or persons or in any other manner, that the same latter legacies thereof shall take place after the former legacies for twelve years executed and performed and not before (for such was my meaning from the beginning), any thing to the contrary in any wise notwithstanding. And whereas I have given and bequeathed to the poor people of the parish of Saint Mary Magdalen's in Southwark for ever, ten pounds yearly to be issuing out of my houses situate in Bermondsey Street, built upon the causey there, for that I am informed the same legacy is not good in law to continue for ever according to my intent, therefore I do revoke and make void the same legacy, and do by these presents will and devise to William Gardiner and Nicholas Smith, whom I have made mine executors, and to [blank] and to their heirs and assigns for ever, one annual or yearly rent of ten pounds, to be issuing and going out of all my said houses and tenements situate in Bermondsey Street aforesaid,

built upon the causey there, to be paid half-yearly at the feasts of the Annunciation of the Virgin Mary and Saint Michael the Archangel by equal portions, to the intent that the poor inhabitants of the said parish of Saint Mary Magdalen's in Southwark may be relieved therewith. And I do further will and devise that if any default of payment be made of the said rent or of any part thereof at any time or times when it ought to be paid, that then and from thenceforth it shall be lawful for those to whom it is devised as above, their heirs and assigns and every of them, to enter into the said tenements or into any part or parts thereof, and there to distrain for the said rent and arrearages thereof, if any shall be, and the distress or distresses to withhold until satisfaction be made of the said rent and arrearages thereof; and mine hope and desire is that if all the said feoffees save one shall decease, that then the one surviving feoffee shall make a new grant or assignment to others of the same parish and to their heirs and assigns of the said yearly rent, to the intent to continue the payment of the same rent, the better for the good of the poor of the said parish forever. In witness whereof, I, the said William Gardiner to this present Codicil annexed to my will have set my hand and seal the seven and twentieth day of September in the nine and thirtieth year of the reign of our Sovereign Lady, Queen Elizabeth, and in the year of our Lord God One Thousand Five Hundred Ninety Seven. Witnesses hereunto, Nicholas Fuller, Nicholas Chalkeley, George Bacon, George Rooper. Memorandum that the name of Thomas Gardiner was rased and blot out by me William Gardiner, esquire, in the presence of us, Griff: Steuens, Cornelius Tise his mark, George Rooper.
Probatum fuit Testamentum suprascriptum apud London coram venerabili viro Magistro Willielmo Lewyn legum doctore Curie Prerogatiue Cantuariensis Magistro Custode siue Commissario legitime constituto: Octauo die mensis Decembris Anno Domini Millesimo Quingentesimo Nonagesimo Septimo:

Juramento Thome Browne notarij publicj procuratoris Wil-
lielmi Gardiner filij dicti defuncti et Nicholai Smithe armigeri
Executorum in huiusmodi testamento nominatorum Quibus
commissa fuit administratio bonorum Jurium et creditorum
eiusdem defuncti De bene et fideliter administrandorum &c.,
Ad sancta Dei Evangelia Jurat'.
[Marginal Note:]

Duodecimo die mensis Aprilis Anno Domini 1605 probatum fuit huiusmodi testamentum cum codicillo eiusdem defuncti annexato Et commissa fuit administratio &c. Domino
Thomæ Gardner filio naturali et legitimo dicti defuncti et exe-
cutori &c., vt in libro actorum de approbacionibus testamen-
torum plenius liquet et apparet.

ccli.

[1597, December 22. College of Arms, Funeral Certificates,
I. 16, f.7.]

22 Decem. 1597.

WILLIAM GARDYNER of Barmescy in the County of
Surrey, Esquire, married to his first wife Frances, daughter to
Robert Lucy of London, gent., and had by her issue 3 sons
and 2 daughters viz.:
Christopher Gardyner his son and heir, who married Judeth
daughter and heir of Tho: Sackville of Chedingle in the County
of Sussex, Esquire, by whom he had issue Christopher his son
and heir, now about the age of three quarters, and Frances a
daughter about the age of 2 years, their father being deceased;
Thomas Gardyner second son, married Frances, the eldest
daughter of Ralf Skypworth of Parkbury in the County of
Hartford, gent., by whom he had issue 3 sons and 3 daughters,
viz.: Willm. that died young and Willm. now living about the
age of 8 years, Richard died young, Margaret first daughter
about 9 years old, Frances second daughter aged 5, and
Katheryne third daughter about a year old;

William Gardyner third son, married Mary daughter of Christopher Yelverton of Easton-Malditt in the County of Northampton, Serjeant at Law (and now Speaker of the Parliament), by whom he hath as yet no issue;

Katherine Gardyner eldest daughter, married to her first husband Jhon Stepkyn dwelling in St. Katherine's near London, and had by him issue one son named Jhon about 14 years of age. And after the said Katherine married to her second husband Nicholas Smyth of Westminster in the County of Middlesex, Esquire, by whom she hath issue 3 sons and one daughter, viz.: Christopher Smyth about the age of 11 years, Willm aged 8, Jhon aged 4, and Frances their daughter aged 3.

Anne Gardyner the youngest daughter, married Symon Perott of Sutton-Cofield in the County of Warwick, gent., by whom she hath issue 2 sons and 3 daughters (. . . now widow), viz.: Willm Perott about the age of 8 years, Symon aged 3, Dorothy 13, Frances 11, and Ursula 7.

After the said Willm Gardyner Esquire married to his second wife Margaret, daughter of [blank] Lucas of the City of Gloucester, by whom he had no issue.

The said W^m. Gardyner being of the age of three score years and six departed this transitory life at his house at Barmescy Street in the County of Surrey aforesaid, on Saturday the 26th of November 1597, from whence he was very worshipfully accompanied unto the parish church of Barmescy on Thursday the 22th of December following. The preacher was Doctor Mountfort. The pennon of his arms was borne by W^m. Wayt his kinsman. The helm and crest by Tho: Lant, Windsor Herald. The coat of arms by W^m. Camden, Clarenceux King of Arms, who directed the said funeral. The body borne by six of his own servants. The chief mourner Tho: Gardyner his second son. The two assistants W^m. Gardyner third son and Nicholas Smyth aforesaid, being executors to the defunct of his last will and testament. And in witness that this Certificate is true in all points, we whose names are underwritten have hereunto set our hands the day, month, and year above specified.

Subscribed by { William Gardyner
Nicholas Smyth

Willm Camden, Clarenceux
T. Lant, Windsor.

cclii.

[No date. Probably late Elizabeth or early James. Collections made by Archbishop Ussher. Rawlinson MS. 849, ff. 304^v, 305. That this amusing passage refers to Justice Gardiner of Bermondsey is not certain, but it seems very likely to me.]

AN ANSWER TO MR. TRYSTRAME GAWEN HIS CHALLENGE

The title of the challenge.

That the religion which we profess is no new religion or profession; but if any be new, the Romish Church hath the novelties & not we.

The answer.

Such as know you, Mr. Trystrame, & your employments, do assure me you had this challenge of some minister whom I take to be a Puritan; for the church of England alloweth of fasts & feasts kept in honour of Saints, a thing his stomach brooketh not, as you may gather out of his seventh paragraph; and as for this comparison, I report myself to the late Justice Gardiner, who was wont to say that if the Pope was Antichrist, he was an *old* Antichrist; whereas the Puritans had their beginning from John Calvyn, who lived but the other day; a man infamous for his life, & by law to be burned, had not his bishop & magistrate dealt mercifully with him, as you may read in your countryman Mr. Doctor Stapleton's book entitled *Promptuarium Catholicum.*

WAYTE DOCUMENTS

EDMUND WAYTE

1545/6. Fourth Warden of the Leathersellers' Company. *History . . of Leathersellers of London.* [W. H. Black, (1871), 64.]

1552/3. Second Warden of the same. [Black, *ibid.*]

1552, 14 Sept. His wife Elizabeth buried at Bermondsey. [*Genealogist*, vi, app., 19.]

1553, 20 Oct. Ordered to repair pavement before his tenements in Southwark. [Guildhall, Southwark Courts Leet.]

1554, 18 Oct. Fined 3*s.* 4*d.* for not mending pavement before his tenements on the 'causeye', and ordered to do it. [*Ibid.*]

1555, 6 March. "Item, Edmond Wayte holdeth 7 tenements together late belonging unto Saint George's Church, and payeth yearly for quitrent, 5*s.* . . . . Saint George's Field: Whereof Edmond Wayte claimeth an acre." [*Ibid.*]

1555/6. First Warden of the Leathersellers. [Black, *ibid.*]

1556, 6 Aug. Acknowledged that he owed William Sutton £250, conditioned on the payment of £200 by 12 March next. [Close Roll, 3 & 4 Ph. & Mary. C54/527/18.]

1557, 6 Dec. Buried at Bermondsey. [*Genealogist*, vi, app., 27.]

1558, 24 Oct. Manor of Southwark. Jurors present that Edmund Wayte, a free tenant within the manor, has died since the last Court, and that his son [blank] Wayte, aged 14 or more, is next heir. The heir's hereditaments remain in the hands of his mother, now wife of William Gardener, gentleman, during his nonage, to be applied to his use. [Guildhall, Southwark Courts Leet.]

WILLIAM WAYTE

[?1579, ?1589, 5 Mar.] "William Waight, late citizen and leatherseller of London, son and heir of Edward [*sic*]

Waight, late citizen and also leatherseller of London, deceased," on 5 Mar. 21 [?31] Eliz., leased a house in Bermondsey to John Jefferson for 40 years at a yearly rent of £3. [Chancery Proc., Jas. I. R13/32. Robinson *v.* Pitham, February 1616/7.]

1579/80, Hilary. Between William Gardner, querent, and William Wayte and Joan his wife, deforciants, of 3 messuages, 3 gardens, and 20 acres of pasture in the parishes of St. Mary Magdalen's, Bermondsey, and St. George's, Southwark. Warranted by William and Joan for themselves and the heirs of William to William Gardner and his heirs forever for £220. [Feet of Fines. C.P. 25/Surr. H. 22 Eliz.]

1584, Trinity. Emanuel Cole sued William Waight of London, leatherseller, for debts of £40 and £6, owing on bonds made respectively 13 March and 22 April, 23 Eliz. (1581). [Common Pleas. C.P. 40/1429/1256.]

1589/90, 27 Jan. "Robert Mott. Vicesimo septimo die mensis emanavit Commissio Willelmo Waite nuper marito Joanne Wayte dum vixit proxima consanguinea Roberti Mott nuper de Lambeth in Comitatu Surrey defuncti . . . Ad administrand' bona jura et credita eiusdem Roberti de bene &c. . ." [Prerog. Ct. Canterbury, Admon., 1587–1591, 127.]

1594, Michaelmas. Francis Whyte craves sureties of the peace against John Turner, William Wayghte, Kenelm Hedley, and Elizabeth Roberts, for fear of death, etc. Writ of attachment issued to the sheriff of Surrey, returnable 3 February 1594/5. [Queen's Bench Controlment Roll. K.B. 29/232. William Gardiner was sheriff of Surrey at this time; Kenelm (Kellam) Hedley was a tenant of his, and is mentioned in his will.]

1598, 24 May. Henry Alison, Gardiner's scrivener, deposed on this date in Chancery as follows: "That he remembreth that he was present when one William Wayte, servant to the said William Gardiner, by his master's appointment paid unto one of Sir Nicholas Woodruff's servants, to the use of Sir Nicholas, the sum of £200..." [Chancery Town Depositions. C24/262/62.]

1600, Trinity. In Easter term, Frances Gardiner, a minor, by her guardians John Harborne and John Lloyd, charged William Wayte with wrongfully pasturing cattle on 3 acres of her land at Bermondsey. [Queen's Bench. K.B. 27/1362/1127.]

1602, 26 March. In Chancery, Brooke v. Smyth. Deposition of William Wayte, of St. Mary Magdalen's in Bermondsey, leatherseller, of the age of 47 years or thereabouts. [Chancery Town Depositions. C24/294 pt. 1/5.]

1602, 19 April. In Chancery, Gardiner v. Saunders. Deposition of William Wayte, described as above. [C24/294 pt. 1/30.]

1602, 16 November. Decree in Chancery, Gardner v. Wayte. *Decretum inter Gardner et Wayte.* Where William Gardner of Langham in the county of Surrey, esquire, heretofore exhibited his bill of complaint into this most high court of Chancery against William Wayte of Barmondsey, gentleman, for and concerning the right, title, and interest of and to the rectory and parsonage of Ewell in the said county of Surrey, and of one water-mill, called or known by the name of the Nether Mill, and of two closes and of other lands, tenements, and hereditaments with their appurtenances in Ewell aforesaid, contracted and agreed on by William Gardiner, late of Bermondsey in the said county, deceased, father of the complainant, in his lifetime with Henry Saunders of London, gentleman, and Nicholas Saunders of Ewell aforesaid, gentleman, for the sum of £600 paid unto them by the said William the father, who appointed and caused the assurance and conveyance of the premises to be made in the names of the said William the son and the said defendant Wayte, whereby the said Henry and Nicholas

Saunders did grant, bargain, and sell the premises to the complainant and defendant as persons in trust by the said William the father to the only use and behoof of the said complainant and defendant in fee simple; the said complainant by his said bill further declaring that although the said William the father always intended that the ordering and disposition of the premises should be at his own appointment (albeit the conveyance was made as is aforesaid), and manifested the same sundry times before credible witnesses, that the said complainant and defendant were but persons trusted to his use, and did before his death by his last will and testament dispose and bequeath the premises to the complainant and his heirs, yet the said defendant Wayte, finding himself joined with the complainant in the said indenture whereby the premises were conveyed, did give forth speeches that he would have and keep the moiety of the premises to his own use, and denied to convey and assure his interest therein to the complainant, contrary to the intent and meaning of the said William Gardiner deceased, and contrary to all right, as by the said bill remaining of record in this Court more at large appeareth; and whereas the said defendant Wayte made three several answers to the said bill, and did thereby confess that the said William Gardiner the father did purchase by deed of bargain and sale enrolled in this Court the said rectory in the name of the said complainant and defendant, and denied that he ever knew of any trust touching the said purchase or of any trust of conveying the said premises at the disposition of the said Willian Gardiner, but referred himself therein to such proofs as the complainant should make thereof, as by the said several answers remaining of record likewise in this Court more at large appeareth; and whereas the said complainant thereunto replied, and the parties thereupon being at a full and perfect issue, witnesses were examined thereupon in this Court; and publication being thereof granted, a day for the hearing, ordering, and adjudging the said cause in question was by this Court appointed; at which day, forasmuch as upon the entering into the hearing of the matter in the presence of the counsel learned on both parts for and touching the parsonage of Ewell aforesaid with the mill and other lands in the bill mentioned, it appeared unto this Court, by an order made the first of June last upon the hearing of the matter upon a bill wherein the said Wayte was then complainant against the said Gardiner now plaintiff, demanding amongst other things the moiety of the said parsonage, mill, and lands, that upon the hearing of that cause this Court was then satisfied by proofs then read upon the said Wayte's own bill that the said parsonage, mill, and lands were purchased by the father of the said William Gardiner, though the assurance thereof was taken in trust in the names of the said now plaintiff and defendant, and that all the money which was paid for the same was paid by the plaintiff's said father, and that he by his will devised the same to the plaintiff and his heirs, and that yet nevertheless, for that the said Wayte's counsel then supposed that he could make better proof to the contrary upon the now plaintiff's bill, whereupon no publication was then had, the said Wayte had then liberty to examine what witnesses he would touching the said matter of trust; but with this, that if upon the further hearing of the cause upon the now plaintiff's bill the matter should fall out against the said Wayte, then he should pay unto the now plaintiff good costs for that delay; and for that the said Wayte's counsel did then allege that the said Wayte had not since that time examined any other witnesses touching this cause than before were examined, and submitted the ordering of the cause to this Court in discharge or excuse of the payment of the said costs, whereupon this Court did discharge the said defendant of any such costs, it is therefore, this present term of St. Michael, that is to say on Tuesday [16 November 44 Eliz. (1602)], by the right honourable Sir Thomas

Egerton, knight, Lord Keeper of the Great Seal of England
and the Court of Chancery, ordered, adjudged, and decreed
that the said plaintiff, his heirs and assigns, shall and may
from henceforth have, hold, and quietly enjoy the said parsonage, mill, and lands without let, suit, or interruption of the
defendant or any claiming from, by, or under him or by his
means or procurement, according to the plaintiff's title made
by his bill; and it is also by the said Lord Keeper and Court of
Chancery ordered, adjudged, and decreed that the said defendant shall at the costs and charges of the plaintiff make such
conveyance and assurance thereof to the plaintiff and his heirs
as his counsel shall devise, discharged of all encumbrances
done by him the said defendant. [Chancery Decree Rolls.
C78/102/16.]

JUSTICE GARDINER'S SONS

Christopher Gardiner

1582. Christopher Gardiner of the Inner Temple, London,
gentleman, jointly bound with another in £50 to John
Barnarde. [Close Roll, 24 Eliz. C54/1144.]

1583, 17 Dec. Bound in £400 to John Duncombe of Moreton,
Bucks, esquire.

1584, Michaelmas. Judgment of £61, debt and damages,
awarded against him at suit of William Browne, citizen
and mercer of London. [Queen's Bench. K.B. 27/1291/206.]

1585/6, Hilary. In prison for debts owing to Henry Bannester
and others amounting to £313:13:4. [Queen's Bench. K.B.
27/1296/295.]

1591. John Fleette of the Inner Temple, gentleman, against
Elizabeth Springe. Suit to stay an action on a bond at
the common Law. Plaintiff was jointly bound with Chris-
topher Gardiner for the latter's debt to John Springe of
London, deceased, defendant's late husband. [Requests
Proc. 206/28.]

1596, Michaelmas. Between Nicholas Smyth, esquire, and William Waight, querents, and Christopher Gardener, gentleman, and Judith his wife, deforciants, of 8 messuages, 4 gardens, and 42 acres of land in Bermondsey, Redrith, and Camberwell, warranted against the deforciants and the heirs of Christopher for £160. [Common Pleas. Notes of Fines, Surrey.]

THOMAS GARDINER

1599, 27 July. Thomas Gardyner of Peckham, Surrey, gentleman, and Frances his wife, for £240 sold to Thomas Gryme of London, skinner, and Joan his wife, tenements in Water Lambeth and Lambeth, Surrey. [Close Roll. C54/1636.]

1605/6, 6 February. James Buddowe, one of his Majesty's footmen, against Sir Thomas Gardiner and two other newly-created knights. For himself and other footmen and porters, Buddowe sues for the customary fees which Gardiner and the other defendants, "of a stubborn and wilful resoltion", have refused to pay. [Chancery Proc. James I. C2 Jas. I/B33/12.]

1612, 10 November. David de Marteleyre et al. against Sir Thomas Gardiner et al. Concerning Bermondsey Grange and land used for whiting linen cloth. [Chancery Proc. James I. C2 Jas. I/M22/4.]

WILLIAM GARDINER

1597/8, 4 February. Charles Howard, esquire, and Charitie his wife, late wife of Richard Leech, esquire, against William Gardiner and Nicholas Smith. To recover an annuity of £50. [Chancery Proc., Eliz. C2 Eliz./H9/59.] Depositions in this suit. [Town Deps., Chanc. C24/262/62.]

1598, Easter. William Gardiner, gentleman, and Nicholas Smith, gentleman, against Luke Lanckford et al. Concerning St. Saviour's Grange, Bermondsey. [Exchequer Bills and Answers. E112/Eliz./Surrey 70.]

1598, 12 May. George Maxy of Southukenden, Essex, gentleman, against William Gardiner, gentleman, and Mary his wife. Concerning Lagham Park, Godstone, Surrey, demised by defendants to plaintiff. To protect plaintiff's title by lease. [Chancery Proc., Eliz. C2 Eliz./M3/21.]

1598, Easter. Surrey. Christopher Yelverton, serjeant at law, and Henry Yelverton, esquire, demandants, against William Gardener, esquire, and Mary his wife. The manor of Lagham *alias* Langham Park: 6 messuages, 1 dovecote, 6 gardens, 700 acres of land, etc., in Godstone, Wolkensted, Tandridge, and Crowhurst. [Recovery Rolls. C.P. 43/Easter 40 Eliz./Surrey.]

1598, Easter. Surrey. The same demandants against William Gardener, esquire. 60 messuages, 20 gardens, and 3 acres of pasture in the parish of St. Mary Magdalen, Southwark. [*Ibid.*]

1599, 20 October. Robert Smyth of Bromley, Middlesex, esquire, against William Gardyner et al. The 'James' brewhouse and other tenements in Bermondsey Street. Relief against bond for performance of covenants in deed of bargain and sale. [Chancery Proc., Eliz. C2 Eliz./S18/40.]

1599, Michaelmas. William Gardyner, esquire, against George Etheridge, on an action of trespass for felling timber in Lagham Park. [Queen's Bench. K.B. 27/1358/360d.]

1600, Trinity. The same against the same on another similar charge. [Queen's Bench. K.B. 27/1362/316.]

1599/1600, Hilary. Thomas Grymes of London, gentleman, sues William Gardner, esquire, on a debt of £100. [Queen's Bench. K.B. 27/1360/929.]

1600. William Gardyner, esquire, and Nicholas Smith, esquire, against the President and Scholars of Magdalen College, Oxford. Concerning the lease of tenements in St. Olave's, Southwark. [Requests Proc. Req. 2/210/12.]

1600–1601. William Gardiner, esquire, against William Fro-

monds and Nicholas Saunders. Concerning the value of
Saunders's inheritance. Depositions. [Chancery Town
Deps. C24/283, C24/294 pt. 1/30.]

1602. William Brooke and Agnes his wife against Frances
Smyth, widow, and Robert her son. Depositions on behalf
of plaintiffs. [Chancery Town Deps. C24/294 pt. 1/5.]

1602. Millicent Saunders, Thomas Wright, et al., against Marmaduke Dawney, William Gardyner, et al. [Star Chamber
Proc. St. Ch. 5/S80/1.]

1602, May. George Etheridge against William Gardiner and
Nicholas Smith, for riot and forcible entry on Lagham
Park, tried at Special Sessions at Godstone. [Hawarde,
Les Reportes del Cases in Camera Stellata, pp. 139ff.]

1602, June and July. The same against the same, in Chancery.
Deposition, 6 July 1602, of Robert Glue of St. Olave's,
Southwark, bricklayer, aged 27. "That in May last he (this
deponent) and Water Franklyn, at the request of Mr. William Gardener, did take view of the said house [in Lagham
wherein Etheridge dwells], and of the gatehouse, brewhouse, and other buildings belonging unto it . . . and . . .
did also survey and make an estimate of the several de-
cays . . . in the house at the postern gate of Lagham Park
wherein William Harlinge dwelleth, and in three other
houses there . . ." [Chancery Town Deps. C24/296/35.
Further depositions. C24/296/26.]

1602, Trinity. William Gardyner and Nicholas Smyth against
Judith Phillippes *alias* Gardyner and William Wayte.
Plaintiffs allege that defendants, in an effort to impede the
execution of the will of William Gardiner, esquire, deceased, have brought false charges against them before
Dr. John Gibson, Master of the Prerogative Court of Canterbury. They say, *inter alia*, that the testator, by his will
made 1 September 1597, left to William Wayte, senior, a
lease of some lands and tenements in St. George's Fields

made to George Dalley, and 200 marks; and to Wayte's four children, £50 apiece. That afterwards, on 1 November 1597, he put William Wayte, senior, out of his will, and abridged the bequests to the Wayte children to £40 each. [Queen's Bench. K.B. 27/1374/362.]

1602/3, Hilary. Lord Mayor and Citizens of London against William Gardyner and Nicholas Smyth. Two debts of £10 each owing since 20 March 1595/6 by William Gardyner, senior, deceased. Satisfaction of £21 for debts and damages acknowledged by plaintiffs. [Queen's Bench. K.B. 27/1377/300d.]

1603, 13 May. William Gardner of Surrey created Knight Bachelor at the Tower. [Shaw, *The Knights of England*, ii, 109.]

1603, Michaelmas. Sir William Gardiner against Richard Johnson, gentleman, of Southwark, for debt of £15. [Common Pleas. C.P. 40/1707/216d.]

1603, Michaelmas. Sir William Gardyner, knight, against Sir Thomas Gardyner, knight, concerning the estate of William Gardyner, esquire, deceased. Depositions. Among them is this deposition of Alice, wife of John Arnold of St. Olave's, Southwark, dyer, aged 55: [at the signing of a lease made by Justice Gardiner to her husband] "she besought the said William Gardener (in respect of the great fine) that he would be good landlord to her and her husband; whereunto he answered in these or the like words viz.: 'I will be no worse landlord unto you than I have been, and I hope you shall find as good a landlord of my son William (meaning the complainant) when I am dead and rotten.' " [Chancery Town Deps. C24/322/50, 51.]

1605, 19 November. Sir Thomas Gardyner of Camberwell, against Sir William Gardyner. Dispute over the executorship of Justice Gardiner's will, and the right to lease Bermondsey Grange. [Exchequer of Pleas. E13/437/18.]

1607/8, 11 February. Marmaduke Dawney of Sessay, Yorkshire, gentleman, against Sir William Gardiner et al. Lands in Sutton Coldfield, Warwickshire, late of Simon Perrott. [Chancery Proc., James I. C2 Jas.I/D3/17.]

1607/8, 11 February. William Skeffington of Fisherwick, Staffs., esquire, against Sir William Gardner et al. Lands in Sutton Coldfield, Warwickshire, late of Simon Perrott. [*Ibid.*, S5/51.]

1610, 18 June. Sir Alexander Clifford of Ewell, Surrey, husband of Jane, late wife of Luke Guido *alias* Ward, against Sir William Gardiner, J.P., et al. Violent resistance to distress for rent charged on the manor of Lagham *alias* Langham, and lands in Godstone, Tandridge, and Crowhurst, by Nicholas Saunders of Ewell, esquire, in 1591. [Star Chamber Proc., James I. St. Ch. 8/99/25.]

1616. Thomas Cole of Hampreston, Dorset, esquire, and Frances his wife, late wife of Robert Smyth, against Sir William Gardener et al. Property in Southwark late of William and Agnes Brooke. [Chancery Proc., James I. C2 Jas.I/C19/37.] Depositions in this suit, among which is that made 24 January 1617/8 by Helen Medland of St. Olave's, Southwark, widow, aged 50, printed in part above, pp. 66–67. [Chancery Town Deps. C24/445/20.]

1617. Sir William Gardener of Lagham, Surrey, against Sir Nicholas Saunder, Dame Elizabeth his wife, and Henry Saunder his brother. Concerning the parsonage and mill in Ewell. [Chancery Proc., James I. Bill of complaint, C2 Jas.I/G15/21. Answer, C2 Jas.I/G6/25.]

1618, 26 August. Will of Sir William Gardiner of Lagham Park, Surrey. Proved 4 March 1621/2 by Dame Mary Gardiner. [Prerogative Court of Canterbury, Savile 25.]

1622, 16 May. Inquisition post mortem of Sir William Gardiner. [Inq. Post Mortem, Chancery and Wards. C142/394/75 and Wards 66/76.]

EXTRACTS FROM LAY SUBSIDY ROLLS

E 179

185/224. 1547 Bermondsey
      Edmonde Waite in goods £35 . 46s. 8d.
      William Gardyner in goods £35 . 46s. 8d.
      [Justice Gardiner's father.]

185/230. 1547 Southwark
      Bp. of Winchester's Liberty
      Robert Motte in goods £10 . . . 10s.

[Wayte's wife Joan Tayler was Mote's next-of-kin.]

185/240. 1549 Bermondsey
      Rychard Gardener in goods £10 . . 10s.
      [Justice Gardiner's elder brother.]
      Edmonde Wayte in goods £40 . . 40s.

185/276. 1556 Bermondsey
      William Gardyner in lands £20 . . 40s.
      [Justice Gardiner.]
      Edmond Wayte in goods 100 marks £4:8:10
      [100 marks is £33:6:8.]

185/310. 1576 Bermondsey
      John Strangman gent. in lands £20 53s. 4d.

[Gardiner swore the peace against Strangman in 1577.]
      Martin Manley in goods £3 . . 5s.
      [Frances Luce's brother-in-law.]
      Kellam Hedley in goods £3 . . . 5s.
      [See Gardiner's will, and William Wayte,
        document dated 1597, Michaelmas.]
      William Gardiner in lands £20 . 53s. 4d.
      [An assessor for the parish, and 'high col-
        lector' for Brixton Hundred. His collec-
        tion, paid into the Exchequer Oct. 11,

1576, was £120 100s. 20d.—B.M. Addl.
Ch. 39978, m. 4.]

186/354. 1593 Bermondsey

†*exoneratur* William Gardiner Esquier
in lands £40 . . . . £8

186/349. 1593 Southwark

William Gardiner Esquier in lands £25   £5
[In this year Gardiner served as a Com-
missioner for the Subsidy in Southwark.
He was therefore discharged of his pay-
ment in Bermondsey, and was assessed in
Southwark. The foregoing entries show
that he saved himself £3 by the change.]
Southwark
The Clink
Philip Hensley £10   . . . . 26s. 8d.
[Henslowe, an assessor for the Liberty.]
Paris Garden
Frauncis Langley £20 . . . . 53s. 4d.
[An assessor for Paris Garden.]

186/360. 1594 Bermondsey

†William Gardiner Esquier in lands £40 £8
["Discharged here because he answers in the
Borough of Southwark."]

186/362. 1594 Southwark   £4

William Gardyner esqr £20   . 53s. 4d. [sic]
[Still a Commissioner for Southwark, and
thus dodging his tax of £8 in Bermondsey,
Gardiner managed this year to lower his
own assessment in Southwark from £25 to
£20. But after the list was drawn up other
Commissioners objected to his action, and
hoisted him to £30; thereby obliging him

to pay £4 instead of £2:13:4; a definite increase, but still far from the £8 he should
have paid in Bermondsey. Gardiner's
tricks to cheat the Queen were not hidden
from his neighbours.]

Southwark

The Clink

    Phillipp Henslowe £10 . . .   26s. 8d.

[An assessor for the Liberty.]

Paris Garden

    Frauncys Langlie £20 . . .   53s. 4d.

[An assessor for Paris Garden.]

186/347. 1595 Bermondsey

    William Gardiner Esquier in lands £40

                              £5:6:8

186/369. 1598 Bermondsey

    William Gardiner gent. in lands £10   40s.

[Justice Gardiner's younger son and executor.]

    William Wayte in goods £3 . . .   8s.

186/368. 1599 Bermondsey

    [Similar to foregoing.]

186/370. 1598 Southwark

    Frauncys Langley Esquier £20 . 53s. 4d.

    [Langley has risen to 'esquire' by being
joined in the Subsidy Commission for
Southwark with Edmund Bowyer, Bartholomew Scott, and others.]

The Clink

    Exoneratur Phillipp Hensloe £10   26s. 8d.

186/375A. 1599 Southwark

    Frauncis Langley £20 . . .   53s. 4d.

    [A Commissioner.]

The Clink

    Phillipp Henchlowe £10 . . . 26s. 8d.

186/368. 1599 Camberwell

    Edmond Bowier Esquier in lands £20   £4

    Bartholomewe Scott esquier in lands £20 £4

Peckham

    Thomas Gardner gent. in lands £5   20s.

[Justice Gardiner's eldest surviving son.]

186/376. 1600 Bermondsey

    William Gardiner gent. in lands £10   40s.

    William Waite in goods £3 . . .   8s.

186/377. 1600 Southwark

Paris Garden

    Francis Langley in goods £15 . . 40s.

[Langley has been dropped from the Commission, and his assessment has fallen by a quarter. We know from other sources that he was less prosperous than he had been.]

GARDINER'S COAT OF ARMS

Note of Grant: Addl. MS. 26,702, f. 142ᵛ, MS entitled 'Arms in trick granted by Sir C[hristopher]Barker, H. VIII-Ed. VI.'; Harl. MS. 1507, f. 101ᵛ, 'Wᵐ Gardner of Barmondsey street per Ro[bert] Cook Clar[enceux]'.

In Trick: Harl. MS. 1414, f. 120ᵛ; Harl. MS. 1422, f. 14: 'Willm Gardener of Bermondsey streete per R[obert] C[ook] Cl[arenceux]'; Addl. MS. 18,594, f. 228; Addl. MS. 19,521, f. 225.

In Trick with Lion Crest: Stowe MS. 693, f. 9: 'Wyllm Gardyner of Barmonsey in Surrey'; Harl. MS. 1475, f. 51ᵛ; Addl. MS. 17,439, f. 90ᵛ: 'Gardiner of Barmondsey street'; Addl. MS. 26,702, f. 142ᵛ; Addl. MS. 12,444, f. 51: 'Sʳ Thomas Gardener of Peckham in Surry'; ibid., f. 90ᵛ: 'Christopher Gardiner.'

In Trick with Unicorn Crest: Harl. MS. 1459, f. 64: 'of Gardener of London et Surry'; Harl. MS. 1475, f. 207: 'of Sʳ Tho: Gardner Kᵗ Surry'.

Impaled Arms in Trick: (Gardiner impaling Lucy.) Harl. MS. 5849, f. 63ᵛ (second part of MS.); Stowe MS. 587, f. 1ᵛ.

GARDINER AS JUSTICE OF PEACE AND OF THE *QUORUM*

Extracts from the records of the Surrey clerks of Assize (P.R.O., Assizes 35/19, 22-40).

William Gardiner was commissioned as justice in 1580. First pricked of the *quorum* in 1581, he continued in that body until his death in November 1597, with the exception of the summer of 1594 when he was noted 'egrotus', and of the year September 29, 1594–September 28, 1595, when he served as High Sheriff of Surrey and Sussex. The figures below represent the number of prisoners (at the semi-annual gaol-deliveries) committed respectively by Gardiner and his neighbour fellow-justices.

		William Gardiner of Bermond-sey	Edmund Bowyer of Camber-well	John Scott of Camber-well	Robert Livesey of Streatham
1580	Summer .	5	1	..	..
1580/1	Winter .	5	6	11	1
1581	Summer .	2	1	6	..
1581/2	Winter	*missing*			
1582	Summer	*list of prisoners missing.*			
1582/3	Winter .	5	..	3	..
1583	Summer .	16	1	2	1
		Bowyer and Livesey jointly committed 6 more.			
1583/4	Winter .	15	1	..	2
1584	Summer .	13	6	1	..
1584/5	Winter .	5	6	..	2
1585	Summer .	18	7	..	..
1585/6	Winter .	8	2	..	1

		William Gardiner of Bermond- sey	Edmund Bowyer of Camber- well	John Scott of Camber- well	Robert Livesey of Streatham
1586	Summer .	16	2	..	1
1586/7	Winter .	17	8	..	..
1587	Summer .	missing.			
1587/8	Winter .	18	2	..	2
1588	Summer .	8	2	..	1
1588/9	Winter .	11	7	..	..
1589	Summer .	4	7	..	..
1589/90	Winter .	18	6	..	..
1590	Summer .	17	3	..	..
1590/1	Winter .	8	15	..	2
1591	Summer .	3	6	..	4
1591/2	Winter .	13	6	..	3
1592	Summer .	14	6	..	..
1592/3	Winter .	missing.			
1593	Summer .	missing.			

				Bartholo- mew Scott of Camberwell	
1593/4	Winter .	7	8	9	..
1594	Summer .	8	5	3	..
1594/5	Winter .	8	12	11	..
1595	Summer .	Sheriff	17	2	..
1595/6	Winter .	1	17	8	..
1596	Summer .	missing.			
1596/7	Winter .	19	21	4	..
1597	Summer .	15	12	10	..
	Totals .	297	193		

This table bears eloquent testimony to Gardiner's exceptional activity as justice of the peace. His impressive total of committals, far larger than that of his nearest competitor, Edmund Bowyer, over the same number of years, shows that his district was the thickly-settled and turbulent borough of Southwark.

In view of the discovery that Shakespeare's figure of Justice Shallow contains more than one hit at Justice Gardiner, it is tempting to look for Mr. Justice Silence in the person either of Edmund Bowyer or of Bartholomew Scott, both of whom lived in Camberwell. Little love was lost between Justice Bowyer and Justice Gardiner in the spring of 1597. Gardiner tried to steal a piece of land from Bowyer, who characterized his companion on the Bench as 'covetous and insatiable'. After Gardiner's death, his widow Margaret married, as her fourth husband, Bartholomew Scott—who had already buried two wives, one of whom was the widow of the martyred Archbishop Cranmer. Scott died childless, leaving Peter Scott, a nephew and foster-child, as his heir. I expect that more material will be found for the lives of these justices and neighbours of Gardiner. Whether any likeness to Master Silence will be revealed in either of them remains to be seen. In the present limited state of our knowledge it would be quite unjustifiable to indulge in theorizing.

2 B

JUSTICE GARDINER'S SONS ENTERED AT THE INNER TEMPLE

1581, Nov. Christopher Gardiner, Bermondsey. Son and heir of William Gardiner. Died *vitâ patris*.

1587, Nov. Richard Gardiner, Bermondsey, Surrey. Eldest son [sic] of William Gardiner. Died *cœlebs*.

1591, Nov. William Gardiner, Bermondsey. Younger son of William Gardiner. Knighted.

JUSTICE GARDINER'S GRANDSON

1614, Nov. Christopher Gardiner, Sandplace, Dorking, Surrey. Eldest son of C. Gardiner, a Member of the Inn. Born 1596.

— W. H. Cooke, *Students admitted to the Inner Temple, 1547–1660* (1887), pp. 101, 119, 130, 208.

GARDINER GENEALOGY

Gardiner pedigree put together from the following sources, supplemented by manuscript legal records in the Public Record Office: William Gardiner's Funeral Certificate, College of Arms, I. 16, f. 7; William Gardiner's will, P.C.C. Cobbham 113; B.M. Addl. MS. 14311, f. 79ᵛ; Bodl. Rawl. MS. B75, ff. 116-117; Bodl. Rawl. MS. B429, f. 143; Harleian Society, i (1869), 87; Surrey Archaeological Society, *Collections*, xi (1893); Registers of St. Mary Magdalene, Bermondsey, pr. *Genealogist* vi-ix; G. S. Steinman, 'Account of the Manor of Haling, Croydon, Surrey', in *Collectanea Topographica et Genealogica*, iii (1836), 14ff; Manuscript Registers of the Parish Church of Dorking, Surrey.

EXTRACTS FROM THE REGISTERS OF ST. MARY MAGDALENE, BERMONDSEY, PRINTED IN *THE GENEALOGIST*, vi-ix

1549, 8 June *Bur.* William Gardynarde ffarmor of Burmondsey grange

1552, 14 Sep. *Bur.* Elizabeth the wife of Edmund Wayte

1555, 8 June *Chr.* ffrances Waight

1557, 6 May *Mar.* Raffe Inglish and ffryswighe Askew

1557, 30 Oct. *Bur.* Alice the daughter of Raffe Inglish

1557, 6 Dec. *Bur.* Edmund Wayte

1558, 1 Mar. *Chr.* John the son of Raffe Inglish

1558, 7 June *Mar.* William Gardyner and ffrances Waight

1558, 22 Nov. *Bur.* Joan the daughter of Rauffe Inglish

1558, 18 Dec. *Bur.* Rachell Luce

1559, 6 Jan. *Bur.* William the sonne of Wm Gardyner

1559, 23 Jan. *Bur.* John the son of Rauffe Inglish

1559, 31 Mar. *Bur.* Christian the dau. of Margery Gardiner

1560, 16 Mar. *Bur.* John Wayte

1560, 3 Apr. *Chr.* W^m the sonne of William Gardyner

1560, 17 Apr. *Bur.* William the sonne of Wm Gardyner

1560, 15 June *Mar.* John Tompson and Alice Bowyer

1560, 3 July *Mar.* Thomas Sheppard and ffriswide English

1560, 26 Sep. *Chr.* John Wayte

1561, 15 June *Bur.* Elizabeth Waighte

1563, 31 Jan. *Bur.* Thomas the sonne of Wm Gardynar

1563, 17 Oct. *Bur.* Tho: Sare

1565, 1 Apr. *Chr.* Katherine the daughter of Wm Gardyner

1566, 17 Dec. *Chr.* Agnes the daughter of William Gardyner

1568, 16 Mar. *Chr.* William the sonne of Wm Gardyner

1568, 29 Aug. *Mar.* James Chibball and Jane Chare

1569, 20 Feb. *Bur.* W^m the sonne of Wm Gardyner

1570, 6 Aug. *Mar.* Wm Tory and Jane Gardyner

1571, 24 June *Mar.* Nicholas Gardyner and Alice Armorer

1572, 27 Jan. *Chr.* Wᵐ Gardyner

1572, 28 Mar. *Bur.* Alice Gardyner

1572, 20 May *Bur.* Mother Sare

1572, 7 Oct. *Bur.* Mary Gardyner

1572, 18 Nov. *Bur.* Mathew Gardyner

1572, 14 Dec. *Bur.* Robert Gardyner

1573, 12 July *Mar.* Thomas Sare and Jane Vicars

1573, 31 Aug. *Mar.* Martin Menley and Sara Luce

1573, 30 Sep. *Chr.* Jo: Gardner

1574, 17 Apr. *Chr.* Rebecca the daughter of Martin Manly

Missing, April 1574–December 1581.

1581, 18 Dec. *Mar.* Mʳ Jo. Stepkin and Mʳˢ Katherine Gardyner

1582, 1 Jan. *Chr.* Mary the daughter of Wᵐ Gardyner

1582, 4 Mar. *Chr.* Nicholas the sonne of John Gardyner

1582, 15 Apr. *Mar.* Heugh Joanes and Jane Sare

1582, 15 Apr. *Chr.* Mary daughter of Martin Manley

1582, 27 May *Mar.* Mʳ William Gardyner and Mʳˢ Margaret
Abraham

1582, 3 June *Chr.* Wᵐ the Sonne of William Wayte

1582, 27 Nov. *Bur.* Mary the daughter of Wᵐ Gardyner

1583, 25 Jan. *Bur.* William Gardyner a child

1583, 13 May *Chr.* Jane the daughter of Martin Manley

1583, 4 July *Mar.* Mʳ Symond Parratt and Mʳˢ Anne Gardner

1583, 5 Sep. *Bur.* Mary the daughter of Martin Manley

1583, 8 Sep. *Chr.* Wᵐ the sonne of Wᵐ Wayt

1583, 22 Sep. *Chr.* John the sonne of Wᵐ Gardener

1584, 15 May *Bur.* William the sonne of William Wayte

1584, 24 May *Chr.* Margaret the daughter of Martin Manley

1585, 1 Feb. *Mar.* Thomas Gardener and Ellyn Smyth

1585, 23 May *Chr.* Margarett the daughter of John Gardener

1585, 23 June *Mar.* Mr Nicholas Smyth and Mrs Katherine Stepkin

1586, 20 Feb. *Chr.* William the sonne of Wm Gardyner

1586, 4 Mar. *Bur.* William the sonne of Wm Gardyner

1586, 18 Apr. *Chr.* Margarett the daughter of Wm Wayte

1586, 28 Aug. *Chr.* Joane the daughter of . . . Manley

1587, 12 Feb. *Chr.* Sara the daughter of Martin Manley

1587, 30 Apr. *Chr.* Katherine the daughter of William Gardyner

1587, 28 May *Bur.* Robart Gardyner

1587, 12 Oct. *Bur.* Sara the wife of Martyn Manley

1588, 6 Jan. *Chr.* William the sonne of John Gardyner

1588, 9 Sep. *Bur.* Katherine the daughter of Wm Gardiner

1588, 10 Nov. *Chr.* John the sonne of William Wayte

1589, 25 May *Chr.* Mary the daughter of William Gardyner

1590, 9 Apr. *Bur.* W^m the sonne of Mr Tho: Gardner

1590, 8 July *Bur.* William the sonne of Jo: Gardner

1590, 12 July *Chr.* W^m the sonne of Mr Tho. Gardyner

1591, 13 May *Bur.* Rich. the sonne of Mr William Gardyner

1591, 1 Nov. *Mar.* John Lee and Annis Walker

1592, 21 May *Bur.* Margarett Luce

1592, 27 May *Chr.* Richard the sonne of Mr Thomas Gardner

1593, 28 Jan. *Mar.* Symon Lapyn and Margarett Gardener

1593, 14 Mar. *Bur.* Winifred Gardyner widdow

1593, 8 Apr. *Chr.* William the sonne of William Gardner

1593, 10 Sep. *Bur.* Mary the daughter of William Gardyner

1593, 14 Oct. *Chr.* ffra: and Annis the daughters of Wm Wayght

1593, 9 Nov. *Bur.* Annis the daughter of William Wayte

1593, 10 Nov. *Bur.* ffran: the daughter of Wm Wayte

1594, 11 June *Mar.* Mr Christopher Gardner and Mrs Judeth Sackfeld

1595, 9 Feb.   *Chr.*   Christopher the son of Wm Gardner
1595, 1 Nov.   *Bur.*   ... the sonne of William Gardner Smyth
1597, 22 Dec.   *Bur.*   William Gardner Esq.   /
1598, 6 Jan.   *Bur.*   Mother Gardner
1603, 29 Aug.   *Bur.*   William and Jone Waite [29 others buried
                                  the same day.]
1604, 30 Aug.   *Bur.*   Mr. William Stere *parson*
1607, 22 Feb.   *Chr.*   An the dau. of John Gardner
1609, 18 Apr.   *Chr.*   Marie the daughter of the right worship-
                                  full Sir Willm Gardner
1609, 28 Apr.   *Bur.*   John Gardner poore cons:

Note: A Francis Langley appears in these books as follows: on
26 Dec. 1599, bur. a son William; on 18 May 1602, chr. a son
John; on 2 Aug 1602, bur. a son William; on 9 Sep. 1604, chr. a
son William; on 27 Nov. 1608, chr. a son Francis.

This Francis Langley, who was a 'laborer' (cf. P.R.O., K.B.
29/243/3*d*), is not to be confused with Francis Langley of
Paris Garden.

THE END